365 Days of Health, Wellness and Weight Loss Prayers

Cathy Morenzie

GUIDING LIGHT PUBLISHING

Published: November 2024

Isbns:
(print) 978-1-990078-57-6
(digital) 978-1-990078-58-3
(audio) 978-1-990078-59-0

Published by: Guiding Light Publishing
46 Bell St, Barrie, ON, Canada, L4N 0H9

Note: The information in this book is for educational purposes only and is not recommended as a means of diagnosing or treating illness. All situations concerning physical or mental health should be supervised by a health professional knowledgeable in treating that particular condition. Neither the author nor anyone affiliated with Healthy by Design dispenses medical advice, nor do they prescribe any remedies or assume any responsibility for anyone who chooses to treat themselves.

Cover design by: KimMonteforte.com

Contents

Other Books and Audio Books by Cathy Morenzie

The Breakthrough Method:
Your Guided Path to Weight Loss God's Way

Weight Loss, God's Way: 21-Day Devotional

Breakthrough with Prayer & Fasting

Fit & Fearless, God's Way

Get Active, God's Way

Healthy Eating, God's Way

Love God, Lose Weight

Pray Powerfully, Lose Weight

Spirit-Filled & Sugar-Free

Stay Steadfast, God's Way

Stress-Free, God's Way

Thankful Heart, Healthy Body

The Word on Weight Loss

Weight Loss, God's Way:
Low-Carb Cookbook and Meal-Plan

healthybydesignbooks.com

Introduction

I n a world filled with constant busyness and countless distractions, it's easy to overlook the importance of our health. We often take our well-being for granted, assuming it will always be there, supporting us as we go about our daily lives. But what if we approached our health with the same intentionality we bring to other areas of our lives? What if we recognized that each day is a precious gift, an opportunity to honor and steward our bodies?

One fateful April 15th, during one of our Saturday morning Bible studies, Psalm 90:12 leaped off the page: "Teach us to number our days, that we may gain a heart of wisdom." Since that moment, I've been on a journey to understand what it means to number my days. God has shown me that every day is a divine assignment filled with purpose. Each sunrise brings a fresh opportunity to carry out the work He has set before us.

Our energy and vitality are crucial in fulfilling this assignment. When we prioritize our health, we are better equipped to pursue our passions and impact those around us.

This book, *365 Days of Health, Wellness, and Weight Loss Prayers*, is born from my desire to align health with faith and share the wisdom God has imparted to me. It invites you on a year-long journey of intentional prayer and reflection, focusing on your health. Each day, as you read or listen to the 90-second prayer and communicate with God, you can tap into a fountain of grace and divine guidance that will transform your physical, mental, and spiritual well-being.

Within these pages, you'll find daily prayers, affirmations, and meditations addressing various aspects of your health. Whether you're on a weight loss journey, seeking to become more active, overcoming emotional eating, or desiring greater well-being, these prayers will guide you in connecting with your Heavenly Father.

365 Days of Health, Wellness, and Weight Loss Prayers will bless you far beyond the physical. When you intentionally bring your health before God, you cultivate a deeper awareness of your body, learning to listen to its needs and care for it with love. Through prayer, you invite God's healing, peace, and balance into your life, recognizing that your health journey is intertwined with your spiritual growth.

Each month, we will explore a specific topic related to well-being, allowing Scripture's wisdom to penetrate deep within your soul. Through intentional prayer, you will invite God to transform your life, renew your mind, and empower you to honor your body as a temple of the Holy Spirit.

As you commit to this year of praying for your health and well-being, I pray that you will experience a shift in your relationship with your health and your Heavenly Father. Embrace each day as a fresh start—a chance to realign your thoughts, actions, and priorities with God's will for your health.

Remember, you are on assignment every day, entrusted with the stewardship of your health. Let these daily prayers be your companion, guiding you toward a vibrant, abundant, and purposeful life. Open your heart, engage in prayer, and watch as miracles unfold in your health and well-being.

Blessings on your journey,

Cathy

Acknowledgements

A few years ago, one of my dear friends, Geri L. Parisella, dedicated her time and effort to help me compile these prayers from all of our programs and courses. After many iterations and edits, it is finally here, birthed through much prayer and life experiences. I want to extend my heartfelt thanks to Geri for her countless hours of work. I also want to thank Brenda Fagan for her editing expertise, and of course, my husband and editor, Preston. May our prayers and cries to God be a blessing to everyone who prays them.

January

PLAN
PRAYERFULLY

Welcome to a New Year! As you enter this first month, embrace the ease and peace that come from partnering with God as you set your intentions and plan your health goals.

In a world that often promotes unrealistic goal-setting and outcomes, it's easy to feel disheartened and discouraged when your aspirations seem out of reach. However, by shifting your focus toward God and inviting Him into your planning process, you open yourself to His wisdom and guidance, which far surpass your limited understanding.

These prayers will remind you to fix your gaze on the Source of all provision, ensuring that God is at the center of all your planning. By aligning your intentions with God's divine will, you cultivate a deep sense of peace, purpose, and fulfillment throughout your journey.

Throughout this month, you will explore heartfelt prayers that help you navigate the complexities of setting and pursuing your health goals. These prayers are designed to inspire you to seek God's divine inspiration, wisdom, and strength as you make choices that support your physical, mental, and emotional well-being.

Let's embark on this sacred path together, surrendering your plans to the Lord's wisdom and guidance. May these prayers move you from a place of goal-setting to goal-getting!

January 1
Setting Godly Goals

"But I have raised you up for this very purpose, that I might show you my power and that my name might be proclaimed in all the earth."

Exodus 9:16 NIV

Dear Lord, my companion and guide, thank You for the New Year. I eagerly anticipate partnering with You on my health journey. I invite You in! Instead of worldly resolutions that often fall short, I commit to staying connected to You, recognizing that apart from You, I can do nothing (John 15:5).

Help me set Godly goals that are aligned with Your will and purpose for my life. In the past, my self-centered goals have hindered my progress and led to disappointment. I seek Your guidance as I write down my goals, co-creating a vision for my health that honors You. With Your presence, I move from fear to faith, knowing that You are my strength and foundation.

May my goals glorify You and be grounded in Your truth. Let my health journey be a testament to Your spirit within me, shaping me in Your image and reflecting Your love to the world (Romans 8:29).

As I enter this new year, I see it as a fresh chapter. Empower me to live out my goals daily, keeping my mind fixed on You (Isaiah 26:3). Grounded in You, I anticipate the blessings and growth this year will bring. Amen.

January 2
Plan Prayerfully

"Commit your work to the LORD, and your plans will be established."

Proverbs 16:3 ESV

Dear Omnipresent God, sovereign over all creation, I come before You in reverence, acknowledging Your intimate knowledge of my weaknesses and tendencies, especially in pursuing my health goals. I recognize that without Your guidance, I can easily lose my way. Forgive me for the times I have planned without seeking Your counsel. Help me understand that true wisdom lies in bringing all my desires to You in prayer, recognizing that prayer alone isn't a magical solution but a channel through which I present my concerns and aspirations (Philippians 4:6).

As I set my health goals for this year, I surrender them to Your capable hands. Establish my plans according to Your perfect will, guiding me toward success and fulfillment (Jeremiah 29:11). I seek abundant health, long life, and immeasurable joy, trusting that Your purpose for me is good.

In this new season, I stand ready to receive Your blessings. In faith, I lift my voice in prayer, placing all my hopes and goals before You. May Your will be done in my life, and may Your name be glorified in every step I take. Thank You, Lord, for the assurance that You are with me in this journey. Amen.

January 3
The Power of Your Word

"Your word is a lamp for my feet, a light on my path."
Psalm 119:105 NIV

God of Creation, I thank You for Your life-giving Word that guides me each day, illuminating my path. As I plan my health goals for this year, I come humbly before You, seeking Your wisdom and direction. Let Your Word be the solid foundation in all I do, reminding me to integrate it fully into every aspect of my life, including my health.

Your Word is a living testament of love and guidance. It gives me life, strength, purpose, and direction. In moments of doubt or temptation, remind me that You are by my side (Psalm 23:4), providing the comfort and assurance I need.

As I make my plans, I am reminded that Your purpose prevails over my own. Your Word is alive in me, sharper than any sword, capable of transforming my thoughts and actions. It invigorates my spirit, strengthens my body, and guides my steps.

Help me to place my faith in You, knowing that through Christ, I can achieve all things with Your Word as my foundation (Philippians 4:13). I commit this journey to You, trusting in Your perfect will. In Jesus' name, I pray. Amen.

January 4
The Power of My Words

"May these words of my mouth and this meditation of my heart be pleasing in your sight, LORD,"
Psalm 19:14 NIV

Dear Lord, my Rock and Redeemer (Psalm 18:2), my true desire is found in You. Thank You for entrusting me with a significant role in my life and in the lives of others. May my words today be affirming and edifying, reflecting the time I spend with You. Let them carry power, authority, and impact, emulating Your living Word (John 6:63) as I grow more like You each day.

Your Word teaches that life and death reside in the tongue (Proverbs 18:21). Help me speak life over myself and others. Remind me that harsh words won't motivate me or inspire me to take action; I cannot shame or guilt myself into getting healthy. Instead, kindness and compassion foster good health. May my heart be Your dwelling place, filled with love and grace.

Empower me to use my creative power to build myself up with positive thoughts and words. I choose not to dwell on the past but to remember Your faithfulness and the good plans You have for my future. Today signifies new beginnings, and I declare that I walk in freedom and excellent health, relying on Your strength and guidance. Thank You, Lord, for the gift of life and the opportunity to reflect Your love in all I say and do. In Your name, I pray. Amen!

January 5
Supernatural Revelation

"Where there is no vision, the people perish."
Proverbs 29:18 KJV

Lord, Your Word highlights the importance of vision. Thank you for opening my eyes! Just as a clear vision is vital for life, so is health for the journey ahead. I aim to grasp the vision you've set for me, which includes my health goals. With unwavering faith, I'll pursue it (Habakkuk 2:2).

The vision You give me goes beyond my wants and wishes. It's supernatural, coming directly from you and it will enable me to fully embrace my health journey with determination and focus. Father, make me sensitive to Your leading, guiding my choices for both vision and health. Let me fix my gaze on You, seeking strength in every step toward my health goals. Grant me courage to walk the path of a healthy life ordained by You.

Thank You for the assurance that I am blessed as I heed wisdom's instruction (Proverbs 12:5). This year will be one of seeking You, surrendering my will, and experiencing joy, peace, and freedom encompassing body, mind, and spirit. I'm filled with anticipation, knowing that aligning health goals with Your vision will reveal wonders. In Your visionary name, guide and empower me on this journey towards optimal health. Amen.

January 6
Running Toward My Vision

"And the Lord answered me: 'Write the vision; make it plain on tablets, so he may run who reads it.'"
Habakkuk 2:2 ESV

Dear Lord, God of promise. You are the faithful God who keeps covenant and mercy for a thousand generations with those who love You and keep Your commandments (Deuteronomy 7:9).

Today, I humbly confess that in the past, I have set goals but lacked the drive and determination to pursue them wholeheartedly. You have given me the desire to be not only a visionary but also a victor. And I pray that this year, I will not only conceive dreams but also have the courage to pursue them relentlessly.

When people ask me how I have achieved my health goals this year, let my words be a testimony of Your unfailing love, grace, and favor. Let me speak of Your healing power and the strength working in me. Holy Spirit, I invite You to be my guide each day.

Lead me step by step, from glory to glory, as I run towards the prize You have set before me (1 Corinthians 9:24)I surrender my dreams and aspirations to You, Lord. May my actions honor You. With You by my side, I'm confident I will overcome every obstacle as I run towards my vision. Thank You for Your unwavering love and strength. In Jesus' name, Amen.

January 7
Focus on Praise

"Give thanks to the LORD, for he is good; his love endures forever."

1 Chronicles 16:34 ESV

Dear Faithful God, you are deserving of all praise. Your love knows no limits, and through it, You reveal Your true essence as love and goodness itself (Psalm 103:8). While Your boundless love is beyond my comprehension, I seek to experience it more each day. My heart overflows with gratitude for everything You've done and continue to do in my life, from the smallest blessings to the greatest miracles.

As I plan out this year, I fix my gaze on Your goodness, knowing that You are the source of every good and perfect gift, including my health and well-being. In moments of discomfort, discouragement, or despair, I will choose to give You praise, for I recognize that praise unlocks Your presence. In that sacred space, restoration and renewal reside, allowing me to experience Your healing touch.

I praise You as the Good Shepherd guiding my physical, emotional, and spiritual health (Psalm 23:1). In this new season, I will never stop giving You praise. I thank You for guiding me toward restoration (Jeremiah 30:17) as I walk in union with Your Spirit toward wholeness. In Jesus' name, I offer this prayer with heartfelt praise and thanksgiving. May my life be a continual reflection of Your goodness, and may I spread Your love and grace to those around me. Amen.

January 8
Teach Me Lord

"Teach us to number our days, that we may gain a heart of wisdom."

Psalm 90:12 NIV

Dear Sovereign Lord, Your presence permeates every aspect of my life, both big and small (1 Chronicles 29:11), and You govern with perfect knowledge and power (Isaiah 11:2). Today, I invite You as my ultimate teacher, asking for Your wisdom to help me prioritize my health each day. I long to make choices that reflect Your love and purpose.

I'm weary of making unhealthy choices that do not serve my best self. Instead, I rise with determination to glorify You in my body. May my thoughts, actions, and intentions align with Your divine purpose. Remind me of Your strength in moments of weakness and doubt (Isaiah 41:10), assuring me that I am never alone in this journey.

Help me grasp the connection between my choices and the abundant life You have planned for me. Let me find joy in nourishing my body, staying active, and nurturing my well-being. With Your guidance, I will honor the vessel You've entrusted me with (1 Corinthians 10:31).

Guide me to steward my time, my health, and my life with Your wisdom and grace. In the name of Jesus, who embodies wisdom, I pray. Amen.

January 9
Seeking You, First

"But first and most importantly seek (aim at, strive after) His kingdom and His righteousness [His way of doing and being right—the attitude and character of God], and all these things will be given to you also."
Matthew 6:33 AMP

Dear Lord, God of order. I stand on your promise today that as I go about Your business (Luke 2:49), You have my back. What a relief that I don't have to spend this year running around on high alert, trying to figure out how to live a healthy life. I've tried, and it's exhausting, not to mention, impossible.

Thank You for teaching me how to order my life so I make time for what's important. Instead of wasting time today on things that have no eternal value, let me focus on what You've assigned me to do and leave the rest behind. And let me do it all as unto You (Colossians 3:23).

I don't have to live under all that weight (literally and figuratively) of orchestrating my own life. Oh Lord, what a delight and a relief that You are telling me that I need not worry about anything (Philippians 4:6-7), ever, because You care for me!

I propose to put and keep You first today and every day. In Jesus' mighty name. Amen.

January 10
Integrity

"The integrity of the upright guides them, but the unfaithful are destroyed by their duplicity."

Proverbs 11:3 NIV

Dear Lord, God of honor and majesty, I come before You with reverence and awe. It is You who spoke and brought forth the magnificent world into existence (John 1:1). Today, I humbly seek Your guidance and strength, as I invite You to transform my intentions into tangible actions this year. Too often, I find myself caught up in discussing what I "want to" or "need to" do, yet fail to take the necessary steps to bring those desires to fruition.

Father, mold me into a person of unwavering integrity, aligning my character with Your divine standards. I am determined to not just desire good health but to genuinely embody it every single day throughout this year. Guard me against excessive planning that hinders progress and obscures Your truth. (2 Timothy 3:7) Grant me the ability to swiftly turn commitments into action, walking in integrity and honoring Your purpose for my life.

As I begin this new chapter, instill within me a resolute and teachable spirit, eager to absorb Your wisdom and promptly apply it. (Proverbs 13:18) May my faith guide me, demonstrating obedience to Your will and consistency in walking with integrity. In Jesus' name, I pray. Amen.

January 11
Praying with Pure Intentions

"You ask and do not receive, because you ask wrongly, to spend it on your passions."

James 4:3 ESV

Lord God, who graciously hears and faithfully answers the prayers of your children. I humbly come before You today, acknowledging that You possess the wisdom to give good gifts to those who seek You (Matthew 7:11). I invite You to search the depths of my heart and uproot any unhealthy desires and intentions within me. Help me seek You with the right motives.

Shape and mold the desires I have for my health and my life, refining me through the fire of Your love. Purify my thoughts, intentions, and actions. Let my hunger be for You above all else. I crave only Your best for me.

Confidently, I approach Your throne, knowing that when I ask anything in accordance with Your will, You not only hear me but also answer my prayers (1 John 5:14). I repent sincerely for the times I have sought even good things, but with impure motives and a misguided heart. With a renewed spirit, I now ask that You grant me the desires of my heart (Proverbs 3:5). In the name of Your beloved Son, Jesus, I pray. Amen.

January 12
Temple Reconstruction

"For which of you, intending to build a tower, does not sit down first and count the cost, whether he has enough to finish it—lest, after he has laid the foundation, and is not able to finish, all who see it begin to mock him, saying, 'This man began to build and was not able to finish?'"

Luke 14:28-30 **NKJV**

L ord, God of wisdom and knowledge. Your infinite wisdom never fails. I know that my body is a temple of the Holy Spirit and that I should honor You with it (1 Corinthians 6:19-20), but I need Your blueprint. Help me to count the costs as I endeavor to care for my body before it's too late. Impress upon me that the actions that I take now will prevent negative consequences in the future.

Your Word says that the body is perishable, but the soul is eternal (1 Corinthians 15:42-44). I know that my physical body will not last forever, but I want to take care of it while I am on this earth. I want to be able to serve You to the best of my ability, which requires optimal health.

This month, as I lay the foundation to rebuild my temple, I invite You in to oversee the entire reconstruction from beginning to end. I stand on Your word that I can do all things through Christ who gives me strength (Philippians 4:13), so I declare that this is my year to rebuild my temple. Thank You for Your constant presence, love, and grace. In Jesus' name, Amen.

January 13
Breaking Unhealthy Cycles

"Therefore do not be foolish, but understand what the will of the Lord is."

Ephesians 5:17NIV

Lord, I thank You for desiring the best for me and holding the blueprint for my best life. Grant me wisdom to walk wisely, making the most of my time and aligning with Your ways.

As I break free from unhealthy cycles and habits of the past, I stand on Your promise that I am a new creation in Christ (2 Corinthians 5:17). Help me release old ways of being and embrace the new creation - designed in Your image.

As I establish my goals, keep me connected to You. I declare the cycle of setting unrealistic expectations, followed by disappointment, and self-condemnation broken in Jesus' name!

Your Word reminds me to trust in You with all my heart and to lean not on my own understanding (Proverbs 3:5-6). Father, I pray that You will guide me and give me wisdom as I create new habits. Help me to surrender my desires and my will to You, knowing that You have a plan and a purpose for my life. I will achieve a healthy mind, body, and weight this year as I align with Your best desires and plans for me. I will achieve all You've called me to achieve. Unhealthy cycles are broken! In Jesus' name, I pray. Amen!

January 14
Thankful in Advance

"... give thanks in all circumstances; for this is the will of God in Christ Jesus for you."
1 Thessalonians 5:18 NIV

Dear Faithful God. I praise You and give You all glory and honor. I ascribe greatness to You (Deuteronomy 32:3). Today, I thank You in advance for the healthy year that lies before me, knowing that You are the source of all good things. Thank You for already going before me and leading me on the right path (Psalm 23:3)

I am grateful for the progress that I am making even though it seems slow. It has not been without its trials and tribulations, but through Your unwavering love and encouragement, I will find the strength to persevere.

As I continue, I humbly ask for ongoing strength and discipline to make daily healthy choices beyond just food, impacting all aspects of my life. May my body be a temple dedicated to worship and service, bringing glory to Your name (1 Corinthians 6:19).

This year, help me to maintain an attitude of gratitude, whether I am experiencing the exhilaration of progress or facing the frustration of feeling stuck. Wherever I find myself, I will never stop giving You praise. In Jesus' name, I pray. Amen.

January 15
Planning with Diligence

"The plans of the diligent lead to profit as surely as haste leads to poverty."

Proverbs 21:5 NIV

L ord God, who graciously hears and answers prayers, I humbly come before You, acknowledging Your wisdom in giving good gifts to those who seek You (Matthew 7:11). As I plan for a healthy year, please examine my heart, revealing and removing any unhealthy desires within me. Grant me what is truly best, aligning my thoughts with Your purpose. I confidently approach Your throne, knowing that when I ask according to Your will, You hear and answer (1 John 5:14). I repent for seeking good things with impure motives, and help me align my desires and health with Your purpose.

Help me understand the importance of being diligent in my planning. Instill in me the discipline to approach my health goals with intention rather than haphazardness. I seek Your strength to do the necessary work of planning, embracing the skill of preparation, and avoiding procrastination. I know that this diligence will benefit me in the long run. In my planning, keep me humble and open to Your leading, so I can surrender my own agenda and trust Your guidance. Let Your Holy Spirit be my constant companion, enlightening my mind and directing my steps. May my diligent planning bear fruit in due season, bringing glory to Your name. In Jesus' name, I pray. Amen.

January 16
Planning with Intention

"Therefore I run in such a way, as not without aim; I box in such a way, as not beating the air; but I buffet my body and make it my slave, lest possibly after I have preached to others, I myself should be disqualified."
1 Corinthians 9:26–27 NIV

Dear Great God, you are a God of intention, and I acknowledge that You have a plan and purpose for my life. My deepest desire is to fulfill this purpose, especially when it comes to caring for my body and health. I am grateful for Your indwelling Spirit, which empowers me with the self-discipline needed to face this journey with assured victory.

Help me remain focused and intentional as I let go of my own ways of getting healthy, which have never worked and never will. Grant me the resilience to resist temptation (1 Corinthians 10:13) and empower me to make healthy choices consistently, even in challenging situations. May I always remember that my body is a sacred temple of the Holy Spirit, deserving of honor through wise and mindful decisions.

Teach me, O Lord, to find joy in physical activity and exercise, and let my motivation stem from a desire to glorify Your name (1 Corinthians 6:20). May I wake each morning with my mind set on prioritizing my health, seeking creative ways to incorporate it into my daily life. In the mighty name of Jesus, I pray, trusting in Your unfailing love and guidance. Amen.

January 17
Stewarding My Time

"LORD, remind me how brief my time on earth will be. Remind me that my days are numbered—how fleeting my life is."

Psalm 39:4 NLT

Dear Precious Lord, Your profound wisdom and knowledge move me to make wise choices about how I invest my time. Grant me the heart of wisdom to recognize when I'm wasting Your precious time. Help me to understand that You've called me to steward my time by making deliberate and purposeful daily choices for a healthy life.

Guide me to set and meet deadlines diligently, understanding that procrastination only hinders progress. Thank you for the gift of 24 hours today, I propose to maximize it as I fulfill my God-given assignment. Your Word emphasizes diligence, and I seek the richness it brings (Proverbs 13:4).

Enable me to make purposeful and intentional choices for a healthy life. I open my heart to Your guidance, and I am submitting my schedule and my perspective on time to You. Lead me in time and health management, aligning with Your will.

I commit to numbering my days and gaining a heart of wisdom (Psalm 90:12). May this year be a testament to making the best use of the time You've given me, investing in my health for Your glory. In Jesus' name, I pray. Amen.

January 18
Little by Little

"Little by little I will drive them out before you, until you have increased enough to take possession of the land."

Exodus 23:30 NIV

Lord God, You're progressive, always leading Your children to higher levels of glory. With a heart full of gratitude, I desire growth in every area, including my health. Recognizing You as a God of progress and transformation, I trust Your guidance step by step.

As You guided the Israelites to conquer the land little by little, I trust You to lead me towards my health goals. I surrender impatience, embracing "little by little" with contentment. I'm learning that lasting transformation occurs with taking small steps consistently. With Your guidance, I'll make better choices—one bite, one meal, one habit at a time.

I trust in You, so I take small steps in faith, not needing to see the entire staircase. As I dedicate myself to strengthening my temple—spirit, soul, and body—I believe I'll grow from glory to glory, aligning with Your purpose (2 Corinthians 3:18).

Lord, I thank You for Your presence and guidance. I thank you for always working in me so that I progressively look more like You every day. May my efforts testify to Your goodness and faithfulness. In Jesus' name, I pray. Amen.

January 19
The Gift of Today

"And on the seventh day God finished his work that he had done, and he rested on the seventh day from all his work that he had done."

Genesis 2:2 ESV

Lord, I thank you for the gift of today. Remind me that each and every day is a gift from You and I have an opportunity to enjoy all that it brings. Please help me make the most of my days (Ephesians 5:15-17), maximizing every opportunity that each day affords me.

Let me never be guilty of wasting Your time. It is such a precious commodity. As I learn the skill of planning, teach me how to put first things (Matthew 6:33) first instead of jumping from thing to thing. Then help me to prioritize and actually stick to my priorities. Teach me to rest when I've done enough so I don't overwhelm or stress myself out. Let me have a healthy work-rest balance today.

Give me the strength to embrace the challenges and blessings of this day with gratitude and joy. May I use this day to serve others, to grow in love and compassion, to honor You through my thoughts, words, and actions, and lastly to see the ability to move my body as a gift from You. Today, I embrace the opportunity to live a healthy life with purpose and joy, in alignment with Your best for me. In Jesus' name, I pray. Amen.

January 20
Rejoice in This Day

"This is the day that the Lord has made; let us rejoice and be glad in it."

Psalm 118:24 ESV

Heavenly Father, today I will rejoice in this day that You have made! And no matter what I may be feeling, I will make the choice today to walk in joy. I find joy in the simple acts of eating, moving, and resting. I rejoice in the strength and vitality that You have given me to live this day in alignment with You.

When I am tempted to despair, remind me that You always go before me (Deuteronomy 31:8) and strengthen me. When trials come, help me to keep my eyes and my mind fixed on You (Hebrews 12:2 because that's where I will find focus, strength, clarity, and peace for this journey. When I'm losing motivation and feel like giving up, let me keep rejoicing in You.

I rejoice in the knowledge that my health is a blessing from You, and that You are the ultimate source of my wellbeing. So, with thanks in my heart, I surrender this day to You. Be the first thought on my mind when I wake up and let me end the day with a smile on my face because You are Lord of my life. And as I seek You first (Matthew 6:33), let my praise usher me straight into Your presence. In Jesus' name. Amen.

January 21
My Steps are Ordered

"The heart of man plans his way, but the Lord establishes his steps."

Proverbs 16:9 ESV

Dear Lord, thank you that You have established my steps and the path I need to take this year to live a healthy life. I come before You today with a humble heart, seeking Your guidance, Your order, and direction on my health journey. You are the author and finisher of my faith, and I trust that You have a plan and purpose for my health and my life.

I'm excited to spend more time with You, to grow, to learn (Matthew 11:29), and to experience Your Spirit leading me and guiding me in everything that I do. Continue to guide me to make wise choices when it comes to my diet, exercise, sleep, and stress management this year. With each step, each day, and each decision, I will rely on Your guidance and love. Thank you for Your grace and mercy.

Help me to overcome any challenges or obstacles that threaten to take me off the path, and give me the wisdom (Proverbs 3:13) to find the right tools that will keep me on course. Show me when my plans are getting in the way of Yours and lovingly bring me back to You. Thank you, that my steps are ordered by You. In Jesus' name. Amen.

January 22
Prayer for Strength

We have this hope as an anchor for the soul, firm and secure.

Hebrews 6:19 NIV

Dear Jehovah-Tsuri – my rock, you are the source of strength and wisdom (Philippians 4:13) Admittedly, I'm wavering in my belief that I can actually accomplish my goals. Please grant me the determination to keep prioritizing my health each day, even when challenges and setbacks come. As the self-doubt arises, let my hope be anchored to You.

I invite Your Holy Spirit to empower me and keep pointing me to the truth that my body is Your temple (1 Corinthians 6:19-20). In times of temptation or discouragement, I ask for Your hand to guide me back to the path I've chosen. Let Your Word be a constant source of inspiration, reminding me that I am fearfully and wonderfully made (Psalm 139:14) in Your image.

Father, today I commit my health goals to Your loving hands. With Your help, I am confident that I can do all things in Your son's name Jesus Christ, who gives me strength (Philippians 4:13). I declare that I can make meaningful changes and honor the body You've entrusted to me. Thank you for walking beside me on this journey and for being my ultimate source of strength. In Jesus' name, I pray. Amen.

January 23
Prioritizing Prayer

"As soon as I heard these words, I sat down and wept and mourned for days, and I continued fasting and praying before the God of heaven."
Nehemiah 1:4 ESV

Dear Lord, I come before You today pouring out my heart to You in prayer. Without You, I am nothing (John 15:5), and I cannot achieve anything on my own. I commit to planning, daily prayer, seeking Your guidance, and relying on You completely for my health and well-being.

Like Nehemiah, who fasted and prayed before planning his strategy, I'm seeking Your guidance and favor. I want to make prayer my first line of defense, my immediate response to cravings, temptations, laziness, and apathy.

Lord, I commit to praying Your Word over my health and seeking Your wisdom (James 1:5) and guidance daily. Help me be honest and humble in my prayers, trusting in Your unfailing love and mercy. Teach me that prayer and planning are not mutually exclusive but essential to my victory in health and life.

I pray that, whether on the mountain-top or in the valley, I will always seek You first in prayer. In Jesus' name, I pray. Amen.

January 24
Planning in Spite of Your Fears

"I was very much afraid."

Nehemiah 2:2 NIV

Dear Lord, Your Word says 'fear not,' (Isaiah 41:10) and You command me to not be anxious for anything (Philippians 4:6). I release the fear of failure, the fear of overwhelm, the fear of disappointment, and all other fears that have kept me from achieving my health goals.

I cast my cares on You because You care for me (1 Peter 5:7). Keep reminding me that You always go before me, so there is no reason to fear. As I plan, teach me to act despite my fears. I don't need to master or overcome them; I need to remember You are with me.

Thank You for being my health, strength, and shield. Thank You for always going before and behind me. As I kick off this year, teach me how to recognize when fear is stopping me from moving toward my health goals. Show me when I want to run to food instead of feeling fear, and help me understand that in those moments, it's really You that I'm craving. Remind me that the comfort and fulfillment I seek cannot be found in food or distractions, but only in Your presence and love. I choose faith instead of fear and Christ over my cravings. In Jesus' name. Amen.

January 25
Growing Through Resistance

"Dear friends, do not be surprised at the fiery ordeal that has come on you to test you, as though something strange were happening to you."

1 Peter 4:12 NIV

Lord, I thank you for giving me a realistic picture of what this health journey will be like: simple, but not easy. I am grateful for the strength and resilience that You are giving me to face any obstacles that may come my way. Help me to remember that resistance and challenges are opportunities for growth and transformation and that through Your guidance and strength, I can rise above any difficulties.

Keep reminding me that resistance and challenges will mature me (Romans 5:3-4), strengthen me, and draw me closer to You. I purpose to stay focused on my health goals, to resist the temptation to give up or give in to despair, and to remain steadfast in my commitment to this health journey. My assignment today is to pray at all times (Ephesians 6:18), be proactive, and be obedient to how Your Spirit is leading and guiding me.

May Your love and grace sustain me through every trial and challenge, and may I emerge from this journey stronger, wiser, and more faithful than ever before. In Your holy name, I pray. Amen.

January 26
Rising Above Mediocrity

"Then this Daniel was preferred above the presidents and princes, because an excellent spirit was in him; and the king thought to set him over the whole realm."
Daniel 6:3 KJV

Dear God of Excellence, I thank you that the same spirit that You gave Daniel is also in me. As I plan this year, teach me how to do it in excellence. As I take steps in faith every day, let me never take unnecessary shortcuts or look for quick fixes but let me do everything with excellence as unto You (Col. 3:23).

Teach me how to take my time and put the right systems and structures in place. You are a God of order (1 Cor. 14:33) and do not operate in chaos as I've been guilty of in the past. Father, help me to slow down and put the proper plans in place now so that I don't have to keep circling the same mountain because of my impatience and lack of diligence.

This year, I commit to rising above the level of mediocrity. I rise to excellence and know that when I operate in this spirit, I reflect Your glory and bring honor to You. I will soar with wings as eagles, I will run and not be weary, and I will walk and not faint as I surrender this journey to You (Isaiah 40:31). In Jesus' name, I pray, Amen.

January 27
Planning without Distractions

"Teach me your way, Lord, that I may rely on your faithfulness; give me an undivided heart, that I may fear your name."

Psalm 86:11 ESV

Dear Father in Heaven, I am grateful for the gift of faith and the assurance that You are with me always. Help me navigate through the daily distractions that sabotage my desire to become healthier. Grant me the strength and discipline to eliminate anything hindering my progress as I plan to live out this year in the best health possible. Binge-watching TV and social media, trivial arguments, and overthinking—I call them out by name and cast these unhealthy distractions out of my life.

Help me discern between the essential and trivial, recognizing that my time and energy are valuable resources. In moments of temptation, remind me of Your promise that I will reap a harvest if I do not give up (Galatians 6:9). Grant me an undivided heart, focused solely on Your will, so I can prioritize what truly matters.

I choose to fix my gaze upon You (Heb. 12:2), knowing that as I prioritize Your presence in my life, distractions will fall away. In the mighty name of Jesus, I pray. Amen.

January 28
Planning Protects from the Prowler

"Be sober-minded; be watchful. Your adversary the devil prowls around like a roaring lion, seeking someone to devour."

1 Peter 5:8 ESV

Dear Lord, my shield and protector, thank you for the wisdom that teaches me how to be proactive. As a sentry stands on guard, I will protect my mind (2 Corinthians 10:4).

You have provided for my safety from the wiles of the enemy (James 4:7), but I have a responsibility to put plans in place and live under the protection of those plans. Help me take Your commands seriously and stay vigilant against my adversary who is on the prowl. I have victory over him in the mighty name of Jesus.

Empowered by Your strength, I embrace the role of a planner, putting on the armor You provide (Ephesians 6:13) to engage in a victorious spiritual battle. I resist negative thoughts and doubts that attempt to rob me of the healthy lifestyle You desire for me.

Lord, as I abide under the shadow of Your protective plans, grant me discernment and courage. In moments of weakness, remind me of the victory already secured in Jesus Christ. May my actions align with Your will, and may this journey bring honor to Your name. In the mighty name of Jesus, I pray. Amen.

January 29
Planning Prevents Poor Performance

"Many are the plans in the mind of a man, but it is the purpose of the Lord that will stand."
                                        Proverbs 19:21 ESV

Thank You for the gift of this new day and the opportunities it brings. As I embark on this journey toward improved health and well-being, I recognize that my results will be directly tied to my efforts, which depend on how much I've planned and prepared. Help me, Lord, to be diligent in my efforts and to approach my goals with intention and purpose (Proverbs 21:5).

Guide me to create a realistic plan that aligns with Your will for my life (Jeremiah 29:11). Remind me that each step I take is important and that preparation is key to achieving my desired outcomes. When I feel overwhelmed, help me remember that proper planning prevents poor performance (1 Corinthians 14:40).

I make a steadfast commitment to finish this month and this year with resolute strength and to keep on planning. As I put in the work and trust in Your guidance, may I remain focused and motivated, knowing that with You, I can accomplish what I set out to do. Thank You, Lord, for Your unfailing love and the strength You provide as I strive for better health. In Jesus' name, I pray. Amen.

January 30
Progress in Motion

"For I know the plans I have for you, declares the LORD, plans to prosper you and not to harm you, plans to give you hope and a future."
Jeremiah 29:11 NIV

Dear Heavenly Father, I come before You, acknowledging that You are my Creator and Sustainer (Psalm 100:3). Thank You for the gift of this day and the opportunity to reflect on my health journey. I recognize that progress requires diligence and intention, and I ask for Your guidance as I evaluate my goals and achievements.

Help me to celebrate the small victories while also recognizing areas that need adjustment. I know that growth often comes from reassessing my path and being open to change (Isaiah 43:19). As I reflect on my progress, grant me the wisdom to discern what is working and what needs improvement.

May I not become discouraged by setbacks but instead view them as opportunities for growth. Teach me to remain steadfast and committed to my health goals, trusting in Your plan for my life. I ask for Your strength and encouragement to move forward with confidence.

Thank You, Lord, for being my source of motivation and inspiration. As I align my efforts with Your will, may I flourish in my health and well-being. In Jesus' name, I pray. Amen.

January 31
Planning for a Year of Peace and Health

"Be anxious for nothing, but in everything by prayer and supplication, with thanksgiving, let your requests be made known to God; and the peace of God, which surpasses all understanding, will guard your hearts and minds through Christ Jesus."

Philippians 4:6-7 NKJV

Dear Heavenly Father, I come before You today with a heart full of gratitude and a desire to live a life of health and peace, not just for this year but for all the days of my life. I am grateful for Your clear instructions on how to take control of my thoughts (2 Cor. 10:5) and plan my days so that I can experience Your health and peace in my spirit, soul, and body.

Lord, I acknowledge that in this health journey, I will face trials and tribulations (John 16:33), but You have made a way for me to navigate them all and have Your peace guarding my heart and mind. I thank You for the gift of Your Son, Jesus Christ, who is my Prince of Peace.

Father, I pray for Your guidance in maintaining my newfound habits of prayerful health planning. I appreciate this month as an opportunity for a supernatural rewiring of my mind. With certainty, I acknowledge that with You on my side and inside me, I possess the resources to face every challenge in health and life. In Jesus' precious name, I pray. Amen.

February

BOUNDERIES ARE BLESSINGS

This month's prayers are dedicated to exploring the importance of boundaries in your health journey. Through prayer, God can show you what boundaries you need to erect and help you maintain them. Establishing and maintaining healthy boundaries are essential for your overall health and well-being.

These prayers will also highlight how having clear boundaries can simplify the process and enhance your results. Throughout this month of reflection, you will come to understand that boundaries are not restrictions but blessings.

As you navigate your busy life, it's easy to become overwhelmed and lose sight of your boundaries. You may find yourself caught up in the demands and expectations of others, neglecting your own self-care. However, by setting clear boundaries around your health, you can reclaim your God-given power and create space for self-care and improved health, allowing God to help you establish these boundaries in your life.

Boundaries serve as protectors of your physical, mental, spiritual, and emotional health. They establish limits on what you are willing to accept and the behaviors necessary to live a healthy life. When you set and uphold these boundaries effectively, you create an atmosphere of respect, understanding, and trust within yourself.

Throughout this month of prayers, I invite you to explore the wisdom of boundaries, drawing confidence from God's Word. May these prayers guide you toward a deeper understanding of boundaries as blessings and empower you to navigate your health journey with grace, gratitude, and unwavering determination.

February 1
Holy Spirit-Inspired Boundaries

"For the kingdom of God is not a matter of eating and drinking, but of righteousness, and peace and joy in the Holy Spirit."

Romans 14:17 NIV

Heavenly Father, I bless and magnify Your holy name, giving You all glory, praise, and honor as I enter a new month. I acknowledge the crucial role of boundaries in living a healthy and fulfilling life. Grant me the wisdom to recognize and apply them wisely, especially in matters of my health.

I desire to experience the fullness of Your kingdom, understanding that boundaries are vital for achieving this. I acknowledge that I eat even when I'm full and often remain inactive when my body is craving movement. Strengthen my resolve, Father. I thank You for the gift of the Holy Spirit, who brings wisdom, peace, comfort, and righteousness (John 14:26). Guide me in putting boundaries around food and drink, honoring You with my body (1 Corinthians 10:31).

This month, I surrender my desires, fears, and weaknesses in setting health boundaries to You. Open my eyes to the ways in which boundaries protect and nurture my soul. I pray in the mighty name of Jesus, who exemplified healthy boundaries during His time on earth in everything He did. Amen.

February 2
A Simple Boundary: Love Myself

"Jesus replied: 'Love the Lord your God with all your heart and with all your soul and with all your mind.' This is the first and greatest commandment. And the second is like it: 'Love your neighbor as yourself.'"
Matthew 22:37-39 NIV

Dear God of Love (1 John 4:8), I abide in Your love, drawing close to You with all my worries and cares. I confess past struggles with health boundaries, and today, I'm thankful for the clear boundary You set: to love myself.

This command reflects the essence of Your boundless divine love, the foundation for a healthy relationship with myself, promoting well-being from the inside out. As I move forward, I seek Your wisdom to apply this boundary of love to all I do, informing my health choices with grace and compassion.

May the understanding of Your unconditional love empower me to honor my temple. In Jesus' name, who exemplified love through sacrifice, I pray for strength, resilience, and unwavering faith to abide by this simple yet profound boundary, shifting from self-loathing to caring for my body (Eph. 5:29). Let Your Word continue to be my compass, leading me to a life that pleases You (Psalm 19:14). In Jesus' name, I pray. Amen.

February 3
All for You, God

"Love the Lord your God with all your heart and with all your soul and with all your mind and with all your strength."

Mark 12:30 NIV

Dear God of all creation, I'm grateful for Your unwavering love and guidance. Create in me a pure heart and renew a steadfast spirit (Psalm 51:10) - a heart that is sold out for You and You alone.

As I purpose to erect boundaries in my health, show me how to love You with all my heart, soul, mind, and strength. Help me remove distractions that hinder my wholehearted devotion to You and fill my heart with unwavering love for You.

Teach me to love You intensely "with all my heart," sincerely "with all my soul," intuitively "with all my mind," and fiercely "with all my strength" and energy.

With Your love guiding me, I commit to self-nurturing with kindness and compassion, honoring the temple You've entrusted to me. I put feet to my words and let my actions display my love for You as I honor You with my body (1 Cor 6:20). I'm all in this year, Father—no holding back, floundering, or second-guessing whether You are worthy of it all (Rev 4:11). Thank You for enduring love. In Jesus' name, I offer this gratitude-filled prayer. In Jesus' name, I pray. Amen.

February 4
Keeping the Good In and Bad Out

"You are free to eat from any tree in the garden; but you must not eat from the tree of the knowledge of good and evil, for when you eat from it you will certainly die."

Genesis 2:16-17 NIV

Dear God of Creation, thank you for the wisdom in the boundaries You set for us in the Garden of Eden. I acknowledge that Your boundaries are designed to help me keep the good in and the bad out of my life.

In my health journey, I've realized I've had it backward, consuming unhealthy foods and neglecting the nourishment of the good ones. Father, guide me to reverse this pattern. Help me erect new health boundaries that align with Your wisdom and principles for a healthy life. Instill in me a genuine craving for nutritious foods and a disdain for those that harm my body.

Empower me to put the right boundaries in place, transforming my taste buds and inspiring creativity in my cooking. Let me be intentional about glorifying You with my food choices (1 Cor. 10:31). May I learn to savor the goodness of the foods You've provided, honoring the temple You've entrusted to me. I pray for strength, discipline, and a renewed mindset as I embark on this journey. In Jesus' name, I pray. Amen.

February 5
Boundaries and Self-Control

"A person without self-control is like a city with broken-down walls."

Proverbs 25:28 NLT

Heavenly Father, Author of life. I come before You, acknowledging my need for Your guidance. I feel a lack of control and yearn for the walls of self-control to be built around me, shielding me from temptations and distractions that hinder my well-being. Hem me in so that I can experience Your safety and protection (Psalm 139:5).

Grant me the spirit of self-control in various aspects of my life, including eating habits, exercise, sleep, and stress management. Help me align my actions with Your divine purpose, recognizing that my body is a temple of the Holy Spirit (1 Corinthians 6:19-20).

Empower me to overcome moments of temptation and persevere through challenges. Remind me constantly that You are with me, providing strength and support (Isaiah 41:10). I purposefully set boundaries to protect my health and rebuild the walls of my temple this year. May these actions bring glory to You, the Giver of life. In the name of Jesus, who exemplified discipline and self-control, I pray. Amen.

February 6
Boundaries and Integrity

"Better is a poor person who walks in his integrity than one who is crooked in speech and is a fool."
Proverbs 19:1 ESV

Dear Lord, I thank You for this day and for the gift of walking in the truth of who You created me to be. As I align my boundaries with my values, my desires, and with You, I can effortlessly maintain them because I walk in Your strength (Ephesians 6:10). Let my health boundaries look the same whether I'm by myself or with a crowd.

Guide me to live as a committed person of steadfast integrity, never betraying myself (1 Peter 2:9). As I walk in alignment with Your truth, I am empowered to be honest about both the quality and quantity of food that nourishes my body. Teach me to eat to live, not live to eat.

I am grateful that in You, I discover wholeness and completeness (Colossians 2:10). I live solely for an audience of One, seeking to please You above all else. Thank You for the immeasurable grace, love, and mercy that flow abundantly into my life. May Your name be forever praised, and may my unwavering commitment to living in alignment with my values and honoring You endure for all eternity. In Jesus' name, I pray. Amen.

February 7
Thankful for Boundaries

"Behold, You desire truth in the innermost being, And in the hidden part You will make me know wisdom."
Psalm 51:6 NASB

Dear Lord, thank you for illuminating the importance of establishing boundaries for my health and well-being. While boundaries may currently feel like barriers hindering my enjoyment of life, I recognize that they exist to bless and protect me. Your boundaries safeguard my temple from illness and harm, so I desire to change my perspective so I can see them as You do.

You, in Your intricate and wonderful creation of my body (Psalm 139:14), guide me to discern what is beneficial and what is not for this temple. Your desire is for truth in my innermost being, and in the hidden parts, You promise to reveal wisdom.

Thank you for the strength and courage You grant me to prioritize my health, even when it requires saying 'no' (Matthew. 5:37). Your discernment allows me to recognize when to rest, decline certain activities, and choose nourishing foods. I am thankful for Your guidance to consistently maintain these boundaries. May I continually seek Your truth and wisdom in every decision I make. In the name of Jesus, I pray. Amen.

February 8
Boundaries that Motivate

"In everything, I showed you [by example] that by working hard in this way you must help the weak and remember the words of the Lord Jesus, that He Himself said, 'It is more blessed [and brings greater joy] to give than to receive.'"

Acts 20:35 AMP

Father God, You are great and greatly to be praised. Today, I pray for guidance in establishing boundaries that I can maintain. Lord, grant me the wisdom (James 1:5) to strike a balance between establishing boundaries that keep me safe and healthy while also guarding me against losing my focus on you.

Let my boundaries around food prioritize nourishing my body with foods that provide energy and vitality instead of bondage and restriction. Guide me in establishing boundaries for physical activity that excite me rather than burden me. Let stewardship of my temple be a driving force to maintain my boundaries.

And may the boundaries I establish align with my values and purpose. I decree and declare that my motivation flows solely from You, my Heavenly Father. In You, I find strength to persevere and the inspiration to reach for my goals (Psalm 18:29). In the name of Jesus, who empowers me with His strength, I pray. Amen.

February 9
Boundaries and Obedience

"See, I am setting before you today a blessing and a curse—the blessing if you obey the commands of the Lord your God that I am giving you today; the curse if you disobey the commands of the Lord your God and turn from the way that I command you today by following other gods, which you have not known."
Deuteronomy 11:26-28 NIV

Dear God of Power, help me to understand that boundaries are not limitations, but rather a loving guide for my life. As I learn to establish health boundaries in my life, help me to surrender everything to You, trust You with all my heart, and lean not on my own understanding (Proverbs 3:5-6).

Forgive me for those times when I disobey You and keep me from repeating patterns that don't serve me. I thank You for Your grace that covers me as I heal from past traumas, grow in faith, and learn to trust You more. I renounce every agreement I've ever made with the spirit of rebellion in my life, and I agree right now with the spirit of obedience (1 John 5:3).

By Your Holy Spirit and not through my own willpower, I walk in Your ways and walk out the freedom I have to say 'no' to besetting sins. I resist the devil (James 4:7). I surrender my own desires and submit to Your perfect will that strengthens me. In Jesus' precious name, I pray, Amen.

February 10
Discovering Freedom in Boundaries

"The boundary lines have fallen for me in pleasant places; surely I have a delightful inheritance."
Psalm 16:6 NIV

B less you today, God of favor. I am grateful for Your kindness and love. I appreciate Your desire to establish me and show me favor (Psalm 106:4). Thank you for assuring me that the boundary lines You have established for me have fallen in pleasant places. In these pleasant places, I find not only comfort and security but also opportunities for growth and fulfillment in alignment with Your divine purpose.

Lord, I come seeking Your help. Sometimes, I view boundaries as bondage, especially when something I desire is on the other side. Please help me rethink what true freedom is and where it is found. As I meditate on Your Word, I'm reminded of Your servant David's contentment within the boundaries You set for him.

I yield to the freedom You are already working in my life (Philippians 2:13). I acknowledge that I am dead to sin (Romans 6:11) and alive to You, God. I am grateful for this reality.

May You be glorified in every aspect of my life. I surrender my desires and ambitions to Your will, recognizing that Your ways are higher and better than mine. I am free indeed (John 8:36). In Your holy and matchless name of Jesus, I pray. Amen.

February 11
Clearing the Way

"So put to death and deprive of power the evil longings of your earthly body [with its sensual, self-centered instincts] immorality, impurity, sinful passion, evil desire, and greed, which is [a kind of] idolatry [because it replaces your devotion to God]."

Colossians 3:5 AMP

Dear Faithful God, I thank you for Your powerful Word, a two-edged sword able to cut straight to the heart of the matter (Hebrews 4:12). While I don't consciously want anything to replace my devotion to You. I admit that at times, my desires lead me astray.

I acknowledge that greed, in all its forms, is a kind of idolatry, replacing my devotion to You. I confess placing food, alcohol, mindless TV watching, unrestricted social media, the scale, and even my desire for the ideal body above my love for You. I repent of this idolatry and seek Your forgiveness as I bring them to Your throne of grace. Help me erect boundaries around anything that replaces You as Lord of my life. I trust Your love, knowing You won't ask me to relinquish true blessings.

Reveal anything hindering my intimate relationship with You. Search me, know my hidden parts (Psalm 139:23), and shine Your light on them, breaking their power. May my devotion be unwavering. In Jesus' mighty name, I pray. Amen.

February 12
Mastered Only By You

"I have the right to do anything," you say—but not everything is beneficial. "I have the right to do anything"—but I will not be mastered by anything."
1 Corinthians 6:12 NIV

Dear Master, thank you for providing everything I need to live a Godly life (2 Peter 1:3). I submit to You. Help me prioritize what is beneficial and healthy for my body over everything else.

Father, I confess to yielding to desires that override my better judgment (Philippians 3:3) such as over-indulging in unhealthy habits disregarding their impact on my well-being. Today, I surrender these tendencies to You. Grant me the spirit of self-control. I declare that I make wise choices (2 Timothy 1:7). I will not be mastered by anything but You. Let that boundary guide my daily actions.

Thank You that I don't need to muster up strength or willpower, but rely on Your Holy Spirit, allowing the fruit of self-control to manifest. As I navigate choices, help me discern what honors You, recognizing nourishing foods and life-giving choices like adequate rest and physical activity.

With Your help, I can overcome any obstacle and live a life that glorifies You. Thank You for Your guidance my Lord, Master, and Saviour. In Jesus' name, I pray. Amen.

February 13
Giving God the Glory

"So, whether you eat or drink, or whatever you do, do all to the glory of God."

1 Corinthians 10:31 ESV

Dear Lord, I thank you for creating me so wonderfully complex, I'm in awe of Your perfect design (Psalm 139:14). You created me to worship You. Giving You glory transforms even my mundane tasks into sacred moments of worship and peace. Reframing eating and movement as opportunities to glorify You changes everything. Thank You for this new perspective, a simple boundary guiding me daily and bringing purpose to my life.

Forgive me for the subtle ways I seek approval from others or in things to make myself look or feel good instead of glorifying You. May I always carry the understanding that You care about every detail of my life, no matter how small (Psalm 139:16).

In all I do, including honoring my temple, You remain my foremost priority. I declare that my actions and intentions shine a light on Your glory, even this consecrated time with You right now. Let this awareness guide me, aligning every choice with the purpose of glorifying Your name. In the glorious name of Jesus. Amen.

February 14
Boundaries That Protect My Goals

"I press toward the mark for the prize of the high calling of God in Christ Jesus."

Philippians 3:14 KJV

Heavenly Father, I come before You with gratitude for the goals You've placed on my heart. I recognize that achieving these goals requires consistent habits, and these habits are safeguarded by the boundaries You've set for me. Your wisdom guides me in understanding that the path to success is paved with disciplined routines.

Grant me the strength to adhere to the habits that align with these goals, and may these habits become a testament to Your faithfulness and guidance in my life. Let me cling to Your word every day as my food (Jeremiah 15:16) I am encouraged to press on towards the goal for the prize of the upward call of God in Christ Jesus, as I recognize the spiritual significance of this health journey (Philippians 3:14).

Lord, I anchor my goals in Your divine purpose, seeking to honor You through the habits and boundaries I establish. May my pursuit of these goals be a testimony to Your grace and the transforming power of consistent habits guarded by Your loving boundaries. In Jesus' name, I pray. Amen.

February 15
Demolishing Mental Strongholds

"For the weapons of our warfare are not of the flesh but have divine power to destroy strongholds."
2 Corinthians 10:4 ESV

Dear God of Power and Might, I thank You for the divine power You have given me to demolish strongholds (Luke 10:19). You are always fighting for me. When I'm frustrated or stuck in a rut of "stinkin' thinkin'", help me remember that You have given me the authority to use Your all-powerful arsenal to be victorious!

Help me Lord to not sit back passively, fearfully fretting that I will get taken out or be overpowered. Remind me that boundaries keep me safe and protected. Greater is the one on the inside of me (1 John 4:4)! Today, I use my authority in Christ to push back against the darkness (Isaiah 59:19) and tear down strongholds.

I erect firm boundaries around my thoughts and will not give the enemy access to my mind. Negativity, all-or-nothing thinking, victim mindset – all mental strongholds are broken! In Jesus, I have the power to think new thoughts, to take every thought captive and make it obedient to Christ (2 Corinthians 10:5). I decree that I am healthy. I declare that my body is strong. I have the power to make healthy choices! In the name of Jesus, Amen.

February 16
Practice Over Perfection

"Whatever you have learned or received or heard from me, or seen in me—put it into practice. And the God of peace will be with you."

Philippians 4:9 NIV

Dear God of Peace, Your peace keeps me from trying to figure everything out in my own strength. Your peace keeps me showing up each day with a spirit of curiosity and openness. Grant me the wisdom to apply the lessons I've received from Your Word and observed in others.

I seek Your grace to understand the power of practice. My flesh keeps telling me that I have to do it perfectly but striving to be the best keeps getting in the way of Your best for me. Remind me that Your power is made perfect in my weakness (2 Corinthians 12:9).

I acknowledge that I am a work in progress and embrace the journey of continual growth. Release me from the pressure of perfection, and instead, let me find joy in progress. Every effort contributes to my development. Grant me the grace to focus on practice rather than perfection, rejoicing in each step forward.

Guide me to release the pressures of striving for flawlessness and instead focus on progress. May I find joy in the small victories, knowing that every effort counts and contributes to my personal development. I pray all this in Jesus' name, Amen.

February 17
Catching Foxes

"Catch for us the foxes, the little foxes that ruin the vineyards, our vineyards that are in bloom."
                                    Song of Solomon 2:15 NIV

Dear Loving God. You care about every single detail of my life, even the little things I often overlook. Today, help me master the mundane and be vigilant in recognizing and addressing the small distractions, temptations, and compromises that can slowly erode my boundaries.

I acknowledge that it is often the seemingly insignificant choices and actions that add up over time and eventually wear me down. Give me Your wisdom to discern the little foxes that may try to infiltrate my daily walk with You and sabotage my goals, habits, and boundaries. Help me to guard my heart above all else, for it is the wellspring of life (Proverbs 4:23).

I will store up Your Word in my heart so that I will stay on Your path and avoid sinning (Psalm 119:11). When my faith is failing, remind me that Your strength is made perfect in my weakness. In Your strength, I will faithfully guard my vineyard, tending to it with diligence so that it may bloom and bear fruit for Your glory. In Jesus' precious name, I pray. Amen.

February 18
Guided by Grace

"—continue to work out your salvation with fear and trembling, for it is God who works in you to will and to act in order to fulfill his good purpose."
Philippians 2:12-13 NIV

Dear Mighty God, I thank You for the stirring within me to diligently pursue growth. I am grateful that Your grace guides me on this health journey, encompassing not only my spiritual but also my physical and emotional well-being. Grant me the wisdom and strength to navigate this path with reverence and determination.

Father, I recognize that true transformation stems from Your divine intervention. Empower me to align my desires with Your will and to take action in accordance with Your purpose (Romans 12:2). I surrender my aspirations to You, trusting that Your guidance will lead me toward fulfillment.

As I embark on this journey, I seek Your constant presence and guidance. Strengthen my resolve to persevere, even in the face of challenges and setbacks. Remind me that You are with me always, guiding my steps and ensuring that my efforts bear fruit (Psalm 37:23). May my commitment to maintaining healthy boundaries reflect Your goodness and faithfulness in my life. Thank You for Your unwavering love and strength. In Jesus' name, Amen.

February 19
Living One Day at a Time

"Therefore do not be anxious about tomorrow, for tomorrow will be anxious for itself. Sufficient for the day is its own trouble."

Matthew 6:34 ESV

Dear Lord, Jehovah Jireh, I bow before You, humbled by the depth of Your provision and grateful for Your constant presence in my life. Thank You for guiding me to live day by day, step by step trusting in Your perfect timing. When I get anxious, I feel Your gentle guidance, reassuring me that I need not carry the burden alone. You remind me of the futility of over-worrying, over-thinking, and over-planning and tell me to not be anxious for anything (Philippians 4:6-7).

With each sunrise, may I awaken with a renewed commitment to living within my health boundaries. Through the highs and lows, may Your grace be my anchor, reminding me that in every moment, I have the opportunity to choose health and practice self-care.

Heavenly Father, forgive me for my moments of doubt and self-reliance. Just as You care for the birds in the air, You will also care for me (Matthew 6:25-26). Let my daily steps be guided by Your wisdom, my spirit be lifted by Your grace, and my heart be filled with gratitude for the chance to honor You through the daily choices I make. In Jesus' name, Amen.

February 20
The Boundary of Rest

"The LORD is my shepherd, I lack nothing. He makes me lie down in green pastures, he leads me beside quiet waters."

Psalm 23:1-2 NIV

Dear God of Comfort. You are the Father of mercies and God of all comfort (2 Corinthians 1:3-4). In the midst of the busyness, daily pressure, and demands, You invite me to rest in You.

Father, in this fast-paced world, I recognize the necessity of rest for my physical, mental, and spiritual well-being. Grant me the wisdom to prioritize rest, finding moments of stillness for rejuvenation and peace.

Help me resist constant busyness and seek serenity in Your love. The more rested I am, the stronger I will be to stay within the healthy boundaries You have set for me. Thank You for this insight and wisdom.

Lord, I pray for the discipline to establish healthy rhythms of rest in my life. Help me to surrender my anxieties, worries (1 Peter 5:7), and striving into Your capable hands, knowing that You are the one who sustains me. May I find rest and rejuvenation in Your presence, for it is in resting in You that I am truly refreshed (Matthew 11:28). In Jesus' name, I pray. Amen.

February 21
Heart Protection

"Above all else, guard your heart, for everything you do flows from it."

Proverbs 4:23 NIV

Dear Lord, my protector, I'm desperate for Your guidance. You cover me with Your feathers (Psalm 91:4); constantly infusing me with Your wisdom to keep me safe and secure. I am grateful for Your steadfast love and care.

Help me remain firm in the boundary You've set for me—to guard my heart above all else. Grant me discernment to recognize harmful thoughts, attitudes, and behaviors that threaten my well-being. Strengthen me with Your Holy Spirit, empowering me to resist negativity or toxicity seeking to infiltrate my heart.

I now understand that true change begins in my heart. Open the eyes of my heart, Lord, so I may see Your truth (Ephesians 1:18). From my heart flows love, dreams, passions, and desires—it is the gateway to my being. By protecting it, I align with Your will, understanding that without Your guidance, maintaining boundaries is futile (James 1:14).

May Your Word illuminate my path as I guard my heart and maintain healthy boundaries. Thank You for Your unwavering faithfulness and for always providing the strength and wisdom I need. In Jesus' name, I pray. Amen.

February 22
"No" is a Complete Sentence

"But let your statement be, 'Yes, yes ' or 'No, no';
anything beyond these is of evil."
Matthew 5:37 NASB

D ear Daddy, thank you for this day (Psalm 118:24). You never change. You are consistent and resolute and I'm so grateful for the clarity of Your Word and nature. You are not a God of confusion (1 Corinthians 14:33), but of peace.

You know me, Lord, my yes sometimes means "no", and vice versa. I want to stand firm in my convictions, trusting in Your power and goodness. I decree today to establish firm boundaries in my words. 'No' must be a complete sentence without wavering, rationalizing, justifying or back-pedaling. Teach me confidence and integrity in what I say. Deliver me from double-mindedness (James 1:8).

I surrender doubts or guilt from asserting boundaries. Fill me with knowledge that saying "no" is an act of love and self-preservation. Guide me on the path of authenticity, grant me peace living in alignment with my truest self. I feel peaceful ease aligning with Your will and your best for me. Thank You for a sound mind and help me stay focused on You. I declare today that I have the mind of Christ! In His name, I pray. Amen.

February 23
Boundaries and Feelings

"For whenever our heart condemns us, God is greater than our heart, and he knows everything."
1 John 3:20 ESV

Dear Lord, thank you for reminding me that my feelings do not get to vote on whether I should honor my daily boundaries. You are so much greater than my feelings! Too often, I have allowed feelings of shame and guilt to weigh me down and dictate my actions, neglecting the boundaries You have set for me. I repent for making my feelings my Lord and allowing them to rule over me in the place that belongs to You as my only authority. I take dominion over my feelings today in the mighty name of Jesus (Genesis 1:26).

Today, I choose to trust in Your unconditional love and Your sovereignty over my life. Help me to rely on You rather than my fluctuating emotions. When feelings of anxiety or uncertainty arise, grant me the wisdom to bring them to You in prayer with thanksgiving (Philippians 4:6-7).

Give me the patience to pause before acting on my feelings, allowing them to be acknowledged without controlling me. Instead of using food to bury my feelings, I commit to trusting You with my emotions, experiencing the freedom, peace, and joy that Your compassion brings. You are truly awesome! In Jesus' name, I pray. Amen!

February 24
Boundaries and Self-Esteem

"... for you were bought with a price. So glorify God in your body."

1 Corinthians 6:30 ESV

Heavenly Father, I praise You for making me Your beloved child, bought with the precious blood of Jesus. In a world where I often feel devalued, I find comfort in knowing my worth is defined by Your unconditional love. Your Word declares that I am fearfully and wonderfully made (Psalm 139:14), and my worth is high (Proverbs 3:15). Yet, I struggle with low self-esteem, seeing myself as less than.

Help me build boundaries grounded in Your view of me, not the world's. Guide me to release self-deprecating thoughts and embrace my identity in Christ. Teach me to prioritize self-care as an act of worship, understanding it equips me to love myself from a healthy perspective.

As I honor my boundaries, may I grow in integrity and self-esteem, seeing myself through Your eyes. Enable me to glorify You in my body by valuing myself as You do. I surrender my insecurities, doubts, and negative self-talk, trusting Your guidance. Thank You for shaping me into who You've called me to be. In Jesus' name, Amen.

February 25
Boundaries and My Speech

"The tongue has the power of life and death, and those who love it will eat its fruit."

Proverbs 18:21 NIV

L ord God Almighty, I stand in awe of Your presence, recognizing Your power to shape my speech. As Your creation, formed in Your image (Genesis 1:27), I honor You today. I surrender my speech to You, as I see its direct impact on my health boundaries. Embolden me to speak to my mountains and have them move (Matt.11:24)

As I align myself with Your will and embrace the truth of who You say I am, I recognize that when I speak negatively about myself (Ephesians 4:29), I am, in fact, speaking against Your creation. Set a guard over my mouth, Lord; keep watch over the door of my lips. (Psalm 141:3). Today, I repent of this harmful practice, whether done knowingly or unknowingly. I thank You, gracious God, for Your abundant forgiveness and for empowering me to speak life through You.

In the name of Jesus, the source of all grace and mercy, may my words be a reflection of Your love and truth. I surrender my speech to You and I pray that You will continue to mold me into a vessel that speaks words that bring life and honor to You. In Jesus' name, I pray. Amen.

February 26
Boundaries and Time

"For where your treasure is, there your heart will be also."

Matthew 6:21 ESV

Dear Heavenly Father, I approach Your throne with gratitude for the gift of time. I ask You for the wisdom to put boundaries around how I invest it.

I find myself often rushing around like a busy bee, fearful that I don't have enough time or conversely, wasting it by procrastinating in taking action on what You've called me to do. Your Word assures me that I need not be consumed by worry or anxiety (Philippians 4:6). My time is in Your hands (Psalm 31:15) so when I seek You with my whole heart, You will help me to make the most of my time.

Release me from the fear that hinders me from prioritizing my own well-being. Help to get over the feeling that I'm wasting time or that I'm not worth the time investment when it comes to self-care. Grant me the understanding that in order to fulfill Your work in this life, I must be healthy in body, soul, and spirit. I surrender my time to You and commit to using it wisely, in accordance with Your divine plan. Let my time management be a testament to Your glory. In the precious name of Jesus, I pray. Amen.

February 27
Boundaries and Relationships

"A hot-tempered person must pay the penalty; rescue them, and you will have to do it again."
                                        Proverbs 19:19 NIV

Dear Precious Lord, I am grateful for the tender heart You have given me (Matthew 7:11). Yet, I confess that I've allowed this gift to overshadow my own boundaries and jeopardize my health. Today, I seek Your guidance in untangling myself from consuming relationships and situations.

I accept responsibility for my life (Galatians 6:5) and understand that it is not my duty to fix, rescue, or save anyone. I release the spirit of codependency. Grant me the courage to establish healthy boundaries, respecting both my needs and theirs. Help me to love others as You do – unconditionally and wholeheartedly. In Your strength, I am committed to reestablishing these boundaries, allowing me to accept myself and others, trusting in Your restoration (1 John 4:19).

In Your holy name, I pray for strength and wisdom to uphold these boundaries so that I can prioritize my physical, mental, and emotional health while honoring You in my relationships. In Jesus' name, I pray. Amen.

February 28
Establishing New Boundaries

"Therefore, if anyone is in Christ, he is a new creation.
The old has passed away; behold, the new has come."
2 Corinthians 5:17 ESV

Dear God of Creation, You make all things new (Isaiah 43:19). Thank You, Lord, that the new has come! Thank You for this glorious new life, the new heart and regenerated spirit in me that will live on forever with You, no matter what! In the past, I struggled in my own strength to try to maintain boundaries and I failed every time. These new boundaries You've given me the grace to maintain are grounded in Your new covenant so they bring me peace, freedom, and joy. They are for my good and Your glory.

As I live as a new creation in You, I hear You softly whisper to me, "I have loved You all along, with an everlasting love (Jeremiah 31:3), at every age and every stage, I have loved the same. Fully. Totally. Completely. I welcome all of You."

As I walk in my bold boundaries, they are not burdensome (1 John 5:3). I am so excited to enjoy this new life together with You as You help me honor my health boundaries. I decree that I am healthy and whole in my new life in Christ, in His holy name. Amen.

February 29
The Wisdom of Boundaries

"Whoever trusts in his own mind is a fool, but he who walks in wisdom will be delivered."
Proverbs 28:26 ESV

Lord, I love Your Word! I love that You've written a road map for me to follow. Your entire Word is a beautiful boundary that I happily commit to living within. You've given me Your word for wisdom, guidance, correction, for instruction in righteousness (2 Timothy 3:16). Like Solomon, I ask You today for wisdom (1 Kings 3:9). Even when Your ways don't seem to make sense to my mind, please help me to lean not on my own understanding and instead, acknowledge You and trust You to make my paths straight (Proverbs 3:5-6).

Continue to bless me with the discernment to recognize when my boundaries are being crossed or violated. Grant me the wisdom to address these situations with grace and firmness for and within myself, allowing for the right balance of both. Guide me to approach these moments with empathy and love, always learning from the blessings in the lessons.

As this month ends, I thank You for helping me to understand how to live within the boundaries that You have set for my health. You have given me a new perspective. Thank You for the wisdom of boundaries, they truly are blessings. In Jesus' name, I pray. Amen.

March

HEALTHY EATING

In a world filled with countless dietary fads, conflicting nutritional advice, and an ever-growing obsession with physical appearance, it is easy to lose sight of the true purpose of nourishment. While the pursuit of a healthy lifestyle is certainly commendable, you may often neglect the spiritual aspect of your relationship with food.

Food is a gift from God, our Father, designed not only to nourish your body but also to be a source of pleasure and joy. However, the stress and pressures of modern life may have led you to develop unhealthy habits and dependencies when it comes to eating. You might seek comfort and even temporary fulfillment in the very sustenance that was intended to sustain you physically and spiritually.

This month, you will seek to cultivate a deeper understanding of your own cravings, recognizing that the yearnings of your soul often extend far beyond food. Through prayer, reflection, and seeking God's guidance, you aim to uncover the true source of your hunger and the depths of your spiritual appetite.

In moments when you feel the pangs of soul cravings, pray to our God who is the source of all satisfaction and fulfillment.

Be blessed with wisdom, strength, and perseverance as you embark on this path toward healthy eating God's way.

March 1
Soul Cravings

"Search me, God, and know my heart; ... See if there is any offensive way in me, and lead me in the way everlasting."

Psalm 139:23-24 NIV

Lord, today I acknowledge You as my comforter and sustainer, satisfying and nourishing my soul, spirit, and body (Psalm 103:5). As I prioritize nourishing my body through eating healthy foods, I invite You to search my heart and reveal what eludes my natural sight (Ephesians 1:18). I have blind spots when it comes to eating healthy so I need Your help.

As You search my heart, root out any offenses within me and unveil the soulish cravings that often lead me astray and tempt me to turn to unhealthy foods instead of seeking You. My heart often deceives me (Jer. 17:9), convincing me that I'm hungry when I'm not.

Lord, I want to hunger for You alone. Teach me to listen to natural hunger cues instead of being led by my emotions.

With You, there is no failure or judgment; there is only love. Shine Your light upon me today, I want to see Your truth. I trust in Your love and safety as I exchange my soul cravings for satisfaction and fulfillment found in You alone. In Jesus's compassionate name, I pray. Amen.

March 2
Heavenly Treasures Over Temporal Pleasures

"Looking at him, Jesus showed love to him and said to him, 'One thing you lack: go and sell all you possess and give to the poor, and you will have treasure in heaven; and come, follow Me.'"

Mark 10:21-22 NASB

Dear Faithful God, You call me to be holy as You are holy (1 Peter 1:16). Thank You for loving me even when my thoughts focus more on my possessions than on Your promises. For me, these possessions are often food. But amidst the temptations, Your grace and mercy always offer me a way out (1 Cor. 10:31). Your divine guidance leads me on a path of righteousness (Proverbs 8:20).

You continuously reveal to me a better way, aligning with Your perfect will. I humbly open my heart to You, allowing Your loving gaze to expose wounds and unhealed emotions that have me choose food over You.

As I wholeheartedly follow You, I find renewed focus, strength, clarity, and peace in my food choices. Forgive me for choosing temporary satisfaction over the enduring fulfillment of a deep relationship with You. I am grateful for Your boundless grace, which forgives and cleanses me (1 John 1:9). Continue to open my heart and grant me understanding of Your ways. Holy Spirit, guide me. In the name of Jesus, I pray, Amen.

March 3
I Am Satisfied

"For he satisfies the thirsty and fills the hungry with good things."

Psalm 107:9 NLT

My good, good Father God (Psalm 103:13), Your goodness surely is running after me (Psalm 23:6). Quench my physical appetites spiritually as You satisfy my thirsty soul and fill my hungry heart with Your goodness! I confess that I have turned to food as a means to fill a void within me when in reality, You are the only one who can truly satisfy my soul.

In moments of weakness and temptation, remind me that You are always near, ready to strengthen and guide me. True satisfaction is found in Your presence, in the depths of Your love and grace.

I surrender my desire for satisfaction in food and place it at Your feet. Grant me the strength and discipline to seek You above all else, knowing that in You, I will find true and lasting fulfillment. Thank You for filling me completely with joy and peace (Romans 15:13). I trust You to meet all of my needs—emotionally, physically, and spiritually. You give me just what I need when I need it so that I am satisfied. In the precious and Holy name of Jesus, I pray. Amen.

March 4
In Step with the Spirit

"So I say, walk by the Spirit, and you will not gratify the desires of the flesh."

Galatians 5:16 NIV

Heavenly Father, I thank You for Your promises. You say that if I walk by the Spirit, that I will not gratify the desires of the flesh. That is my prayer today, Lord. The struggle is real. I'm so tired of my flesh constantly leading me astray (James 1:14) and interrupting my day with its assaults and demands.

That's why I'm so grateful for Your solution. You are such a practical God. You created me as a spirit, with a soul that thinks and feels, and You've encased me in this earth suit called my body. Then You sent Your son to model how it is possible to live as a tripartite being. And just as He had to die, teach me how to die to my flesh daily so that I live in You. As Your spirit quickens my soul (Romans 8:11), like Jesus, I do not have to waste time gratifying every whim and desire that attempts to lead me away– there is a better way.

I have victory today over every temptation as I yield my mind, will, and emotions to walk by the Spirit. In Jesus' name, I pray today. Amen!

March 5
Uncommon Health

"Enter by the narrow gate. For the gate is wide and the way is easy that leads to destruction, and those who enter by it are many. For the gate is narrow and the way is hard that leads to life, and those who find it are few."

Matthew 7:13-14 ESV

Lord, today I thank You for Your leadership. You lead me beside still waters and (Psalm 23:2)always provide a way of escape when I feel trapped (1 Corinthians 10:13). When I feel tempted to veer off the path of healthy eating, You remind me of its consequences.

I desire for healthy eating to be my norm. I declare that I am part of the few who have found the narrow gate – living each day feeling energized, vibrant, and full of Your spirit. Help me resist simple, quick fixes and pacifying myself with food, and remind me of the everlasting satisfaction found in Your presence. So I honor You today. I worship You and give You glory and praise. I thank You that through Your strength I have the power to go against the grain of society and make healthy choices.

In You, I choose the narrow gate. I choose life over death and blessings over curses (Deuteronomy 30:19). In You, I choose nutritious and wholesome foods and eat when my body needs nourishment. I am healthy and whole. In Jesus' name, I pray. Amen.

March 6
Feel It to Heal It

"Be angry and do not sin; do not let the sun go down on your anger, and give no opportunity to the devil."
Ephesians 4:26–27 ESV

Dear Omnipotent Lord, I bless You today. I magnify Your name. I give You all praise, glory, and honor. I thank You that You are so much greater than my feelings. In Your great love, You gave them to me to serve me.

You have granted me the gift of self-awareness so I can pay attention to my feelings and use them as a guide to how I am to respond to situations. Teach me how to have greater self-control and emotional maturity so I can use my feelings responsibly. You created me in Your image and likeness, granting me the power to exercise dominion over all things (Genesis 1:26) including my feelings.

I invite Your help here, Holy Spirit. I pray for a healthy relationship with my feelings, that I acknowledge their existence but do not permit them to rule me. Teach me to feel my feelings instead of feeding them with food. I know that when I feel them, You can heal them if they are too much for me to bear. I come to You trusting that You will minister to any inappropriate feelings today. I surrender my range of feelings to You. In Jesus's name. Amen.

March 7
Ending My Excuses

"But they all alike began to make excuses. The first said to him, 'I have bought a field, and I must go out and see it. Please have me excused.' And another said, 'I have bought five yoke of oxen, and I go to examine them. Please have me excused.' And another said, 'I have married a wife, and therefore I cannot come.'"

Luke 14:18-20 ESV

Dear God of Grace and Compassion. I come before You today with a humble heart, acknowledging that You are a God who sees through all of my excuses. You know the inner workings of my mind and know why I make excuses. In spite of myself, You never leave me or forsake me (Heb 13:5). In Your strength, I can overcome any obstacle (Psalm 18:29).

I confess that my excuses have hindered my ability to have a genuine and intimate relationship with both You and myself. I long to be transparent and honest, laying aside the masks of excuses that I have worn for far too long. Today, I surrender my pride and ego, and I choose to face the truth. I let go of my excuses that keep me from making healthy food choices.

I commit to taking full responsibility for my thoughts and actions that drive unhealthy patterns. I will no longer hide behind excuses or shift the blame onto external situations. Instead, I will take ownership of all my choices. In Jesus' name, I pray. Amen.

March 8
Exposing Laziness

"The soul of a lazy man desires, and has nothing; But the soul of the diligent shall be made rich."
Proverbs 13:4 NKJV

Dear God of Grace, You are full of mercy and compassion. You look past my weaknesses and offer me strength to overcome them. Today, I confront the spirit of laziness that tempts me to choose quick, unhealthy options over diligence and effort in my eating habits. I know from experience that what was quick and easy always had negative consequences. I acknowledge that laziness leads to empty desires and commit to walking in the Spirit (Galatians 5:16), seeking Your guidance in the food choices I make.

Grant me the courage to confront the root of my laziness and remove it from my life. Help me to cultivate habits of diligence and excellence in my approach to healthy eating. Thank You for Your enduring love (Jer. 31:3)and mercy, which empowers me to make positive changes.

May my actions reflect Your goodness, and may I honor You in all aspects of my life, including what I eat. I decree that I am diligent and enjoy the rich rewards of eating healthy wholesome foods. In Jesus' name, I pray. Amen.

March 9
Foods That Heal, Foods That Harm

"Every moving thing that lives shall be food for you. And as I gave you the green plants, I give you every-thing."

Genesis 9:3 ESV

Heavenly Father, I worship and praise Your holy name, grateful for the gift of nourishment that You generously provide. Thank You for guiding me to foods that heal my body and support my well-being. I rejoice in the abundance and diversity of wholesome, colorful nutritious foods You have given me. Teach me what foods to eat and which ones to avoid (Proverbs 25:16). Grant me the discipline to follow this guidance and honor my body as Your temple.

As I approach You, Jehova Raffa (Exodus 15:26), my Great Healer, I pray You will bring healing to my troubled digestive tract and help me to develop a healthy relationship with food. Let me crave healing foods only.

By the authority of Jesus's name, I proclaim my body healed, for You are the ultimate source of restoration and wellness. I surrender the allure of unhealthy choices and embrace Your grace, which sets me free from temporary gratification. Fill me with Your unfailing love (Psalm 33:22) and satisfaction, illuminating each day with joy. In Jesus' name, I pray. Amen.

March 10
Fasting for Optimal Health

"Is not this the fast that I choose: to loose the bonds of wickedness, to undo the straps of the yoke, to let the oppressed go free, and to break every yoke?"
Isaiah 58:6 ESV

Dear Lord, God of wisdom and strength, I thank You that You have provided me with both spiritual weapons (Ephesians 6:12a), as well as, practical strategies to help me walk in the freedom that You died for me to have (Rom 8:3). Lord, I confess that although I understand the countless benefits of fasting, my flesh fights against it.

Today, I seek Your divine wisdom. I ask that You reveal to me what I need to lay down as I make more room within my heart to feast on Your Word instead of physical food. Help me to surrender those things that hinder my spiritual growth and draw me closer to You through fasting. I desire to decrease so that You may increase (John 3:30).

Remind me that You are with me every step of the way, providing strength and sustenance that surpasses any physical food. May Your presence fill every empty space within me as I immerse myself in Your Word and seek a deeper connection with You. In the precious name of Jesus, I pray. Amen.

March 11
Taking Responsibility

"... I have no one to help me into the pool when the water is stirred. While I am trying to get in, someone else goes down ahead of me."

John 5:7 NIV

Dear Lord, I thank You, You are a God who hears me and knows my weaknesses and challenges. You don't leave me alone in my struggles but You are always with me stretching Your loving arms towards me for me to grab hold of.

Thank You for giving me the strength to take responsibility for my actions instead of making excuses, blaming others, or procrastinating, which have all kept me feeling powerless and stuck. Let me hear and obey Your voice as You call me to follow You. Let me walk in Your spirit so I will not give rise to my flesh (Gal 5:16) that is always trying to seduce me into complacency.

I will rise up. I declare that I will take responsibility for everything I eat. Today, like the man at the pool, I pick up my mat and walk into the bright future (Proverbs 23:18) that You have for me.

May my body become a temple of health, vitality, and joy, reflecting Your love and grace. In the Holy Name of Jesus, I pray. Amen!

March 12
Jesus Over Junk Food

"But put on the Lord Jesus Christ, and make no provision for the flesh, to gratify its desires."
Romans 13:14 ESV

Lord, I humbly and gratefully approach Your throne of grace, acknowledging Your infinite power and boundless love. I pray for a fresh revelation of my new nature (Ephesians 4:22) to come alive in me now, Jesus. My flesh cries out for foods that do not serve my body. Processed foods with empty calories seem to call to me but let Your voice be louder inside me.

Like a warm comforting sweater, I put on the Lord Jesus Christ. It's in this covering that I can resist the enemy (James 4:7) when he tries to have me focus on gratifying my desires rather than glorifying You, Father. Whether it's junk food, laziness, or procrastination, I choose Jesus over everything.

Thank You in advance for always providing a way of escape (1 Corinthians 10:13) when junk food calls out to me. You are my refuge, my source of strength, and my ever-present help in time of need. I rely on Your grace to carry me through trials and temptations, knowing that Your love will guide me to victory. In the precious and holy name of Jesus, I pray. Amen

March 13
A Peaceful Health Journey

"The mind governed by the flesh is death, but the mind governed by the Spirit is life and peace."
                                             Romans 8:6 NIV

Heavenly Father, Jehovah Shalom, I humbly come before You, recognizing the power of Your Spirit to bring life and peace to my health journey (Romans 8:6) I am grateful for the victory I have through the blood of Jesus Christ, freeing me from the bondage of unhealthy eating habits and fears associated with my health (Galatians 4:7).

Guide my thoughts, Lord, so that they are centered on You, leading to peace in my food choices (Isaiah 26:3). Help me to see that all my life and existence is in You (Acts 17:28), reminding me that true peace is found in Your presence, not in food.

I praise You, Jesus, for Your unwavering love and faithfulness, which empower me to overcome any challenges on my health journey. With Your grace, I am strengthened to make wise choices and embrace transformation.

Thank You, Lord, for hearing my prayer. I trust that as I continue to seek You and walk in Your ways, my health journey will be marked by peace, joy, and lasting transformation. In Jesus' name. Amen.

March 14
Planning Healthy Meals

"Careful planning puts you ahead in the long run;
hurry and scurry puts you further behind."
Proverbs 21:5 MSG

Dear Lord, I thank You for this day that You have made and I will rejoice and be glad in it (Psalm 118:24). Today I choose planning what to eat over pressure and rest in You over rushing. It has been said that if I fail to plan, then I am planning to fail, and Your word confirms it. I pray for Your guidance in finding new and exciting recipes that will keep me motivated and excited about healthy eating.

Inspire me to explore a variety of flavors and cuisines, so that I can maintain my interest in meal prep. May I find joy in the process of planning as I honor the gift of nourishment that You have given me.

Show me what I will need to let go of in order to make it a priority. Help me to remember that my efforts are not in vain, for You have called me to be a good steward of my body (1 Cor. 6:19). Remind me that as I plan my meals, I am not merely making choices about food but also about honoring and glorifying You. In the loving and mighty name of Jesus, I pray. Amen.

March 15
Victory Over Temptation

"No temptation has overtaken you that is not common to man. God is faithful, and he will not let you be tempted beyond your ability, but with the temptation, he will also provide the way of escape, that you may be able to endure it."

1 Corinthians 10:13 ESV

Hallelujah, Jehovah Jireh, thank You for Your promises! You are always providing for me even when I feel trapped. There is no food so tasty or more irresistible than my desire for You.

I am no match for the powerful diet industry that has hijacked my tastebuds in the name of profit, but You are. Intervene on my behalf, Lord. I know this battle can only be fought on my knees. You know my humanness and in Your great love for me, You have promised to always deliver me.

The thief comes only to steal and kill and destroy(John 10:10), but I refuse to give in to his tactics and temptations. I rebuke all forms of pride that come in and try to tell me that I can handle "just one bite" or "I can do this on my own." Instead, I recognize and submit my weakness to You, grab Your hand, and head for the escape route. Thank You that You always lead me to victory (1 Corinthians 15:57) freedom, and safety. In Jesus' name alone, I pray. Amen!

March 16
Making Wise Food Choices

"Wisdom is the principal thing; therefore get wisdom."
Proverbs 4:7 NKJV

Father God, You are a God of order (1 Corinthians 14:40) and not chaos, of honesty and not deception. Thank You for teaching me how to live wisely and well in Your kingdom. Thank You for giving me the wisdom to know what foods heal my body and what foods will harm it. Help me to choose life over death and blessings over curses every day (Deuteronomy 30:19).

I understand that there are certain realities I must accept if I want to continue on this road. Help me to get real and honest about my food choices, my appetites and my will that wants what it wants when it wants it. Help me to accept that I can not eat unhealthy foods whenever I want. I know that as I realign with Your best for me, then I will learn to make wise choices but until then, I need Your intervention, Lord.

Help me to walk in honesty and integrity with the guidance of the Holy Spirit. I glorify You in my healthy living. In Jesus' name. Amen.

March 17
Honoring My Temple

"I praise you because I am fearfully and wonderfully made; your works are wonderful, I know that full well."

Psalms 139:14 NIV

Dear Lord, Divine Creator, I praise You for creating me fearfully and wonderfully, in Your image (Genesis 1:27). What a privilege and an honor to know that I have been fashioned after You, my God. It also comes with a great responsibility. You have gifted me with this magnificent vessel, a dwelling for Your spirit and the vehicle through which I experience life's wonders such as delicious and nutritious foods.

Grant me the understanding to make food choices that honor this sacred temple. Help me recognize that my body is not just a receptacle to gorge with my indulgences, but a vessel deserving of respect and care. Guide me towards the foods that nourish me —those that energize, heal, and strengthen.

I surrender my desire for instant gratification, knowing that true fulfillment comes from treating my body as a sacred vessel (1 Corinthians 3:16-17). Help me cultivate a balanced relationship with food, where nourishment is both physical and spiritual. With gratitude, I pray in the mighty name of Jesus. Amen.

March 18
Beyond Temporal Treasures

"For where your treasure is, there your heart will be also."

Matthew 6:21 NIV

Father God, today I thank You that You have given me a map to show me the location and position of my own heart. And no matter where I find that it is, I turn it toward You and open my heart to receive Your love, guidance, and direction. Help me to understand that my treasure should not lie solely in earthly desires or fleeting pleasures, but in the pursuit of a healthy spirit, soul, and body (1 Thes. 5:23).

In my quiet times with You, I see the truth – I've treasured food more than You. Forgive me, Lord. Help me to see that when I seek You above all else (Matthew 6:33), I don't have to worry about anything because You satisfy me. You make known to me the path of life; in Your presence, there is fullness of joy; at Your right hand are pleasures forevermore (Psalm 16:11).

Thank You for loving me so much that You empower and encourage me to shift my priorities from earthly treasures to spiritual ones. Continue to change my heart so that I become more and more like You each day. In Jesus' name, I pray. Amen.

March 19
The God Who Hears

"I have called on you, for you will hear me, O God:
incline your ear to me, and hear my speech."
Psalm 17:6 NKJV

Dear el Shama, the God who hears. You listen attentively to my pleas for help, just as You heard Hagar in her distress (Genesis 16:11). I am grateful for Your unwavering assurance that when I call upon You, You will answer me (Psalm 34:4).

Lord, the cycle of giving in to my temptations, feeling condemned, vowing to never do it again, and then falling again is one of the most frustrating parts of my journey. I start the day feeling strong and encouraged, but as the day goes on I just get weaker and weaker until I feel so defeated. That's why I'm so grateful that You hear me. You respond to my cries and deliver me from all my fears, anxieties, worries, proclivities, temptations, and strongholds.

As You unveil Your truths, Lord, I incline my ear to listen attentively (Isaiah 55:3). I commit to continually posture myself at Your feet, eager to receive Your words of peace and wisdom. In Your matchless name, I pray. Amen.

March 20
Hydrated for Health

"... but whoever drinks of the water that I will give him will never be thirsty again. The water that I will give him will become in him a spring of water welling up to eternal life."

John 4:14 ESV

Dear God, my fountain, I come to You in gratitude for the gift of water, essential for sustaining life in my body. You promise that those who drink of Your water will never thirst again reminds me of the vital role water plays in nourishing and refreshing my physical being.

Thank You for the abundance of water on this earth, from the rain that nurtures the soil to the springs that quench the thirst of all living creatures. As I recognize the importance of water to sustain every system in my body, I am reminded of Your divine provision in every drop that hydrates and revitalizes me.

Just as I depend on water to hydrate, nourish, and rejuvenate my physical body, I rely on Your Living Water to nourish my soul and spirit (Matthew 5:6). Help me to drink deeply from both sources, recognizing the interconnectedness of my physical and spiritual well-being.

As I read Your Word, I invite Your Spirit to dialogue with me throughout the day, and as I soak in Your presence, satisfy my thirst for You (Psalm 107:9), Jesus. In Your name, I pray. Amen.

March 21
Never Hungry or Thirsty

"As the deer pants for the water brooks, So my soul pants for You, O God."

Psalm 42:1 NKJV

I honor You today Jehovah Rohi, God my shepherd, I thank You for always leading, guiding, protecting, and satisfying me. You created me with a hunger and thirst for You (Matthew 5:6), and just as a compass points north, You are the true source of fulfillment in my life. Remind me of this when I try to find satisfaction in food instead of seeking You.

Yes, I need food and water for daily life, but I often find myself overindulging, and most of the time I'm eating for boredom, loneliness, or habit. Help me to eat by choice and not be led by my emotions. Satisfy my emotional and spiritual hunger, as I learn how to satisfy my physical hunger with the right foods.

Today, I ask You to connect me with my truest desires for You, my source of life. Illuminate the places where my wires are crossed and my thirst for the infinite has been directed toward broken cisterns I have dug myself, and heal me. And like a good Shepherd (John 10:11) lead me and guide me in all truth. In the name of Jesus. Amen!

March 22
Wise Food Choices

"Wisdom is the principal thing; therefore get wisdom: and with all thy getting get understanding."
Proverbs 4:7 KJV

Dear God of Wisdom, Your Word tells me that Solomon knew the most important thing to ask You for – wisdom. And thank You for extending that same promise to me. You've given me Your rock-solid promise that if I will ask You for wisdom, that You will pour it out willingly.

Today, I specifically seek Your wisdom and understanding to guide me on my health journey, particularly in making wise food choices. Grant me discernment to consistently opt for nourishing and life-giving foods that promote vitality, rather than those that bring harm and decay to my body (Deuteronomy 30:19). In my own limited understanding (Proverbs 3:5-6), I tend to make choices that compromise my well-being, which is why I desperately need Your divine wisdom to instruct me in applying knowledge in the most beneficial way to my life. Help me to merge common sense with Your wisdom, enabling me to navigate my health journey with ease, peace, and grace. I declare and decree that, in the mighty name of Jesus, I will consistently make wise choices not just today, but every day. Amen.

March 23
Eating Clean

"Please test your servants for ten days. Let us be given only vegetables to eat and water to drink. Then compare our appearances with those of the young men who are eating the royal food, and deal with your servants according to what you see."

Daniel 1:12-13 NIV

Dear Lord, I thank You for providing me with a bounty of foods that nourish my body. They are designed specifically for my unique needs, and I'm so grateful for that. You have created me so uniquely and have given me the blueprint for how to care for it. My body is like no other. Teach me to eat clean, nourishing foods that strengthen and heal my body. Give me an appetite for vegetables and other healing foods that will maximize my energy and minimize my aches and pains. Your wisdom is teaching me that although everything is permissible, not everything is beneficial (1 Corinthians 6:12). So help me to accept that while I can eat whatever I want, I should opt for clean, wholesome foods, otherwise, It harms my body and does not honor Your temple (1 Corinthians 6:19). Satisfy me with the foods that honor my temple and please turn my eyes away from all other foods. Make me be the one who accepts what You have for me, and let me celebrate it by giving You glory. In Jesus' name, I pray. Amen!

March 24
I Deserve a Treat

"Have this mind among yourselves, which is yours in Christ Jesus, who, though he was in the form of God, did not count equality with God a thing to be grasped, but emptied himself, by taking the form of a servant, being born in the likeness of men. And being found in human form, he humbled himself by becoming obedient to the point of death, even death on a cross."

Philippians 2:5-8 ESV

Heavenly Father, I thank You for giving me a standard for humility in Your son, Jesus Christ. He came to save the lost by submitting to Your will. I bind and banish the spirit of entitlement in my life and ask You to fill me now with a spirit of humility.

I release the mindset that tells me, "I deserve a treat" or that, "I can do what I want to do when I want to do it." Those are all lies, and I rebuke them in the name of Jesus. My body is Your temple, and I humbly steward it as You will. When the desire for indulgence tries to rise up in me, help me see that I'm attempting to be lord over my own life by dictating what I deserve. When I feel that urge, help me to find a more suitable alternative to meet that need, but most importantly, let me bring that need to You so You can tell me how to satisfy it.

Empty me before You now and fill me to overflowing with Your love and grace. In Jesus' name, I pray. Amen.

March 25
One Bite Won't Hurt

Then you will know the truth, and the truth will set you free."

John 8:32 NIV

Dear Lord, You are the Way, the Truth, and the Life, and as I abide in You, I am set free. I thank You for the gift of discernment, that enables me to distinguish truth from deception. I confess that the allure of temptation and instant gratification often clouds my judgment, and leads me off my intentions to eat healthy. Help me Lord, to overcome the lie that "one bite won't hurt, " and the many others like it that whisper in my ear, urging me to compromise my values and surrender to momentary desires.

Remind me that a single bite, a fleeting moment of weakness, can have far-reaching consequences on my physical health, emotional well-being, and spiritual journey. Grant me the strength to resist the allure of instant gratification and to choose the narrow path (Matthew 7:13-14).

So today I thank You for the freedom that I've found in You as I fix my mind on You and focus on worshiping You in spirit and truth (John 4:24) . Whom the son sets free is free indeed (John 8:36). In Jesus' name. Amen!

March 26
The Gift of Food

*"For everything created by God is good, and nothing is
to be rejected if it is received with thanksgiving, for it
is made holy by the word of God and prayer."*
1 Timothy 4:4-5 ESV

Lord, I thank You for this day and for every gift You generously provide. I will rejoice and be glad in it (Psalm 118:24). I am learning to see food as a gift from You too. In the past, food has been my comfort, my friend, my go-to when bored, or my entertainment but that is changing.

I'm in awe at how You gave food to Your creation to delight our senses, to energize us, to nourish us, to strengthen our bodies, and to sustain us. When I think about the digestive process and how food is converted into energy to sustain me, it's truly mind-boggling. I am grateful for Your unfailing provision that sustains me day by day (Psalm 145:16). Every time I sit down to eat, I will give You thanks, for the miracle of food and how it nourishes me. I am forever grateful for Your love, provision, and faithfulness. May my meals be a reminder of Your goodness and an occasion to give thanks and praise. In Jesus' name, I pray. Amen.

March 27
Taking Authority Over My Food Thoughts

"We demolish arguments and every pretension that sets itself up against the knowledge of God, and we take captive every thought to make it obedient to Christ."
2 Corinthians 10:5 NIV

Dear Lord, Thank You for equipping me with everything I need to reign in my thoughts. I give You my struggle with obsessive thoughts about food, recognizing that it has taken authority over my mind and emotions. I humbly seek Your intervention, knowing that only through Your grace and strength can I overcome this battle.

Lord, I acknowledge that my body is a temple, wonderfully and fearfully made by You. Yet, I have allowed unhealthy thoughts and obsessions to control my actions and distort my perception of nourishment. I confess that I have turned to food for comfort, seeking satisfaction in it instead of turning to You. Even when it seems that my thoughts consume and overpower me, I am learning to lean on You and to believe that it is possible to have the mind of Christ (1 Corinthians 2:16).

I pray for a transformed mind, one that aligns with Your truth. Let Your Word become a shield against negative thoughts and self-condemnation. I choose to think about those things that are true, noble, right, pure, lovely, and admirable (Philippians 4:8). In Jesus' name, I pray. Amen.

March 28
Ditching the Diets

"But the Helper, the Holy Spirit, whom the Father will send in my name, he will teach you all things and bring to your remembrance all that I have said to you."
John 14:26 ESV

Dear Lord, You make all things new (Revelations 21:5) You have sent Your Holy Spirit to help me in all things so I come before You today seeking guidance in releasing my diet mindset. It's all I've ever known, Lord. As far back as I can remember thoughts about my weight and appearance have consumed and preoccupied me, but I'm ready for change.

I call on You today to help me cultivate a healthy and intuitive approach to nourishing my body. Help me let go of restrictive thoughts and beliefs about losing weight and teach me how to listen to my body's signals of hunger and fullness, and to trust myself in making choices that promote overall well-being.

Help me navigate the challenges and triggers that may arise on this journey, granting me the resilience and grace to overcome them without resorting to extremes. My desire is to ditch the diets and live in peace and freedom.

Remind me that I am deserving of a healthy, balanced, and nourishing relationship with food, free from judgment or shame. In Jesus' name, I pray. Amen.

March 29
Overcoming the Spirit of Gluttony

"Their end is destruction, their god is their belly, and they glory in their shame, with minds set on earthly things."

Philippians 3:19 ESV

Dear Lord, God of contentment. I bless You today and I praise Your holy name. You satisfy me with good things. I come to You today in transparency and humility confessing that I have allowed the spirit of gluttony to gain control over my actions and desires. I have indulged in excess, seeking comfort and satisfaction in food instead of finding true fulfillment in You.

Lord, forgive me for using food as an escape from my problems and emotions. Help me to find rest and peace in Your presence and lean on Your strength instead of turning to overeating. I desire to eat in a way that gives You glory (1 Corinthians 10:31) and to honor You with my body, treating it as a temple of the Holy Spirit (1 Corinthians 6:19).

Grant me the wisdom to discern between genuine hunger and the cravings of gluttony. I declare that I have the fruit of self-control (Galatians 5:22-23). I pray for an outpouring of Your Spirit, that I may develop self-discipline to resist the temptations of gluttony. May Your grace and strength be my constant companions on this journey of overcoming gluttony. In Jesus' name, I pray. Amen.

March 30
Ending the Blame Game

"The man said, 'The woman you put here with me—she gave me some fruit from the tree, and I ate it.'"

Genesis 3:12 NIV

Dear most all-knowing and all-seeing God, You see all of me. You know my human nature that tries to blame others like Adam and Eve did. I confess that I have shifted the responsibility for my actions onto others instead of taking ownership and seeking Your help.

Help me to face the truth about my actions and attitudes, taking full responsibility for my choices. Grant me the humility to examine my heart and motives when I am tempted to blame others. Help me to recognize that true freedom comes from acknowledging my own faults and seeking Your forgiveness and transformation.

I renounce all fears that keep me from taking responsibility for my choices and actions and I receive Your perfect love (1 John 4:18). I let go of blaming others or circumstances for my poor food choices. I own what's mine to own without condemnation (Romans 8:1), shame, or judgment. Instead of blaming others, help me to lean on Your strength and seek Your wisdom in overcoming the temptations and challenges I face. May I develop a heart of gratitude and personal accountability, knowing that through You, all things are possible. In Jesus' name, I pray. Amen.

March 31
Forward Progress

"So Joshua said to the Israelites: 'How long will you wait before you begin to take possession of the land that the Lord, the God of your ancestors, has given you?'"
Joshua 18:3 NIV

Dear Lord God, I bless You today. I thank You for this month of surrendering my eating habits to You.

I am more than a conqueror in You (Romans 8:37)! I thank You for all You have revealed to me this month. It has truly shifted my perspective about food. It is a gift from You (Ecclesiastes 3:13) and I propose to treat it as such.

I declare that in the powerful name of Jesus, I am ready to possess the land of health and wholeness! Continue to show me anything holding me back from moving forward in victory into the place of living my life in a right-sized body, with full health, and in the bounty of provision that You have blessed me with.

It's been a powerful month of understanding all the factors that have impacted the way I eat. Let everything that You've revealed to me this month continue to percolate in me and transform the way I think (Romans 12:2). I declare that I am moving forward. I am making progress. I am making choices that are in line with Your best for me and with my goal of a healthy mind and body, and I claim victory in the Holy Name of Jesus, I pray. Amen.

April

GET ACTIVE

This month's prayers are centered around embracing physical activity as a meaningful expression of your faith. As you pray these prayers daily, the Holy Spirit will help you let go of any negative beliefs that may have held you back from embracing physical activity. You will release guilt, shame, or feelings of inadequacy and instead celebrate physical activity as a gift from God. You will learn to engage fully with it and find joy and fulfillment in the movement.

It's easy to fall into the mindset that separates the spiritual from the physical, treating them as two distinct realms. But the truth is, your body is an important part of your spiritual life—it's a sacred vessel that houses the Spirit of God. By recognizing this, you can explore how to integrate your physical self into your worship, especially through exercise.

May this month be a time of revelation and transformation, where the lines between the physical and spiritual blend together, leading you to a more integrated and joyful life. May

God's grace and blessings be upon you this month and always. Amen.

April 1
Rise Up and Walk

"Then Jesus said to him, "Get up! Pick up your mat and walk.

John 5:8 NIV

Dear God of Glory, You are my strength, my rock, and my refuge. You always go before me, paving the way for my journey ahead. As I start this new month focused on moving my body more, I invite You into this new leg of my journey. Lord, I thank You for the gift of this day, for every breath I take (Isaiah 42:5).

This month, I surrender my resistance to exercise to You. Help me to release any fears or doubts that hold me back. Give me the desire to want to move my body as You designed it to move, celebrating its capabilities and honoring the vessel You have entrusted to me. Like the man at the pool, let me hear You calling me to "Rise up" and embrace the gift of movement.

Father, I am aware that I cannot force myself to exercise (Romans 7:15). I ask for Your divine intervention to grant me the discipline and motivation needed to prioritize physical activity in my daily life.

Strengthen my resolve when feelings of inertia creep in, filling my heart with unwavering belief that I am capable of mastering this new skill. I trust that with Your grace, I can become someone who loves to exercise and thrive in my health journey. In Jesus' name, I pray. Amen.

April 2
Clothed in Strength

"She dresses herself with strength and makes her arms strong."

Proverbs 31:17 ESV

Dear Lord, God of strength and power. You are strong and mighty (Psalm 24:8). Thank You for making me so wonderfully complex (Psalm 139:14). I'm in awe of Your perfect design. My heart pumps blood to my entire body; my strong muscles give me the ability to do work, and the flexibility of my joints keeps me supple and limber.

Today I come to You asking to help me strengthen my muscles. Aside from the aesthetics, having strong muscles also makes my everyday activities easier, reduces my risk of injury, and helps me to maintain a healthy weight. Yet, knowing all these wonderful benefits, I still fail to do it consistently.

Grant me the determination and discipline to consistently engage in strength training activities as I seek out ways to incorporate it into my daily life. Help me to overcome any feelings of laziness or fear. Let it become part of my new mindset that I am healthy and strong. May my pursuit of physical strength be rooted in gratitude and reverence for the body You have given me. In Jesus name, I pray. Amen!

April 3
The Discipline of Exercise

"Exercise daily in God—no spiritual flabbiness, please! Workouts in the gymnasium are useful, but a disciplined life in God is far more so, making you fit both today and forever."
1 Timothy 4:6-10 MSG

Dear Father, I bless You today. I surrender everything to You. I long to honor You not only in my spiritual growth but also in caring for the temple You have entrusted to me. Lord, I confess that I have struggled with discipline in the area of exercise.

Help me to develop a disciplined mindset, understanding that self-control is a fruit of Your Spirit working within me (Galatians 5:22). Remind me daily that the discipline I cultivate in my physical routine can spill over into other areas of my life, bringing order and balance. When I lack motivation, remind me that, I can do all things through Christ who strengthens me (Philippians 4:13).

Help me to find joy and fulfillment in the process of physical activity, recognizing it as an opportunity to glorify You by stewarding the body You have given me. May my pursuit of discipline in exercise be an act of worship, an offering of my body as a living sacrifice, holy and pleasing to You (Romans 12:1). May it serve as a testimony to Your transforming power and the renewing work of Your Spirit in my life. In Jesus' name. Amen.

April 4
Rise Up and Go North

"You have circled this mountain long enough. Now turn north."

Deuteronomy 2:3 NASB

Dear God of Progress, You never stop working (Philippians 1:6). I long to adopt that same mindset in my fitness journey. It seems like I do good for a few days or weeks and then something always happens. I get hurt, I get overwhelmed with life, I get complacent or I just get bored. It seems like I can never get past a certain level of fitness and I wonder if I'm destined to stay this way forever.

Grant me the clarity and determination to break free from the self-sabotaging patterns that have held me back. Help me recognize the habits and behaviors that hinder my progress.

Lord, I relate so much to the Israelites. I am sorry for going my own way, and I ask your forgiveness. Do a new thing in me. I can do hard things. I rise up in strength and speak to the mountain before me (Psalm 97:5). I am moving forward as the mountains of complacency, fear of failure, and fear of injury are leveled in the mighty name of Jesus, Amen.

April 5
Reframing My Expectations About Exercise

"Are You the Expected One, or shall we look for someone else?"
Matthew 11:3 NASB 1995

Praise You, Lord, I thank You for Your son Jesus who is the Way, the Truth, and the Life (John 14:6). I recognize that my current mindset may be limiting my progress and hindering my ability to fully enjoy and embrace physical activity. Shift my perspective and help me release any negative beliefs or preconceived notions that may have held me back.

I realize that I see exercise as a necessary evil and a punishment for not taking care of my temple. It is not a chore or a burden but an opportunity for growth, self-discovery, and overall well-being.

Allow me to embrace the process rather than solely focusing on the end results, recognizing that every step forward, no matter how small, is a victory worth celebrating. I surrender my expectations to You, Lord. Reframe my approach so exercise time becomes a time to pray for others who are not afforded this opportunity. I thank You for changing my mindset and allowing me to see my health from Your perspective. In Jesus name, I pray. Amen.

April 6
Making Time for Exercise

"So teach us to number our days that we may get a heart of wisdom."

Psalm 90:12 ESV

Dear God of Favor, I thank You for the gift and the blessing of time. Help me to make the best use of it (Ephesians 5:16). You have granted me 24 hours each and every day to steward. When I think about it, it seems silly that I can't find 30 minutes to move my body, especially when I know that exercise will allow me to be more productive and have more energy.

When I tell myself I "don't have time to exercise," remind me that it's one of the best time investments I can make. Remind me that if I don't invest the time now, I may be forced to make time in the future to deal with the consequences of inactivity.

Lord, help me to incorporate physical activity into the demands of daily life; whether it's waking up a little earlier, or finding pockets of time that I can dedicate solely to physical activity. Enable me to find balance in my commitments and responsibilities, so that I may allocate the necessary time and energy to care for my body as You have called me to do (1 Corinthians 6:19). I surrender my time, my agenda, and my routine to You today. In Your holy name, I pray. Amen.

April 7
Gratitude for The Gift of Movement

*"In everything give thanks; for this is the will of God
in Christ Jesus for you."*

1 Thessalonians 5:18 NKJV

Heavenly Father, source of all goodness and grace, I come before You with a heart overflowing with gratitude. You are the Almighty, the Creator of the universe, whose wisdom and power know no bounds.

Thank You, Lord, for the incredible gift of movement. Your handiwork (Ephesians 2:10) is displayed in every joint, muscle, and nerve as I move. Forgive me, Lord, for the times when I have taken this gift for granted. Help me to see exercise not as a burden, but as a joyful opportunity to honor You with my body. Let me remember those who long for the ability to move, and may their plight inspire me to cherish and steward this privilege well.

Change my mindset from "I have to" to "I get to" exercise. With each step, each stretch, and each moment of physical activity, may my heart overflow with gratitude (1 Corinthians 10:31). Let my movements be a testament to Your goodness and grace. May every motion be infused with praise, every breath a whisper of thanksgiving. In Jesus' I pray. Amen.

April 8
Overcoming Fear of Injury

"Have I not commanded you? Be strong and coura-
geous. Do not be afraid; do not be discouraged, for the
Lord your God will be with you wherever you go."
Joshua 1:9 NIV

Dear Lord my protector, Your Word reminds me that no harm will overtake me and no disaster will come near me (Psalm 91:10) . I stand on Your Word today Father because I live each day with so many fears – When it comes to exercise, I fear that I will hurt myself. Fill me with Your peace (Philippians 4:7), so that I may release the fear that has been holding me captive. Help me to trust in Your sovereignty and Your plans for my life, knowing that You are always with me, guiding my steps– even at the gym.

Let me honor my body by listening to what it needs instead of pushing it beyond its limits or not pushing it enough out of fear. I want that healthy balance that will give me the maximum result. Also remind me that the more I exercise, the stronger my muscles will grow which will decrease my chance of injury. Let me no longer fear the very thing I need the most.

Protect me from any accidents or injuries, and if I do face them, give me the resilience to recover and the faith to trust in Your plan for my healing. I thank You that my strength comes from You (Psalm 121:2). In Jesus' name, I pray. Amen.

April 9
Mastering Self

"A person without self-control is like a house with its doors and windows knocked out."
Proverbs 25:28 MSG

Dear Lord, You have not given me a spirit of fear, but of power, love, and self-control (2 Timothy 1:7). I come before You today with a humble heart, seeking Your guidance and strength as I work to overcome my self-consciousness while exercising. You know the struggles and insecurities I face. Often, I worry about what others may think and find myself comparing my journey to those around me, allowing fear to hold me back from fully embracing the benefits of physical activity.

Grant me the strength to focus on my own journey and progress, rather than comparing myself to others (Galatians 1:10). Remind me that each step I take toward a healthier lifestyle honors the body You have entrusted to me.

In moments of self-consciousness, Lord, I ask for Your peace and assurance. Help me to silence the negative voices that seek to discourage me. I have the mind of Christ (1 Corinthians 2:16), so give me the courage to step out of my comfort zone, challenge myself, and grow in strength and endurance. Thank You for the joy and freedom that come from embracing an active lifestyle. In Jesus' name, I pray. Amen.

April 10
The Easy Yoke

"My grace is sufficient for you, for my power is made perfect in weakness."

2 Corinthians 12:9 ESV

Dear Blessed Assurance, You are my comfort and place of rest. You quiet me with Your love. When I find myself saying "It's too hard," help me to appreciate the gift of my body and to see exercise as an opportunity for growth, rather than a burden. Help me to understand that the effort I put into exercise is not wasted or in vain.

I surrender my struggles with the difficulty of exercise to Your loving care, knowing that with You, all things are possible. There's nothing too hard for You (Genesis 18:14). Remind me that I can do all things through You (Philippians 4:13). As I engage in physical activity, fill me with Your Holy Spirit, guiding my every movement and helping me to find fulfillment and contentment in the journey.

Holy Spirit, show me when I'm making things harder than they need to be by overcomplicating things. And when things are challenging, help me to focus not on the temporary discomfort but on the long-term benefits that exercise brings—strength, endurance, and improved health. I will rise to the challenge and I declare that I can do hard things by taking on the easy yoke of Jesus (Matthew 11:28). In Jesus' name I pray. Amen.

April 11
Overcoming Procrastination

"… making the most of your time, because the days are evil."

Ephesians 5:16 NASB

Dear Father in Heaven, I bless You today. I surrender everything and everyone to You. I love You Lord and I give You all glory, honor, and praise. Lord, grant me clarity and self-awareness to recognize the reasons behind my procrastination. There are so many days when I wake up with every good intention to exercise and it never pans out. I tell myself I'm going to do it later and later never comes. Help me to understand any fears, doubts, or insecurities that may be fueling this behavior. Reveal to me any underlying emotional or psychological factors that contribute to my tendency to avoid getting active and healthier.

I recognize that I cannot overcome procrastination on my own. I need Your divine intervention and grace to transform my mindsets, habits, and behaviors. Guide my every step (Psalm 32:8) and remind me of Your presence when I am tempted (1 Corinthians 10:13) to procrastinate.

I commit myself to Your guidance and surrender my struggles with procrastination into Your capable hands. Thank You for Your unfailing love and patience with me. I believe that, with Your help, I can break free from the chains of procrastination and live a purposeful and productive life. In Jesus' name, I pray. Amen.

April 12
Strengthening My Heart and Lungs

"He gives power to the faint, and to him who has no might he increases strength."
Isaiah 40:29 ESV

Dear Almighty God, Thank You for Your sustaining power (Psalm 55:22). Today, I'm leaning on Your everlasting strength. You are the giver of life and the source of all power and strength.

Lord, I thank You specifically for the benefits of aerobic exercise, which serves as a powerful means to strengthen my heart and lungs and sustain my life. As I move, I am reminded of the miraculous functioning of my heart. It beats tirelessly, pumping life-giving blood to every corner of my body. When I move my body, my heart becomes stronger, more efficient, and better equipped to sustain me throughout my lifetime. Bless me with a strong heart that beats rhythmically and powerfully until I draw my last breath.

Guard my heart from any strain or weakness, and shield my lungs from any harm. I pray that the benefits of cardiovascular exercise extend beyond my physical health. May the increased vitality and energy I gain spill over into all aspects of my life. Strengthen my spiritual resolve, empowering me to run the race You have set before me (Hebrews 12:1) with endurance and unwavering faith. In Jesus' name, I pray. Amen.

April 13
Walking with You

"For in him we live and move and have our being."
Acts 17:28 NIV

Dear Lord, what a beautiful God You are to create me as a temple for Your Spirit, Your Self, to dwell inside. What a wonder that You are omnipresent and simultaneously personally with me every second – I'm astounded! It humbles and excites me to know that in You, I live and I move and I have my being. I am nothing without You, and I can do nothing apart from You (John 15:5).

Give me the desire to move as often as possible and let me start with walking as much as my body allows me to. With each step, I surrender my worries, burdens, and anxieties to You, Lord (1 Peter 5:7). I offer up my prayers, my hopes, and my dreams, trusting that You hear and guide me along my journey. The steady rhythm of my footsteps aligns with the beat of my heart, reminding me of the eternal rhythm of Your love and grace.

As I walk, I find peace and tranquility. It is during these precious moments that I can fully embrace Your love and guidance, feeling Your gentle whispers in the breeze and seeing Your beauty in every tree and flower along my path.

Thank You, loving Father, for the gift of movement. As I walk, lead me closer to You with each step I take. In Your holy name, I pray. Amen.

April 14
Baby Steps

"Therefore, my beloved brothers, be steadfast, immovable, always abounding in the work of the Lord, knowing that in the Lord your labor is not in vain."
1 Corinthians 15:58 ESV

Dear Patient Father, I bless You today. I surrender everything to You. I will wait on You Lord (Isaiah 40:31) instead of running ahead of You. Lord, You know in my eagerness, I sometimes find myself expecting immediate results. Remind me of the value of patience and perseverance. You have taught me that patience is a virtue (Galatians 5:22), and I acknowledge that true growth takes time.

Teach me that my success will come from daily consistent and gradual improvements. Let me not worry about how fast everyone else is making progress and focus instead on my own unique path and abilities. Help me to recognize that small steps forward are still steps forward, and worth celebrating. Grant me the humility to accept setbacks and challenges as opportunities in, with, and through You (James 1:2-3).

Reassure me when I get frustrated with the pace of my results. Help me to find joy in the process, to be grateful for every step I take, and to honor You in all that I do. In Jesus Loving and merciful name, I pray. Amen.

April 15
Cultivating Peace in the Pain

"No discipline seems pleasant at the time, but painful. Later on, however, it produces a harvest of righteousness and peace for those who have been trained by it."
Hebrews 12:11 NIV

Dear Lord, thank you that You love me enough to want to discipline me. You are my good Father, and Your desire to shape and mold me comes from Your deep Fatherly love. Though discipline is not comfortable in the moment, I know it's for my good. Your discipline guides me to the best possible outcome for my life. In the past, I have sometimes fought Your refining work, and I am sorry.

Just as physical exercise challenges and strengthens my body, Your discipline challenges and strengthens my character, faith, and relationship with You. And just like how Your discipline, although sometimes painful, corrects and purifies me, the same goes for my experience with exercise. When I feel like quitting or giving up, remind me that the temporary pain has a purpose and if I endure, I will reap a harvest (Gal 6:9).

Hallelujah! Lord, You love me too much to leave me in pain (Hebrews 12:6). Thank You for the unfailing love You show me through teaching me discipline. I pray to grow in it and from it, in Jesus's holy name. Amen.

April 16
Giving Thanks In All Ways

"... always giving thanks to God the Father for every-
thing in the name of our Lord Jesus Christ."
Ephesians 5:20 NIV

Lord, Your Word says that whatever I do in word or deed I am to do it in Your name (1 Cor. 10:31). I'm understanding that 'whatever' includes exercise and fitness activities. This completely changes the way I approach my days in the best way! With this newfound understanding, I realize that taking care of my body is not merely an obligation or a task to be checked off my to-do list; it is a privilege. I have the honor of tending to the vessel that You have entrusted to me, Your sacred temple.

You are the Way, the Truth, and the Life (John 14:6), and I pray for Your perspective in every area and aspect of my life. I am so thankful that no area of my life is too small or too insignificant to You, Lord, and that You want to be invited into all of it. I don't have to exercise– I GET to exercise. And as I do these things, I maintain a heart of gratitude, remembering to give You all thanks, glory, honor, and praise. Thank you for this revelation, Lord. In Jesus' name, I pray. Amen.

April 17
Me to You

"Let me hear Your lovingkindness in the morning; For I trust in You; Teach me the way in which I should walk; For to You I lift up my soul."

Psalm 143:8 NASB

Heavenly Father, You are love and I open myself to taste and see (Psalm 34:8) Your lovingkindness today. I am Yours and You are mine (Song of Songs 2:16), and I lift up my soul to You, Lord. I am so thankful that You are worthy of all of my trust, and I give it to You today; I give *me* to You today!

Instead of just jumping on the last fitness craze, let me come to You and learn from You. How are You guiding me to take care of my temple today? Does it need to rest? Does it need to sweat? Maybe You're telling me to stretch. I am listening and tuning in. I admit that I don't often do this, but I will pay attention today. I'm eager to glean from You and to walk in Your ways. Open up the eyes of my heart (Ephesians 1:18) to know Your guidance and give me the will to stay in step with You.

Today, I respond by loving You back and following You anywhere You lead in my fitness journey and in all areas of my life. In Jesus's name, I pray. Amen.

.

April 18
Nothing is Impossible

"Truly I tell you, if you have faith as small as a mustard seed, you can say to this mountain, 'Move from here to there,' and it will move. Nothing will be impossible for you.'"

Matthew 17:20 NIV

Dear Way Maker, thank you for Your Word that reminds me that nothing will be impossible for me when I put my trust in You. I apply this truth to my commitment to move my body each day. Your Word is always right and always true. I do believe, and please help me with my unbelief (Mark 9:24).

I decree, in the mighty name of Jesus, that the mountains of dis-ease within my body, the burden of negative thinking within my mind, and the resistance to change shall be moved. I am a new creation in Christ, the old has passed away (2 Corinthians 5:17). I stand today upon the unshakable foundation of your promises.

Lord, I affirm that nothing is impossible for me when I walk alongside You. I am grateful for Your presence, Your strength, and the assurance that You are working in my life. May my commitment to exercise be a testament to Your faithfulness and a reflection of Your transforming power. In the name of Jesus, I trust and pray. Amen.

April 19
My Spiritual and Physical Walk

"... but those who wait upon the LORD will renew their strength; they will mount up with wings like eagles; they will run and not grow weary; they will walk and not faint."

Isaiah 40:31 ESV

Holy, strength-giving Father in Heaven, thank you for Your promises! I'm in awe of Your unfailing love and faithfulness. You are the source of my strength (Exodus 15:2) and endurance. I surrender myself, my journey, and my entire life into Your capable hands.

Lord, I am beginning to see the beautiful harmony between the physical and the spiritual. You have designed us as holistic beings, intricately connected in body, mind, and spirit (Genesis 2:7). As I strive to walk both spiritually and physically, I ask for Your guidance and empowerment.

You promise to lift me up, to revitalize my weary soul, and to empower me when I am weak (Psalm 73:26). I lean on Your everlasting arms, knowing that in You, I find the strength I need each day walk both spiritually and in the natural.

I am grateful for Your constant presence and unwavering undergirding. With You by my side, I am confident that I will be victorious. In Your mighty name, I pray. Amen.

April 20
Experiencing God's Presence During Exercise

Let every activity of your lives and every word that comes from your lips be drenched with the beauty of our Lord Jesus, the Anointed One. And bring your constant praise to God the Father because of what Christ has done for you!

Colossians 3:17 TPT

Heavenly Father, I thank you for the gift of movement and the ability to exercise. You are the giver of all good things (James 1:17). Lord, forgive me for my over-emphasis on weight loss. Grant me a greater perspective on physical activity.

Open my eyes to the numerous benefits of exercise beyond just physical appearance. It also boosts my mood, increases my energy levels, and reduces stress and anxiety, so I can be fit and equipped to be used by You (2 Timothy 2:21). Lord, I surrender my preconceived notions about exercise and invite You to reshape my mindset. Show me how to integrate movement into my daily life in ways that bring glory to Your name.

Whether it's dancing, hiking, cycling, or stretching, may every movement be an act of worship unto You. May Your presence be felt in every step, jump, and stretch, reminding me of Your love and faithfulness. In Jesus' name, I pray, Amen.

April 21
Fully Renewed

"He fills my life with good things. My youth is renewed like the eagle's!"

Psalm 103:5 NLT

Dear Good Good Father, Your mercy endures forever. I thank you for Your undying love for me. I thank you for filling my life with good things and for renewing me each and every day. The old life is gone and the new is here with You (2 Corinthians 5:17), and I declare that I am renewed!

I confess that envisioning a healthy and active life feels challenging. Worrying and obsessing about my weight and health is exhausting. Though my hope may have faded, I recognize that today is a fresh beginning! I commit myself to declare Your Word until it resonates deep within my being.

Thank You, Lord, for reminding me that every good and perfect gift originates from You (James 1:17). I acknowledge that all the goodness in my life is a direct result of Your grace and provision.

I surrender my worries, doubts, and fears to You, and I trust that You will guide me toward a life filled with joy, health, and contentment. I pray all of this in the name of Jesus, my Savior and Redeemer. Amen.

April 22
Healed and Whole

"From time to time an angel of the Lord would come down and stir up the waters. The first one into the pool after such disturbance would be cured from whatever disease they had."

John 5:4 NIV

Dear Jehovah Rapha (Exodus 15:26), You are the source of all healing and restoration. I thank You for the sacrifice You made, so that I can experience true health, healing, and wholeness (Isaiah 53:5).

Today, I humbly embrace Your offer of true restoration as I do my part. I choose to move my body each day and take care of it. I embrace an active lifestyle. I claim wellness, wholeness, and healing in every aspect of my being, and I declare it boldly in the powerful name of Jesus. Satan, take notice of the victory that is mine!

I acknowledge that I have not always walked out my healing perfectly, but I find comfort and assurance in knowing that Your grace and mercy surpass my imperfections. You are greater than my failures and weaknesses, and Your power is made perfect in my weakness (2 Corinthians 12:9).I decree and declare that I am healed, healthy, and whole, in the name of Jesus, my Savior and Healer. Amen.

"I pray that the eyes of your heart may be enlightened in order that you may know the hope to which he has called you, ..."

Ephesians 1:18 NIV

Dear God of Power and Might. I bless You today. I surrender everything to You. Lord, I pray that You would open the eyes of my heart (2 Kings 6:17) and grant me a deep understanding of the hope to which You have called me. Help me to comprehend the incredible purpose and potential that resides within me (Ephesians 2:10). May this knowledge ignite a passion within my soul to actively care for the physical vessel You have given me.

Today, I surrender my body to You and ask for Your guidance to engage in regular physical activity to strengthen my body and renew my energy so I can live fully.

Father, ignite a fire within me, motivating me to rise above excuses, doubts, and discouragement (Isaiah 40:31). Grant me the discipline to consistently prioritize my physical well-being and to persevere when I lack motivation. Enlighten and empower my every step, every movement I make. Use me, God, as a vessel that radiates Your light, bringing glory to Your name through a healthy and active life.

In the mighty name of Jesus, I pray. Amen.

April 24
Rejoicing in my Sacred Temple

"Whatever you do [no matter what it is] in word or deed, do everything in the name of the Lord Jesus [and in dependence on Him], giving thanks to God the Father through Him."
Colossians 3:17 AMP

Dear Blessed Assurance, I thank you for the gift of today. I come before You with a humble heart, seeking Your help in reframing how I think about exercise, so that I may see it not as a burden but as a form of worship—a way to honor the temple You have blessed me with. Help me to find joy in caring for my body.

Grant me the wisdom to embrace the uniqueness that resides within me, understanding that I am a reflection of You (Genesis 1:27). May I find joy in the intricacies of my physical form and see it as an opportunity to serve You and others with love and compassion. I surrender my body to You, recognizing that it is a sacred vessel indwelled by Your Spirit (Romans 8:9).

Heavenly Father, I thank You for the opportunity to realign my thinking and find delight in caring for the temple You. May my physical activity be an offering of praise and gratitude to You. Grant me perseverance, discipline, and joy in each step I take, knowing that through exercise, I honor You and draw closer to You. In Jesus' precious name, I pray. Amen.

April 25
Overcoming Weariness by Your Power

"But David pursued, he and four hundred men, for two hundred who were too exhausted to cross the brook Besor remained behind."

1 Samuel 30:10 **NASB**

Dear Almighty God, You clothe me in strength and dignity (Proverbs 31:25), I thank You for strengthening me during the hard times of this health journey. I understand that this life is a marathon, and not a sprint; that I must gird up myself spiritually, mentally, and physically. In doing so, I will steward my energy wisely and allow You to sustain me when I am weary. The healthier I am, the more stamina I will have to endure physically demanding days. I want the energy to do what You've called me to do. I don't ever want my physical abilities to be a hindrance or limitation.

And I admit, sometimes, weariness overtakes me. I get tired! But, I will not give in. I will rely on Your strength to run this physical and spiritual race with endurance (Hebrews 12:1)

By Your power, Lord, today I yield to Your Holy Spirit and not to my flesh. I truly am dead to sin and alive in You (Romans 6:11). I thank You for boundless energy that strengthens my witness and draws others to You. In Jesus' holy Name, I pray. Amen!

April 26
A Spirit First Approach

"Afterward Jesus found him in the temple and said to him, "Behold, you have become well; do not sin anymore, so that nothing worse happens to you."
John 5:14 NASB

Dear Creator God, thank you that You are concerned with my entire being – spirit, soul, body (1 Thessalonians 5:23). And I am grateful to know the truth of my creation, that I'm not one-dimensional: I'm a complex, fearfully, wonderfully (Psalm 139:14) made tripartite being made with love and for love by You!

Lord, I recognize that Your true transformation begins as I align my spirit with Yours. That is the starting place of all breakthroughs. Forgive me, I've had it backward, I tried to force myself to exercise and get healthier believing that it would change me on the inside, but Your way is an inside-out approach, not the other way around. My body obeys my mind, but my mind obeys my spirit, so all change must start with my spirit man. What a revelation!

I thank you for healing my inner man. Your ways are so much higher than mine (Isaiah 55: 8-9). In Jesus' name. Amen!

April 27
Stretching Towards Wholeness

"I press toward the mark for the prize of the high calling of God in Christ Jesus."
Philippians 3:14 KJV

Lord, I come before You today with a heart full of gratitude for the gift of flexibility both metaphorically and physically. You designed our bodies with remarkable abilities to move, to bend, and to flex. Just as my muscles and joints require regular physical stretching to maintain strength and flexibility, my soul needs to be stretched to reach its fullest potential in You.

As I engage in physical exercise and stretching, grant me discipline and perseverance to stay committed to a regular routine. May I approach each session with gratitude, recognizing that this time is not only an investment in my physical health but also an opportunity for spiritual growth.

Lord, just as my physical body needs to be stretched to prevent stiffness and improve performance, I recognize that my soul needs spiritual stretching to prevent stagnation and deepen my relationship with You. Help me to step outside of my comfort zone, to embrace new challenges and experiences that will stretch my faith and enlarge my capacity to love and serve others. In the name of Jesus, I pray. Amen.

April 28
Divine Balance

"By the seventh day God had finished the work he had been doing; so on the seventh day he rested from all his work."

Genesis 2:2 NIV

Dear Loving Father, I come today seeking Your guidance and strength in finding a harmonious balance between exercise and rest. Like a see-saw, I often feel so unbalanced. I'm inactive for long stretches of time and then I feel guilty and will go hard for a bit only to peter out again. I need Your divine balance, Lord.

In the midst of my striving, help me to remember Your invitation to find rest in You (Matthew 11:28). When my rest turns to slothfulness, motivate me to not only get moving again but to stay active. Teach me to discern when my body needs to rest. Guide me in embracing the gentle rhythm of work and rest.

May Your Word be a lamp to my feet and a light to my path (Psalm 119:105), giving me wisdom and discernment. Grant me strength, perseverance, and the ability to listen to my body's needs. In Your holy name, I pray. Amen.

April 29
Avoiding the Comparison Trap

"We saw the Nephilim there (the descendants of Anak come from the Nephilim). We seemed like grasshoppers in our own eyes, and we looked the same to them."

Numbers 13:33 NIV

Dear God of Creation, I bless You today. You are so worthy to be praised. Father, help me avoid the comparison trap. I want to see myself as You see me, neither greater nor lesser, but with true humility. Let me walk in the truth of my identity, focusing on You and developing the unique qualities You have placed within me.

Help me to not look around at what anyone else is doing, to instead focus on what physical activities are best for me, based on my unique body, needs, and energy requirements. Teach me that my path does not have to look like anyone else's. My assignment is to listen to how You're leading me and please You and no one else (Galatians 1:10).

Your Word instructs me to love my neighbor as myself (Matthew 22:39). Lord, I align myself with this truth and resist the enemy's attempts to undermine my self-love. I decree that as I learn to love myself with the same love You have for me, I will embrace

my unique health journey, free from comparison, and grounded in love. In Jesus' name, I pray. Amen.

April 30
Submitted, Sober, and Centered

"Be alert and of sober mind. Your enemy the devil prowls around like a roaring lion looking for someone to devour."

1 Peter 5:8 NIV

Dear God, my protector (Psalm 121:5), thank you once again for Your clear instructions on how to live a victorious life. I am immensely grateful that You have not left me stumbling in the dark to figure it out on my own. You have sent me a helper to lead and guide me in all truth (John 14:26).

As I conclude this month of focusing on my physical activity, I thank you for the valuable lessons You have taught me. It has been truly eye-opening, especially in understanding that exercise can be an act of worship.

Now, it makes more sense why the enemy always tries to discourage me from prioritizing physical activity. He would rather have me idle on the couch and indulge in unhealthy habits, but I rebuke those temptations in the name of Jesus. Thank you for keeping me safe from his schemes. He is a deceiver (John 8:44), and I refuse to grant him access to my life today.

Help me put into practice what I've learned (Philippians 4:8-9) this month and empower me to remain sober, alert, vigilant, and watchful. I offer this prayer in Your Son's name. Amen.

May

LET GO, LET GOD

This month's prayer focus on the theme of "Letting Go and Letting God." These prayers are designed to help you surrender your health journey to God and draw closer to Him. The concept of letting go and letting God refers to releasing our worries, fears, and control over certain areas of our lives, and instead, entrusting them to God's guidance and care.

Each prayer will revolve around surrendering your physical and emotional well-being to God's hands. They will encourage you to let go of any anxieties or burdens you may carry regarding your health and place your trust in God's ultimate plan for your life.

This month, you will be invited to cultivate a deeper sense of trust in God's providence. You will be encouraged to release your desires for a specific outcome and instead embrace God's perfect timing and purpose in your health journey. This surrender will enable you to experience a greater sense of peace, knowing that God is with you every step of the way.

As you let go of control, you create space for God to work in your life, allowing His grace and healing to flow through you. Letting go and letting God will empower you to embrace a mindset of surrender, trust, and faith in your health journey. They will remind you that God's love is unconditional and His plans are perfect, even if they differ from your own expectations. Be encouraged.

May 1
You See it All

"You know when I sit down or stand up. You know my thoughts even when I'm far away."
Psalm 139:2 ESV

I come to You today El Roi, the God who sees me (Genesis 16:13) and who has numbered the hairs on my head (Luke 12:7) and counts my every tear. You know the motivations and root of my thoughts. You know all my, "what if's," "how do I," "why didn't I," "I wish," "I should have," and "I can'ts."

I surrender all these thoughts to You and believe that You will teach me how to take every thought captive and make them obedient to Christ (2 Corinthians 10:5). Right now that concept feels like herding cats! But I know You are faithful and You are changing the way I think.

So I thank You for reminding me that You see me and You are with me right here, right now. Nothing I do shocks or surprises You and in spite of my actions, You promise to never leave me or forsake me. So I take a deep breath, smile and keep on going. It's good to be seen and known by You. In Jesus' name I pray. Amen.

May 2
Have Your Way, Lord

"Our God is in heaven; he does whatever pleases him."
Psalm 115:3 NIV

Almighty God of heaven, You reign forever and ever, from generation to generation. You are never constrained by anything, and that's why I put my trust in You.

I declare that I "Let Go, Let God" with confidence and boldness. I cease striving and trust You. As I move forward in pursuit of my health goals, I commit to keeping the phrase "Let Go, Let God" in the right context. It is not an excuse for inactivity but rather an acknowledgment that in my own strength, I'm not able to overcome these strongholds I face. Remind me that to "let go" is not a reason to be lazy or run from my responsibilities.

I cast my cares on You because I know that You care for me (1 Peter 5:7). Show me what to let go of; empower me to submit them to You. As I begin this month, I let go of all the faulty patterns, and belief systems that hold me back and keep me from submitting to You. Continue to remind me that Your ways are higher than my ways (Isaiah 55:8), and Your dreams are better than my dreams. In Jesus' mighty name, I pray. Amen.

May 3
Letting Go of Limitations

"Therefore humble yourselves under the mighty hand of God, that He may exalt you in due time, casting all your care upon Him, for He cares for you."
1 Peter 5:6-7 NKJV

Dear God of Perfection, In Your perfect nature, I find grace and guidance. Today, I humbly approach You with a heart that seeks transformation.

Shine Your light upon the depths of my heart (Psalm 139:23), revealing any resistance or reluctance I may unknowingly harbor towards You and Your Word. Help me overcome the limitations of my own thinking, and rescue me from the despair and self-defeating beliefs that often hold me captive.

In moments of frustration or when I find myself trapped in negative thought patterns, I take comfort in knowing that I can call upon You for assistance. Rather than attempting to solve everything independently, I trust in Your renewing power to reshape my mind and guide my thoughts.

Thank you, Lord, for the ongoing renewal of my thoughts, as You replace them with Your divine perspective. I willingly submit myself under Your mighty hand (1 Peter 5:6). In this surrender, I find rest and peace, knowing that Your grace encompasses me. With gratitude and humility, I pray, trusting that You will hear and respond. In the mighty name of Jesus, I pray. Amen.

May 4
Use My Weapons

"We use God's mighty weapons, not worldly weapons, to knock down the strongholds of human reasoning and to destroy false arguments. We destroy every proud obstacle that keeps people from knowing God. We capture their rebellious thoughts and teach them to obey Christ."

2 Corinthians 10:4-5 NLT

Dear Lord, Your way is perfect and Your word is true (Psalm 18:30.) What a contrast to my ways and my thoughts that seem to hold me captive. I feel like I can hold my attention for about 5 seconds before my mind goes off course. It's so frustrating that self-defeating thoughts are constantly jumping in and out of my head, and I feel so powerless to control them.

Lord, today, I will use my weapons; such as the double-edged sword of Your Spirit to fight this battle (Hebrews 4:12). They are mighty for the pulling down of strongholds. When I waiver, remind me that lies and toxic thoughts have no place in my mind. I have the mind of Christ (1 Corinthians 2:16) and I allow only thoughts that are of You to take root today!

I trust that as I cling to You and Your Word, I will be reminded to use my weapons to renew and transform my mind, allowing me to live according to Your perfect plan. In the mighty name of Jesus, I pray. Amen.

May 5
I am Set Apart

"Who is like you, O Lord, among the gods? Who is like you, majestic in holiness, awesome in glorious deeds, doing wonders?"

Exodus 15:11 ESV

Dear Holy God, separate and set apart. There is no one else like You. What a blessing to know that You call me to be holy as You are holy (1 Peter 1:16). Sometimes the truth of my past mistakes is too painful or shameful to face. I thank You that in those moments, You remind me that I am forgiven and all my shame is gone (Psalm 32:5). I am holy!

You restore me to wholeness and remind me that there is no condemnation for those who live in alignment with You (Romans 8:1). What a relief to know that Your grace covers me and washes away my sins.

Lord, help me grasp the depth of what it means to live a life set apart for You. Show me that holiness is not just about avoiding certain actions or behaviors, but it is a surrender of my whole being to Your will. Remind me that being healthy IS holy! May my daily actions in my health and life be a reflection of what it means to be set apart for You. In Jesus' holy name, I pray. Amen.

May 6
New in You

"Therefore if anyone is in Christ, he is a new creature; the old things passed away; behold, new things have come."

2 Corinthians 5:17 NASB

Lord, God of redemption and reconciliation, I humbly come before You, recognizing Your power to make all things new (Isaiah 43:19). You are constantly at work, bringing forth newness and transformation in every aspect of my life, including my health. You are guiding me toward a new way of living, one that is not dictated by my old reactions, unhealthy emotions, or negative thought patterns.

Help me discern which feelings and emotions are beneficial, leading me closer to You, and which ones keep me going in circles. I surrender my old ways of thinking to You knowing that You can help me change the way I think (Romans 12:2). Grant me the wisdom to let go of the mistakes of the past and the uncertainty of the future, as I focus my thoughts solely on the present moment, where Your guiding hand is at work (Matthew 6:34).

As I draw near to You, Lord, You continue to make all things new within me and around me. May Your transformative power shine brightly in my life, illuminating my path and guiding me closer to Your perfect will. In Jesus' name, I pray. Amen.

May 7
I Release My Grip

"If you want to be perfect, go, sell your possessions and give to the poor, and you will have treasure in heaven. Then come, follow me." When the young man heard this, he went away sad, because he had great wealth."
Matthew 19:21-22 NIV

I call out to You today, Yahweh, the God who saves. (Psalm 68:20) I recognize that I have been seduced by the allure of possessions, power, and pride, and I acknowledge that these worldly attachments have hindered my connection with You. But today, I come before You, ready to surrender them all.

I fear the uncertainty of who I will become without these earthly crutches, like excess food or alcohol. What if the pain becomes unbearable? These anxieties flood my mind and overwhelm me. But, in the midst of my trembling, You call me to cast my burdens upon You (Philippians 4:6), assuring me that You will provide me with rest and peace beyond my understanding.

I release my grip on everything that does not bring glory to Your name, entrusting all my weaknesses, worries, doubts, and insecurities into Your capable hands. I trust that You will be my strength when I am weak, my comfort in times of distress, and my guide when I feel lost. In the mighty name of Jesus' I pray. Amen.

May 8
Entering God's Rest

"For we who have believed enter that rest, as he has said, "As I swore in my wrath, 'They shall not enter my rest,'" although his works were finished from the foundation of the world."

Hebrews 4:3 ESV

Heavenly Father, You are the source of all comfort (2 Corinthians 1:3) and the One who leads me beside still waters, restoring my weary soul (Psalm 23:2). In the midst of my daily challenges and afflictions, You are my refuge and strength.

I release any confidence in my own strength and surrender control to You. Take full reign in my life. Guide my thoughts, calm my restless mind, and grant me peace when I feel over-whelmed with life. I release the lies and societal notions that, "I'm good," "I got this," "I can't handle it." The truth is, I can't and although I've been doing the best that I can, it's worn me out. I'm desperate to enter Your rest, Father.

I am grateful for the amazing exchange You offer—my burdens for Your peace. May Your spirit of peace wash over me, saturating every part of my being. You are the source of all comfort, the giver of peace beyond understanding, and the provider of everything I need so I receive Your gift of rest today. In the Matchless name of Jesus, I pray. Amen.

May 9
Promise Keeper

"I will make you into a great nation, and I will bless you; I will make your name great, so that you will be a blessing. I will bless those who bless you and curse those who curse you; and all the families of the earth will be blessed through you."

Genesis 12:2-3 NIV

I call out to You today as my Waymaker and Promise-keeper. Your Word never fails (Luke 1:37). It will always accomplish what You desire and achieve the purpose for which You sent it (Isaiah 55:11).

When the enemy tries to tell me who I am not, remind me of Your promises. And, when the enemy tries to tell me what I am. Remind me of Your promises. And when my own mind tries to betray me and remind me of all my past flaws and mistakes, I stand on Your Word instead. You're bigger than the lies of the enemy. You're bigger than the memories of my past failures and disappointments. With You, my future is bright (Proverbs 23:18). My identity is grounded in You and so is my hope.

So today, I exchange my doubt, discouragement, and despair for Your promise of hope. I give You all my anxiety, my worries, and my overwhelm and I remember Your promises for me. They will stand to a thousand generations (Deuteronomy 7:9). In Jesus' name, I pray. Amen!

May 10
Ruling my Feelings

"The heart is deceitful above all things, and desperately sick; who can understand it?"

Jeremiah 17:9 ESV

I honor You today God of truth (Deuteronomy 32:4) Your truth sets me free from all the lies I've believed and the feelings that lead me astray. You are so much greater than my feelings!

I've been dragged around by them into all kinds of situations that have left me full of shame and guilt. In many ways, God, I have made my feelings my Lord and let them rule over me in the place that You belong as my only authority. I've done what I hate (Romans 7:19) so many times because of my feelings—usually trying to avoid the ones that feel awful, but sometimes just to enjoy the ones that feel great.

Today, I am trusting in Your unconditional love and in the knowledge that I can feel my feelings without feeding them with food. Give me the patience to pause before acting on them, allowing them to realign with my spirit. Continually remind me that my feelings were meant to serve me and not the other way around. Thank you for the gift of my feelings and the ability to bring them under subjection! In Jesus' name. Amen!

May 11
Deliverance from Double-mindedness

"But let him ask in faith, with no doubting, for the one who doubts is like a wave of the sea that is driven and tossed by the wind. For that person must not suppose that he will receive anything from the Lord; he is a double-minded man, unstable in all his ways."

James 1:6-8 ESV

Lord, Your promises are yes and amen (2 Corinthians 1:20). You are ever-faithful to do what You say You will do. Yet, I still live with a double mind, feeling like the waves of the sea that are driven and tossed by the wind. I truly want to believe Your Word, but something my mind keeps telling me otherwise. I desperately want peace, Lord. I want to wake up and not think about my weight or stress about what I'm going to eat or what clothes are going to hide my body.

So just for today, help me keep my mind fixed on You (Isaiah 26:3). You give me the stability and peace I seek. You lift me out of the pit of despair and set my feet on solid ground and steady me as I walk in step with You (Psalm 40:2).

Today, I let go of all the negative thoughts that do not glorify You. I let go of everything that keeps me feeling double-minded. I take every thought captive and I bring them to obedience (2 Corinthians 10:5). I choose to stand in Your truth alone. In Your son's name, I pray. Amen!

May 12
Letting Go of Overwhelm

"Be still, and know that I am God; I will be exalted
among the nations, I will be exalted in the earth."
Psalm 46:10 ESV

I call on You today my God of peace, Jehovah Shalom. You promise to exchange Your rest for my weariness (Matthew 11:28) Yet, I often feel like a hamster on the wheel going 100 miles an hour, but never getting anywhere. I feel like I can never catch up, which has made me turn to food for comfort as a temporary escape. When I'm overwhelmed I just don't care anymore.

So today I let go of everything that keeps me in a state of overwhelm. I release that spirit of lack that tells me I need to do more, be more, give more, and think more. Remind me that I am enough because my sufficiency comes from You (2 Corinthians 12:9).

Help me find peace in the present moment, knowing that You have equipped me with all I need for the day. Fill my heart with the understanding that my worthiness is not determined by my accomplishments or the expectations of others, but by the love and grace You freely bestow upon me. Thank you, Jehovah Shalom, for Your unwavering presence in my life. In Your precious name, I pray, Amen.

May 13
Letting Go of Procrastination

"Look carefully then how you walk, not as unwise but as wise, making the best use of the time because the days are evil. Therefore do not be foolish, but understand what the will of the Lord is."

Ephesians 5:15-17 NIV

Dear Sovereign Lord, You know everything and see everything. I bless You and give You all glory, honor, and praise today. You are King and Lord over my life. Let Your will be done (Matthew 6:10).

Father, I seek Your kingdom above all else (Matthew 6:33) because it gives me perspective and helps me prioritize. I trust You and I want Your best for me. It is my desire to be in good health, but I often procrastinate on taking action. Pluck procrastination out at its root Father God. Whether it's time management tools or encouragement from others, guide me in overcoming this sabotaging spirit.

Remind me that the temporary discomfort is far worth the long-term gains (Hebrews 11:25). Let me work as unto You (Colossians 3:23) and focus on what You've called me to do without hesitation or delay. It's a new day and I will move forward in faith, trusting You to be my motivation and inspiration. I boldly declare and commit to let go of procrastination today in Your Son's holy and precious name. Amen!

May 14
Letting Go of Guilt and Shame

"Even if we feel guilty, God is greater than our feelings, and he knows everything."

1 John 3:20 NLT

Dear omniscient God who knows and sees everything including every feeling I have and will ever feel (Psalm 139:4). Lord, You know that I constantly struggle with feelings of guilt and shame. I'm constantly judging myself and I feel like I always come up short. I feel like I'm either letting myself down, letting others down, or letting You down.

In these times of inner turmoil, remind me that I am doing the best I can. Help me to let go of these feelings after they have served their sole purpose which was to guide me back to You. You have given me dominion over everything (Genesis 1:18) on this earth including my feelings. My feelings serve me, not the other way around.

When the devil or even my own mind tries to come and make me feel guilty, remind me that there is no condemnation in those who are in You (Romans 8:1). And help me to remember that a spirit of guilt or shame will never motivate me to change my unhealthy habits. The only thing that will bring me lasting change is abiding in You (Colossians 3:4). In Jesus' name I pray. Amen.

May 15
Letting Go of Control

"And he said to them all, If any man will come after me, let him deny himself, and take up his cross daily, and follow me.

Luke 9:23 ESV

I bless You today, almighty God, creator of heaven and earth (Genesis 1:1). Thank You for showing me how to live in You (Acts 17:28). I admit that it's the opposite of what I've been striving for. I want to be in control and You call me to let go of control. I want to satisfy my flesh and You tell me to deny myself. Your ways are so much higher than my ways (Isaiah 55:9)!

You know my uncanny knack for taking over and needing to control situations. Thank You for reassuring me that I can relinquish that Jezebel spirit. You are in control and that's all that matters. You promise to do all the heavy lifting as I cast my cares on You (1 Peter 5:7). Strengthen me so I can live a life of worship to You through submission and sacrifice.

Grant me the strength to continually release my need for control and embrace Your guiding hand. As I walk this path of surrender, may my life become a testament to Your glory, shining brightly as an act of worship and devotion. In Jesus' Name I pray. Amen.

May 16
Letting Go of False Perceptions

*"We saw the Nephilim there (the descendants of Anak
come from the Nephilim). We seemed like grasshoppers
in our own eyes, and we looked the same to them."*
Numbers 13:33 NIV

Dear Lord, God of truth. You are the way, the truth, and life (John 14:6) When You say that I am fearfully and wonderfully made, I believe it! You say I am no longer a slave, but an heir (Galatians 4:7). I am Your workmanship, created to do good works. (Ephesians 2:10) I stand only on Your truths.

Father, help me to see myself as You see me. When I look in the mirror, I'm not always happy with the reflection staring back at me. I've believed lies about myself for so long that it's hard to believe that I am more than what I see and believe.

Today, I release all faulty perceptions of myself and only claim who I am in You. Let Your thoughts be my thoughts (Isaiah 55:8). I focus on living in the image of who You created me (Genesis 1:27) to be and reject the enemy's lies that try to tell me that I am not who You say I am. Thank You for renewing my mind and transforming me by the power of Your Spirit. In the mighty name of Jesus, I pray. Amen.

May 17
Letting Go of Codependency

"For am I now seeking the approval of man, or of God? Or am I trying to please man? If I were still trying to please man, I would not be a servant of Christ."
Galatians 1:10 ESV

Dear Mighty God. You sent Your humble son Jesus to serve (Matthew 28:20), not to be served— what a perfect model of love. I thank You for also blessing me with a tender heart to be sensitive to other people's needs and hurts, but somewhere along the line, I let this gift become a stumbling block. Somehow, I started putting other people's needs before my own in an unhealthy way and it's robbing me of living a healthy life.

I come to You today, Lord, to help me to separate myself from all the people and situations that I've entangled myself in. It's not my job to fix, rescue, or save anyone.

I take responsibility for my life only and I give others space to make their own choices (Galatians 6:5). Help me to love others as an outpouring of Your love for me (John 15:12). Give me the courage to face my own challenges and strongholds and hold space for others as they do the same. I'm free to accept myself and others trusting that You will restore and renew each of us. I release the spirit of codependency, in Jesus' Name. Amen.

May 18
Letting Go of Disappointment

"And we know that for those who love God all things work together for good, for those who are called according to his purpose."

Romans 8:28 ESV

Almighty God, You are my strength and shield, a very present help in trouble (Psalm 46:1). I have this pervasive feeling that things will never work out for me. That I will never reach my goal weight, never be loved like I need and never be satisfied. I feel like people are constantly disappointing me and things rarely work out as I want. I know this is not what You say about me.

Lord, Your Word says to trust in You with all my heart and You will give me all I desire (Proverbs 3:5). So today I let go of the lie that things will not work out for me and I trust You. I don't have to be afraid of failure or disappointment.

Help me to believe for Your best in all circumstances. I trust that You will work all things out for my good and Your glory. Remind me that You are the ultimate author of my life's story. Today, I embrace the hope and assurance that You will guide me toward a future filled with fulfillment, love, and satisfaction. In the name of Jesus, I pray. Amen.

May 19
Sanctified Spirit, Soul, and Body

"Now may the God of peace Himself sanctify you entirely; and may your spirit and soul and body be preserved complete, without blame at the coming of our Lord Jesus Christ."

1 Thessalonians 5:23 NASB

Dear Holy Triune God. I bless You today in the name of the Father, Son and Holy Spirit. I thank You for creating me in Your image. Like Yourself, You create me as a tripartite being—body, soul, and spirit.

As I get healthy for Your glory, reveal all parts of my being and teach me how they can come together in harmony. Teach me how to make no provisions for my flesh (Romans 13:14) that always wants to take over; align my thoughts with Yours (2 Corinthians 10:5) and keep my mind fixed on You (Isaiah 26:3).

You are a God of order so teach me to live each day according to Your blueprint—my body obeys my mind and my mind obeys my spirit and my spirit is connected to Your spirit. Let Your spirit take control of my mind every single minute of the day so my body will fall in line. Thank You for Your wisdom and revelation knowledge that allows me to live as a healthy person—spirit, soul and body. In Jesus' name. Amen!

May 20
My Body – A Living Sacrifice

"Therefore I urge you, brethren, by the mercies of God, to present your bodies a living and holy sacrifice, acceptable to God, which is your spiritual service of worship."

Romans 12:1 NASB

Lord, You love me so much that You sent Your son to live on earth in a human body (John 3:16). My desire is to be more like Your son Jesus and less like me. Help me to discipline my body like an athlete and keep it under control (1 Corinthians 9:27). When my flesh is tempted in every way, teach me how to overcome by the power of Your Word (Matthew 4:4).

Let me see my physical body from a new perspective. Remind me that this earthly tent houses You, the living God. Help me to let go of the belief that my body is mine to do with as I please. It is Your temple. Let my stewardship of it be honoring and pleasing to You.

When the gap between Your sinless life and the life I live frustrates me. Remind me that it's You that gives health and nourishment to my bones when I put my trust in You (Proverbs 3:8). Thank You for rescuing me (Romans 7:24) from this body that's constantly betraying me. You've got this, Lord, so I can release and let go. In Jesus' Name, I pray. Amen!

May 21
Lover of My Soul

"Now devote your heart and soul to seeking the Lord your God."

1 Chronicles 22:19 NIV

Dear Lord God, lover of my soul (2 Cor 5:15). You breathed life into my body and created my soul (Genesis 2:7). I am one in a billion with my unique soul which houses my, thoughts, feelings, imaginations, desires, and passions. Pierce my soul with Your truth since it's the fulcrum that determines whether I will satisfy my flesh or yield to my spirit. Your word says that it can be divinely guided or deceitfully wicked when unbridled. Let me always choose the latter.

As I walk out my health journey each day, I pray that You guide my soul with Your divine wisdom. Let Your love be the compass that directs my soul's desires, knowing that in Your hands it finds its true purpose, direction, and fulfillment.

Thank You for restoring my soul when I am weak (Psalm 23:3). Your words says that when I seek You with all my heart (soul) then I will find You (Jeremiah 29:13). Wonderful are Your works, my soul knows it very well (Psalm 139:14). In Your name I pray. Amen.

May 22
Your Spirit in Me

"The spirit of man is the candle of the Lord, searching all the inward parts of the belly."
Proverbs 20:27 ESV

Lord, I thank You for Your Spirit that lives in me (Romans 8:9). Let Your Spirit of wisdom and understanding enlighten my mind and open my heart to Your truth. Let Your Spirit of courage guide me and keep me strengthened for this journey. Let Your Spirit of knowledge and reverence help me see beyond myself and embrace a bigger vision of who I am in You. Spirit of God, ignite my faith and help me to rest in You.

Lord, in the presence of Your Spirit, I surrender my will and desires to You completely (Romans 8:6). Help me to align my thoughts, words, and actions with Your divine purpose. May Your Spirit empower me to walk in obedience and to shine Your light in this world. Grant me the discernment to recognize the voice of Your Spirit amidst the noise of the world, so that I make good choices that honor You.

Let Your Spirit's guiding work within me be evident to all, so that I may be a living testament of Your grace and love. May Your Spirit continue to refine me, molding me into the person You created me to be. In all things, Holy Spirit, have Your way in me. I humbly ask this in Jesus' precious name. Amen.

May 23
Dis-ease

"A joyful heart is good medicine, but a crushed spirit dries up the bones."

Proverbs 17:22 ESV

Dear Lord, Jehovah Rafa, my healer. I thank You that healing comes from You. This means that I don't have to waste extraordinary amounts of time trying to figure out how to heal my body in my own strength. You've given me all I need to care for, nourish, and heal my body and it all starts with a heart that is turned towards You.

As I put my trust in You, humble myself before You, and stay away from evil, You will heal my body and strengthen my bones (Proverbs 3:7-8). You have the power to restore and renew, and I believe that Your healing is not only for my physical body, but it's also emotional and spiritual. Help me to make healthy choices (Deuteronomy 30:19) that enrich my life. Your will is that I would have life in abundance (John 10:10), free of illness and disease.

I speak Your Word over my health. I put boundaries around the conversations I have; the shows I watch; and anything that breeds fear and dis-ease into my life. I embrace Your yoke of ease(Matt 11:30). In You I am healthy, happy, and well! In Jesus' name. Amen!

May 24
Just Breathe!

"And when he had said this, he breathed on them and said to them, 'Receive the Holy Spirit.'"

John 20:22 ESV

Dear Lord, breath of life. It's Your breath that sustains me every day. Each time I inhale, I'm reminded of Your presence, awe, and wonder. There's nothing to worry about when I remember that Your breath fills me with life (Job 33:4). Just as You breathed into the disciples and gave them a new life (John 20:22), do the same for me at all times.

And so, I pause right now Lord, and allow Your breath to fill my lungs with air. Let me flow each day with the rhythm of Your breath in me. Every inhale fills me with Your power and every exhale allows me to release all tension, anxiety, angst, and everything that is not of You.

Just as the wind moves effortlessly through the trees, let Your breath move through every aspect of my being, cleansing, purifying, and revitalizing me. In every moment, help me to be attuned to Your presence, allowing Your breath to infuse me with courage, resilience, and unwavering faith. I am eternally grateful for Your constant presence and Your life-giving breath. In Jesus' Holy name, I pray. Amen.

May 25
Healthy Roots, Healthy Fruit

"I pray that you, being rooted and established in love, may have power, together with all the Lord's holy people, to grasp how wide and long and high and deep is the love of Christ,"

Ephesians 3: 17–18 NIV

Dear Master Gardener, thank you for Your Word that I have hidden in my heart so that I will not sin against You (Psalm 119:11). Forgive me for continually picking back up what I keep laying at Your feet. I pray that I would be anchored firmly in the soil of Your love just like a tree firmly planted by a river (Psalm 1:3). I want to bear good fruit that will bring You glory.

Ground me and root me in Your love today. Let me steep in the truth of Your Word so that the weeds of life and the enemy will not crowd out what You're cultivating in me. Till the soil in my mind and make it a fertile place to receive Your truth. Sink my roots deep into Your love so I thrive! Remind me that I already possess all I need in You to bear good fruit a hundredfold (Matthew 13:8) what You planted!

Grant me the wisdom to persevere through seasons of pruning and nourish me with the living water of Your grace. In Your loving care, I find my truest fulfillment. In Jesus' Name, I pray, Amen.

May 26
Faith to Believe

"Now faith is the assurance of things hoped for, the conviction of things not seen."

Hebrews 11:1 ESV

What an awesome God You are, Father! Thank You so much for making the way to a full and forever life in You; for sending Your Son as a ransom to reclaim me. All I have to do is believe and put my faith in that sacrificial transaction and in Your life-saving Son. So simple, but not easy to live out. So I come to You today asking You to increase my faith. Forgive my unbelief Lord (Mark 9:24). I get so stuck in old cycles that sometimes, it does not even occur to me to run to You, but today is a new day.

Thank You for the saving faith You gave me, even if it's only the size of a mustard seed (Matthew 13:32), but You tell me enough, so I believe it. Although it seems slow, I am making progress. I believe that in Your strength, I am letting go of past hurts and traumas and (Isaiah 53:5), I am healed.

Although I don't see it, I believe that You are changing me from the inside out. My hope in You grows stronger each day as I learn to trust You more and cling to Your Word. Help me to fight the good fight (2 Timothy 4:7) to stay in faith, Lord Jesus. In Your trust-worthy name I ask and pray Amen.

May 27
Acceptance

"That is why, for Christ's sake, I delight in weaknesses,
in insults, in hardships, in persecutions, in difficulties.
For when I am weak, then I am strong."
                                        2 Corinthians 12:10 NIV

My Great Defender. You are always fighting for me (Exodus 14:14). I come before You today asking You to help me accept the parts of me I loathe. The constant wishing, wanting, and hoping to change only adds unnecessary burdens to my soul.

Regardless of how my life unfolds, grant me the wisdom to trust that what You provide is precisely what I need for this day (Matt 6:11). Your grace, abundant and boundless, is sufficient for me (2 Corinthians 12:9).

Teach me that acceptance is an acknowledgment of my limitations and an unwavering surrender of my will to Yours, and not a sign of giving up or giving in.

Grant me the grace to accept what is beyond my control, the courage to change what lies within my power, and the insight to discern between the two. Help me embrace all of me, with all my flaws and imperfections, knowing that You love me unconditionally.

May acceptance be my gateway to peace and fulfillment, as I walk hand in hand with You. In Jesus' name, I pray. Amen.

May 28
Release the Resistance

"It was good for me to be afflicted so that I might learn your decrees."

Psalm 119:71 NIV

Dear graceful and merciful God. Thank You for keeping me from stumbling and falling (Jude 1:24) I'm so grateful for a renewed perspective on the resistance- the setbacks, stumbling blocks, and strongholds that get in my way every time I step out into new territory. Help me to see that it is part of the process instead of fighting against it.

Remind me that resistance is to be released, not resisted. Pretending it does not exist or white-knuckling my way through will never be an effective strategy. Let resistance do its perfecting work of conforming me into Your image and likeness (Romans 8:29). Like the pain of lifting weights at the gym, reminds me of the benefits of resistance training, especially when it hurts and I want to quit.

Today, I release and let go of the resistance that tried to stop me from pursuing all You've called me to do and be. What I resist only persists and what I release flows with ease. I will let patience do its work in me so that I may be mature and complete, not lacking anything (James 1:4). In Jesus' name I pray. Amen.

May 29
Awareness

"Examine yourselves, to see whether you are in the faith. Test yourselves. Or do you not realize this about yourselves, that Jesus Christ is in you?—unless indeed you fail to meet the test!"

2 Corinthians 13:5 ESV

Dear God of all truth. You see all things and know all things. You give sight to the blind (Psalm 146:8).

Today, help me increase my awareness. Too often, I'm not even aware of what I'm doing or why I'm doing it. Something will trigger a thought in my mind and off I go like a wind-up doll out of control.

Today, I pause and feel Your spirit in me (Acts 2:4). I will take You with me throughout the day and include You in every detail of my life today. Teach me why I do what I do. Search for my motives. I know that awareness is the starting point of all breakthroughs. Forgive me for acting blindly and grant me the discernment to recognize when I am acting independently of Your will.

Guide me, Lord, that I may walk in step with Your Spirit, aware and attuned to Your voice and sensitive to Your leading. May my every thought, word, and action guide me to greater awareness of my motives and align them with Your divine will for me. In Your holy name, I pray. Amen.

May 30
Pause and Pray

"Be careful for nothing; but in every thing by prayer and supplication with thanksgiving let your requests be made known unto God."

Philippians 4:6 KJV

Lord, You are so faithful. When I call out to You, You always hear me and answer me (1 John 5:15). Before I busy myself with my to-do list, I come before You in stillness and quietness so that I can hear how You're speaking to me.

Help me to practice the power of the pause; those intentional moments when I stop, realign my nervous system, and fix my mind on You (Heb 12:2). Teach me to always pause and pray, as my first line of defense instead of the last resort. May pausing Increase my awareness, so I run to You instead of food or other things that don't satisfy me.

Let daily pauses teach me to slow down, so I don't rush headstrong in battlefields, but rather experience Your peace and presence which guides me to the truth. I believe in the power of prayer, but too often I forget. So today I slow down; I pause and breathe in Your presence; I listen for how You're speaking to me and then I yield to Your spirit. In Jesus' name. Amen.

May 31
God Truly Cares

"When the Lord saw her, his heart overflowed with compassion. 'Don't cry!' he said."

Luke 7:13 NLT

Dear Lord, God of Compassion, You're not sitting in heaven watching me suffer, but You feel what I feel. This truth brings me so much comfort and peace. I thank You for this month of reminding me how much You love me and care for me. I will continue to surrender my health journey and my entire life to You even though sometimes I feel so alone in my struggles.

My challenges seem so petty in the grand scheme of life, but I know that You care about everything that concerns me (1 Peter 5:7). When I want to throw my hands in the air and give up, remind me that You love me with an everlasting love (Jeremiah 31:3).

Your compassion never fails (Lamentations 3:23) and I thank You for a fresh dose every morning and every day. It's in Your anointing that I will move forward today. I will take each day step by step in faith, trusting that You are with me guiding, protecting, and leading me in the right direction (Psalm 23:4). I cast all my worries, cares, and anxieties on You and embrace Your rest (Matthew 11:28). I let go and let God. In Jesus' name, I pray. Amen.

June

SPIRIT-FILLED & SUGAR-FREE

This month's prayers center around the theme of letting go of excess sugar consumption, which has become a significant concern in our lives in this day and age. It is linked to various health issues such as obesity, diabetes, heart disease, and even mental health problems.

The prayers during this month will increase your awareness of the harmful effects of excessive sugar intake and encourage you to seek God's guidance and strength to rid it from your body. It also includes prayers for the strength to resist cravings, the willpower to make healthier choices, and the discipline to stay committed to your goals. You will also pray to be set free from the emotional and psychological aspects of sugar addiction, as you seek God for healing, self-compassion, and a release from the grip of sugar dependence.

By incorporating these prayers into your daily routine, I pray you will cultivate a greater sense of awareness and intentionality when it comes to choosing what to eat each day. Additionally, as you pray, you will begin to discover the deeper motivations behind your eating habits. This journey is not just about reducing sugar; it's about enriching your spirit and fostering a healthier relationship with food. You will learn to lean on God for strength and support, allowing Him to fill the voids that sugar once filled. May this month be a transformative experience where you break free from unhealthy patterns and grow closer to God in the process.

June 1
How Sweet He Is

"It is not good to eat much honey, nor is it glorious to seek one's own glory."

Proverbs 25:27 ESV

Dear Sweet Jesus, You truly are the sweetest gift, and I acknowledge that there are ways in which I have not allowed You to be just that to me. In my pursuit of temporary pleasures, I have turned to sugary indulgences, seeking fulfillment in fleeting sweetness instead of Your everlasting grace.

Lord, I surrender this struggle completely to You. I humbly ask for Your grace and strength to overcome the allure of sugar and to break its destructive hold on my life.

As I spend time in Your word this month, give me wisdom in understanding how to solve this overwhelming problem.. Renew my mind, O Lord, and align my desires with Your perfect will (Philippians 2:13). Today, I draw a line in the sand, breaking the spirit of gluttony (Philippians 3:19) and addiction over me in the chain-breaking name of Jesus.

I declare that I have a spirit of self-control (2 Timothy 1:7). Teach me to find true satisfaction and fulfillment in Your presence, for You alone can satisfy the deepest longings of my heart. In Jesus' Name. Amen.

June 2
Sweet Surrender

"So now the case is closed. There remains no accusing voice of condemnation against those who are joined in life-union with Jesus, the Anointed One."

Romans 8:1 TPT

Dear Father God, creator of all things, thank You for this day, a new opportunity to embrace change and growth. As I embark on the journey of releasing sugar from my life, I am filled with apprehension and fear. The thought of parting with sweets, which have been a constant in my life, fills me with uncertainty and discomfort. But I trust in Your guidance and provision, knowing that true satisfaction is found in You alone.

Your Word reminds me that joy and delight come from feasting on Your truth (Jeremiah 15:16). Help me to find joy and fulfillment in Your presence, Lord. Through faith in Jesus, I am assured that there is no condemnation for those who are united with Him (Romans 8:1). Your grace covers me completely, giving me the confidence to face challenges with strength and resilience.

I declare that Your presence is sweeter than any indulgence, Lord. Empower me to prepare wisely for the journey ahead, guarding against temptation and staying vigilant (1 Peter 5:8). In Jesus' name, I pray. Amen.

June 3
From Sugar to Sweet Success

"Prepare your work outside; get everything ready for yourself in the field, and after that build your house."
Proverbs 24:27 ESV

Dear Lord, You are God who sees me (Genesis 16:13). You know my tendencies and my habits to choose sugar over healthier alternatives. You see all of me, and You love me in spite of my actions. You know I want to finally kick this sugar habit but I don't take the time to do the planning that it will take to be successful. Help me to get ready, to plan and prepare, to shop for the right foods, and take the time to seek out healthy recipes. I need Your guidance and support, Lord. Help me to gather the necessary tools, to create a well-thought-out plan.

In addition to the practical help, thank You for Your Word and Your wisdom for how to set myself up for success. Your Word is a lamp unto my feet and a light unto my path (Psalm 119:105). Your divine wisdom gives me a blueprint for achieving success in all areas of my life, including this one. There is order and peace in everything that is of You (1 Corinthians 14:33).

I am committing today to walking by Your Spirit and learning how to be successful. (Matthew 11:29). In Jesus' sweet name I pray. Amen.

June 4
Slaying the Sugar Giants

"The world is unprincipled. It's dog-eat-dog out there! The world doesn't fight fair. But we don't live or fight our battles that way—never have and never will. The tools of our trade aren't for marketing or manipulation, but they are for demolishing that entire massively corrupt culture."

2 Corinthians 10:4 MSG

All-powerful Lord God, I honor You and magnify Your name. Thank You for another day with You. And thank You for securing victory for me over anything and everything that may rise up against me. I recognize the battle that I'm in. I'm fighting against a diet industry that stays in business by keeping me addicted to sugar. I recognize that I must advocate for my own health because the food industry's agenda does not serve my agenda to glorify You in my body. I am no match for their schemes, but You are!

I cast them all down in the name of Jesus. I am picking up the double-edged sword of Your Spirit (Hebrews 4:12) to demolish the places the enemy has encamped. When I waver, remind me that Your son Jesus has overcome the world. Remind me that I have the mind of Christ (Philippians 2:5), and in the holy name of Jesus, the victory is won.

Thank You, Lord, that I am worth fighting for. Amen.

June 5
Renouncing Wrong Thinking

"We use our powerful God-tools for smashing warped philosophies, tearing down barriers erected against the truth of God, fitting every loose thought and emotion and impulse into the structure of life shaped by Christ."
2 Corinthians 10:5 MSG

Dear Almighty God, I'm leaning on Your leading with an open heart and mind. Thank You for Your powerful arsenal of weaponry You've equipped me with to walk victoriously. This battle to overcome sugar starts in my mind (Isaiah 26:3), not with my flesh.

Lord, help me to recognize and renounce wrong thinking and warped philosophies (2 Corinthians 10:5) that have kept me stuck in this cycle of craving and indulging in excess sugar. I invite Your Holy Spirit to reveal to me the toxic thoughts that keep me running to it instead of You. I declare that every loose thought, emotion, and impulse is now brought into alignment with and obedience to Your truth. I consciously reject the grip of fear that clings to me, preventing me from letting go, and instead, I choose to place my unwavering faith in You. I firmly believe that Your boundless power is more than sufficient to uplift and support me through every challenge, every craving and every temptation. Thank You for the tools to smash and tear down the lies of the enemy. In the name of Jesus, the liberator from all mental bondage, I fervently pray. Amen.

June 6
Trusting God Through Sugar Withdrawal

For the Lord gives wisdom; from his mouth come knowledge and understanding."
Proverbs 2:6 NIV

D ear God of grace and compassion. Today, I come before You with honesty and vulnerability. Lord, I confess that the thought of living without sugar even for just one day feels overwhelming and daunting. Sugar has woven its way into my daily routine, becoming a source of comfort and pleasure. Right now, I struggle to imagine a life without it and the anticipated withdrawal symptoms loom large in my mind. I fear they will overpower me.

Yet, in this moment of uncertainty, I turn to You, my Rock and Redeemer, for I know that in You alone lies my strength and assurance. Grant me the faith to believe that through Your divine power, even the most daunting challenges, including sugar withdrawal, can be overcome (Philippians 4:13). Give me the faith to believe that with You, all things are possible (Matt. 19:26).

I acknowledge that my dependency on sugar has become a stumbling block in my journey of faith and health. Yet, I know that through Your grace and guidance, I can break free from its grip. Strengthen my resolve, Lord, and instill in me a spirit of perseverance and determination. As I surrender this struggle to You, I trust that You will lead me on the path to wholeness and abundant life. In Jesus' name, I pray. Amen.

June 7
Beyond the Bliss Point

"I can do all things through him who strengthens me."
Philippians 4:13 ESV

Dear God of Power and Might, I come before You today, recognizing the power and influence that sugary foods hold over my life. The diet industry, with its clever scientists, have crafted an enticing combination of sugar, fat, and salt known as the bliss point, designed to captivate my taste buds and fuel my cravings. I'm no match for their schemes (2 Cor 10.5). So, I am here to declare that in You, Lord, I find the strength to fight and win the war for my taste buds.

In moments of weakness, when the allure of sugary treats beckons me, remind me of Your faithfulness and the power that resides within me through Your Spirit. You have promised that no temptation is too great for me to bear, for You always provide a way out (1 Corinthians 10:13).

Open my eyes to the deceitful tactics of the food industry, and grant me the wisdom to make informed decisions about the foods I consume. Teach me to find balance and moderation, allowing Your Spirit to lead me in all aspects of my life, including my eating habits. May my choices bring glory to Your name. I pray all this in the name of Jesus Christ, my Savior and Redeemer. Amen.

June 8
Embracing the Sweetness of God's Presence

*"Where can I go from your Spirit? Or where can I flee
from your presence?"*

Psalm 139:7 NIV

I bless You today, Lord. Thank You so much for Your sweet
presence in my life, right here, right now. Please forgive me
for the times I forget that You are always with me. I confess that
I often find myself consumed by worries about the future and
burdened by shame from the past, neglecting the precious gift
of the present moment.

As I journey through this day, I choose to walk hand-in-hand,
step-by-step, minute-by-minute, and second-by-second with
You. I place my trust in Your power to carry me through
each and every moment. Fill me, O Lord, with Your joy and
peace that surpasses all understanding. You came so that I may
experience a full and abundant life (John 10:10), so I ask You
to break the chains of worry and shame that keep me from
experiencing Your sweet presence.

When I get caught up in my self-defeating thoughts, remind
me that You are always with me and always go before me
(Deuteronomy 31:8). I will be strong and courageous because
You promise to be with me wherever I go (Joshua 1:9). Your
presence is all I need. In the name of Jesus, who has conquered
all temptation, I pray. Amen.

June 9
Abundant Nourishment

"And my God will meet all your needs according to the riches of his glory in Christ Jesus."
Philippians 4:19 NIV

Heavenly Father, my Jehovah Jireh. I thank You for always providing for my every need. You know what I need even before I ask (Matt. 6:8). I confess that I often get caught up in the mindset of fixating on what I need to stop doing–like eliminating sugar which is a good thing but today, Lord, I want to shift my focus towards adding healthy and nourishing things instead. Help me to be additive instead of restrictive.

You desire good things for Your children. Your plans are to give me a hope for the future (Jeremiah 29:11). Help me to see that the path to health and well-being is not only about deprivation but about tuning in to how You are guiding me and embracing the abundance of goodness You have prepared for me.

Open my eyes to the vibrant array of fruits, vegetables, whole grains, and proteins that You have provided. Teach me to savor the flavors and nourishment that come from the gifts of Your creation (Gen. 1: 29-30). Delight my tastebuds with new foods and give me a spirit of curiosity to try different foods.

Thank You, Father, for Your love, grace, and provision. May my choices honor You and bring glory to Your name. In Jesus' name, I pray. Amen.

June 10
Freedom from Emotional Sabotage

"Even if we feel guilty, God is greater than our feelings, and He knows everything."

1 John 3:20 NLT

Dear Great and Omnipotent God. You are greatly to be praised (Psalm 45:3). I confess that I have allowed myself to be dragged around by my emotions, leading me into situations filled with shame and guilt. In many ways, I have made my feelings my lord, allowing them to rule over me instead of giving You the rightful place in my life. I humbly ask for Your forgiveness, Lord.

Today, I place my trust in Your unconditional love and in the knowledge that You, who dwell within me, are greater than any force that threatens to overpower me (1 John 4:4). Teach me to tune in to my emotions as messengers that draw me closer to You, instead of saboteurs. Remind me that Your ways are higher and wiser than mine (Isaiah 55:9).

I invite Your healing presence into my life, speaking shalom peace over my entire being, including my emotions and how I respond to them. May Your peace flow through me, bringing regulation to my emotions. Instead of suppressing, avoiding, or feeding my feelings with sugary foods, I choose to trust You with them. In Jesus' name, filled with His peace that surpasses all understanding (Philippians 4:7), I pray. Amen.

June 11
Savoring True Nourishment

*"Oh, taste and see that the LORD is good! Blessed is
the man who takes refuge in him."*

Psalm 34:8 ESV

Good morning, Father, God of all contentment and satisfaction. Today I pray that You would teach me to
recognize what drives my need to snack. Grant me discernment
and self-awareness, Lord. Open my eyes to recognize when
I am using snacking as a means of distraction or to fill an
emotional void. Help me to turn to You in those moments,
seeking comfort, guidance, and fulfillment in Your presence.
Redirect my focus from temporary indulgence to the everlasting satisfaction found in You.

I pray for the fruit of self-control (Galatians 5:22-23) to manifest in my life, empowering me to make wise choices in my
snacking habits. I desire to live by every word that comes out of
Your mouth (Matthew 4:4). Remind me that true sustenance is
found by feeding on Your Word. Your spiritual nourishment
satisfies me far beyond the temporary pleasures of snacking.

Grant me the strength to resist the temptations that arise and
remind me of Your presence and Your power within me. I
trust in Your ability to transform my snacking habits. I stand on
Your wonder-working power. I renew my mind and let go of
my old habits that no longer serve me or glorify You. In Jesus'
name, I pray. Amen.

June 12
Sustained by Grace

"God resists the proud, But gives grace to the humble."
James 4:6 NKJV

Dear God of Grace, Your abundant grace sustains me (2 Cor 12:9) on this journey of giving up sugar. In moments of weakness and discouragement, when I stumble or feel overwhelmed by cravings, Your grace is my refuge and strength. I am reminded that transformation is a process, and though the road may be challenging, You are faithful to carry me through to completion (Philippians 1:6).

Help me, Lord, to embrace humility in this journey. I need Your grace and help (James 4:6). Teach me to lean not on my own understanding but to trust in Your wisdom and guidance (Proverbs 3:5-6). When I stumble, it's Your grace that sets me back on course.

I declare that I will not grow weary in doing good, knowing that in due season, I will reap a harvest if I do not give up (Galatians 6:9). Grant me the wisdom to find a balance between resting in Your grace and actively working towards healthier choices Teach me discipline and self-control, while also extending grace to myself when I struggle. In Jesus' name, I pray. Amen.

June 13
Fix My Focus

"You will keep him in perfect peace, whose mind is stayed on You, because he trusts in You."

Isaiah 26:3 NKJV

Dear Jehovah Shalom. You are my refuge. You are my hiding place. Today, I choose to shift my focus off my problems and surrender my struggle with excess sugar (among other things) to You. I humbly recognize that my own strength is insufficient to change the old programming in my mind. I need Your divine intervention and guidance. In the powerful name of Jesus, I pray. Amen.

Lord, I acknowledge that pathways of worry and anxiety have been deeply ingrained within me and I spend so much time fixated on these thoughts. I repent of obsessing over them and instead of focusing on Your supernatural power. You have overcome the world (John 16:33), and I choose to align my thoughts with Your victorious truth.

I surrender myself completely to You, Lord. Help me to cease striving (Psalm 46:10) and to submit everything to You. I place my worries and burdens at Your feet and think only on what is worthy of praise (Philippians 4:8). I release every lying thought that does not line up with Your Word. Strengthen me each day, renewing my mind (Romans 12:2), and empower me to keep surrendering the stronghold of excess sugar consumption to You. In the powerful name of Jesus, I pray. Amen.

June 14
True Worship

"I appeal to you, therefore, brothers, by the mercies of God, to present your bodies as a living sacrifice, holy and acceptable to God, which is your spiritual worship."

Romans 12:1 ESV

Dear Glorious God, as I come before You today, I lift up my heart in worship and adoration. You alone are worthy of all praise, honor, and glory. I acknowledge Your greatness and sovereignty over all creation (Psalm 145:3).

I am reminded by Your Word that true worship goes beyond Sunday church service. It's every aspect of my life, including what I put in my mouth and how I care for my body. Help me, Lord, to present my body as a living sacrifice, holy and pleasing to You.

As I strive to live spirit-filled and sugar-free, let it be a form of worship unto You. By honoring my body as Your temple, I demonstrate my love and devotion to You (1 Corinthians 6:19-20). May my life be a living testimony of Your goodness and grace. Let my actions speak volumes of Your transformative power at work within me. Guide me in the path of righteousness and lead me in Your ways (Proverbs 3:5-6).

Thank You, Heavenly Father, for the privilege of worshiping You with my whole being. May my life be a sweet fragrance of worship ascending to Your throne. In Jesus' name. Amen.

June 15
Made to Crave

"For he satisfies the longing soul, and the hungry soul he fills with good things."

Psalm 107:9 NIV

Dear God of Comfort and Peace, Today, I come before You with a heart full of gratitude, recognizing that You have designed me to crave You above all else. You have placed within me a longing for Your presence. Help me, Lord, to redirect my cravings towards You and to find my ultimate satisfaction in You alone.

You are the source of all my desires, and You understand the inner workings of my heart. My soul thirsts for You, and my flesh longs for You in a dry and weary land where there is no water (Psalm 63:1). Father, ignite and increase that craving within me– that deep yearning to be in communion with You.

I invite You to deepen my hunger for worship, prayer, and fellowship with Your children. May my cravings for intimacy with You grow stronger as I seek to know You more and to walk in Your ways. Thank You, loving God, for placing within me the innate desire to crave You. I surrender my desires and longings to Your loving hands, trusting that You will fulfill them according to Your perfect will. In Jesus' name, I pray. Amen.

June 16
Unshackled from Addiction, Transformed by Grace

"For sin shall no longer be your master, because you are not under the law, but under grace."

Romans 6:14 NIV

Dear God of Freedom and Grace, I humbly come before You, seeking Your guidance as I confront my addictions (particularly to sugar). I acknowledge the hold it has over me but today I declare that it will no longer be my master.

I will not conform to the world's patterns but to be transformed by renewing my mind (Romans 12:2). Grant me the strength to break free from these shackles, as I understand the complexities of my addiction and find wisdom to overcome it. Your grace is sufficient grace (2 Corinthians 12:9) in my weakness. I trust in Your deliverance, knowing that You hear the cries of Your righteous ones and rescue them from their troubles (Psalm 34:17-18).

Grant me discernment to recognize triggers and patterns, and the strength to develop healthy coping mechanisms. Renew my mind, Lord, that I may see myself as Your beloved child, unshackled and set free by Your grace. Thank You for Your unfailing love and the promise of freedom. Guide me towards victory, Lord, and fill me with a renewed passion for a life that glorifies You. In Jesus' name, I pray. Amen.

June 17
Satisfied

"But clothe yourselves with the Lord Jesus Christ, and make no provision for [nor even think about gratifying] the flesh in regard to its improper desires."
Romans 13:14 AMP

Dear God of Contentment. You satisfy the thirsty and fill the hungry with good things (Psalm 107:9). Remind me today that one bite of sugary foods is too much and that a thousand will never be enough to satisfy the depths of my being. Only Your love, grace, and presence can truly satisfy my soul.

I confess that I have looked to people, places, things, tastes, textures, and volumes of food in my search for fulfillment. But these temporal pleasures will always leave me empty, incomplete, and hungry.

Jesus, You are the bread of life (John 6:35)." Fill me with Your presence, Your truth, and Your love, so that I may be content in You and no longer seek satisfaction from sweets.

Fill me with Your Holy Spirit, that I may find true contentment in Your presence. I trust that as I seek You with all my heart, soul, and mind, You will fill me with Your perfect love and satisfy the deepest longings of my soul. In Jesus' name. Amen.

June 18
Empowered by Divine Discipline

"No discipline seems pleasant at the time, but painful. Later on, however, it produces a harvest of righteousness and peace for those who have been trained by it."
Hebrews 12:11 NIV

Dear Lord, I approach Your throne of grace, seeking Your divine discipline to help me break free from the grip of sugar and embrace a healthier lifestyle.

Your Word reminds me not to despise Your discipline, and not to resent Your rebuke because You discipline those You love (Proverbs 3:11-12). Father, I submit to Your loving discipline, knowing that it comes from Your deep love and desire for my well-being. I understand that discipline may be challenging and uncomfortable, but I trust in the greater purpose it serves in shaping my character and leading me to a life of righteousness and peace. Grant me the perseverance to endure the temporary discomfort for the sake of long-term transformation.

As I embrace Your discipline, I ask for Your guidance and grace in creating healthy habits and routines that support my journey. Grant me the wisdom to make wise food choices, the discipline to engage in regular exercise, and the perseverance to maintain this new lifestyle.

Thank You for helping me to embrace this journey with humility, perseverance, and a heart surrendered to Your will. In Jesus' name, I pray. Amen.

June 19
Embracing Humility

"Set your mind and keep focused habitually on the things above [the heavenly things], not on things that are on the earth [which have only temporal value]."
Colossians 3:2 AMP

Dear Daddy, I come to You in humility today admitting that sometimes I allow my temporal cravings to take me away from You. I repent, renew my mind, and surrender everything and everyone to You. I choose to keep my mind habitually focused on what's important to You, Lord, not on the temporary things that will pass away when this world does.

You must increase and I must decrease (John 3:30). I praise You each day for who You are and for all You've done for me. Help me to continually humble myself before You, recognizing that it is through Your strength and grace that true transformation occurs.

As I focus on You, Lord, I trust that You will lead me on the path of greater health and free me from craving foods that don't serve me. As I humble myself and bring my flesh under Your authority, I know that You will help me (1 Peter 5:6).

May my humble heart overflow with praise and adoration for You. In Jesus' magnificent name, I pray. Amen!

June 20
Embracing Progress, Releasing Perfection

"Are you so foolish? Having begun by the Spirit, are you now being perfected by the flesh?"

Galatians 3:3 ESV

Dear God of love and grace, I thank You that there is not one thing that I could do (or not do) to make You love me any more or any less than You do right now. I confess that I have believed the lie that Your love is fickle and shifty, based on my performance and appearance (1 Samuel 16:7). I apologize for embracing this attitude and for not fully understanding the depth of Your unfailing love.

Yes, I am a new creation, but manifesting it is a process. I am being made more and more into Your likeness each and every day.

Help me to rest in the knowledge that I don't have to be the best, but rather to do my best to follow You every day.

I say "yes" to the progress that comes from allowing You, the potter, to mold me into the likeness of Your image (Rom. 8:29), day by day. I embrace the process and surrender my pursuit of perfection, knowing that You are faithful to complete the good work You have started in me. (Phil 1:6) In Jesus' name, I pray. Amen.

June 21
Changing the Narrative

*"Forget the former things; do not dwell on the past. See,
I am doing a new thing! Now it springs up; do you not
perceive it? I am making a way in the wilderness and
streams in the wasteland."*

Isaiah 43:18-19 NIV

Heavenly Father, In this moment of surrender, I'm asking You to change the untrue stories I tell myself every day. I confess that I have fallen into the lie that I need something sweet when in reality, it is merely a habit that keeps me trapped. Help me to let go of these lies and embrace the transformative power of Your truth.

Father, I surrender my mind to Your redeeming strength. Empower me to recognize the lies I tell myself and replace them with Your promises. Guide me to test and approve Your good, pleasing, and perfect will (Romans 12:2), which leads to genuine fulfillment and joy.

Lord, I release the narrative of the past and the chains that have held me captive. Help me to let go of the story that no longer serves me and open my eyes to the new thing You are doing in my life (Isaiah 43:18-19). Give me the discernment to perceive Your work and the courage to embrace it fully. May my story of freedom from sugar addiction be a testimony of Your power and grace, inspiring others to seek truth and freedom in their own lives. In Jesus' name, I pray. Amen.

June 22
Beyond Temporary Satisfaction

"Beloved, do not be surprised at the fiery trial when it comes upon you to test you, as though something strange were happening to you. But rejoice insofar as you share Christ's sufferings, that you may also rejoice and be glad when his glory is revealed."

1 Peter 4:12-13 ESV

Dear Redeeming God, Your grace and mercy endure forever. You are working all things together for my good and for Your glory. (Romans 8:28). When I'm tempted by sugar cravings, remind me that You always provide a way of escape, a path to overcome (1 Corinthians 10:13).

I surrender my desire for instant gratification and comfort, knowing that the lasting pain of regret is far greater than the temporary discomfort of food cravings. Empower me to endure by relying on Your strength when I grow weak (2 Corinthians 12:9). Thank You for Your steadfast love and the promise of redemption in Christ. I trust in Your grace to guide me through this battle with sugar. Fill me with Your Holy Spirit, who enables me to resist temptation and make choices that honor You.

Lord, I surrender my cravings and my dependence on sugar into Your hands. Renew my mind and transform my desires. Help me to find satisfaction in You alone, knowing that Your love and presence are the ultimate fulfillment I seek. In Jesus' name, I pray. Amen.

June 23
My Food is My Food

"And the Lord will guide you continually and satisfy your desire in scorched places and make your bones strong; and you shall be like a watered garden, like a spring of water, whose waters do not fail."

Isaiah 58:11 ESV

Dear Magnificent God,

Today, I lift my voice in praise to You, the King of kings and Lord of Lords. I acknowledge that I am fearfully and wonderfully made in Your image, designed to crave You above all else. When I'm tempted to compare my diet to others', remind me of Your call to live differently, to glorify You in my body (1 Corinthians 10:31).

Help me understand that my food is uniquely mine, tailored to my body's needs, free from anything that hinders my energy (1 Corinthians 6:19-20). Grant me continued wisdom in discerning what foods are right for me, and keep my focus fixed on You, not on what others are eating (Proverbs 3:5-6). You've crafted me with a unique body, deserving of honor and care.

Lord, I surrender my food choices into Your hands. Remind me that my food is my food. Help me to approach this process with discernment and self-control. Grant me the wisdom to make choices that nourish my body, mind, and spirit. I declare that my food choices are guided by Your Holy Spirit. In the name of Jesus' I pray. Amen.

June 24
Power to Overcome Temptation

"No temptation has overtaken you except what is common to mankind. And God is faithful; he will not let you be tempted beyond what you can bear. But when you are tempted, he will also provide a way out so that you can endure it."

1 Corinthians 10:13 NIV

Dear God, my strength and deliverer, I humbly come before You today standing on Your word that I am free from the grip of sugar addiction. I thank You for the freedom and deliverance You've given me by the power of Your Word.

Lord, I recognize the allure and the hold that sugar can have over me. I confess that at times, I have succumbed to its temptations and allowed it to regain control in my life. But today, I surrender my weaknesses and struggles to You, knowing that Your grace is sufficient for me (2 Corinthians 12:9). I declare that I will remain vigilant and steadfast in my resolve to abstain from the destructive cycle of addiction. Grant me the wisdom and discernment to make choices that honor my body, which You have fearfully and wonderfully created (Psalm 139:14).

Above all, Father, I ask for Your presence to be my constant companion. Fill me with Your Holy Spirit, who empowers me to overcome the desires of the flesh (Galatians 5:16). I am more than a conqueror (Romans 8:37). In Jesus' name, I pray. Amen.

June 25
Accepting Weakness and Finding Strength

"I came to you in weakness and fear, and with much trembling."

1 Corinthians 2:3 NIV

Dear God of Grace and Mercy. I come before You with a humble heart, acknowledging that I have often been harsh with myself, beating myself up for my inability to resist the allure of sugar. Today, I surrender this unhelpful burden to You. You are a compassionate and loving God so I rebuke that spirit of judgment.

Fill me with Your grace. Help me to accept my weakness without judgment or self-condemnation. Remind me that it is through acknowledging my weaknesses that Your strength can be made perfect in me (2 Corinthians 12:9). Teach me to extend the same grace and compassion to myself that You freely offer me.

Fill my heart with the understanding that I am fearfully and wonderfully made (Psalm 139:14). When I stumble and give in to temptation, remind me that there is no condemnation for those who are in Christ Jesus (Romans 8:1). Help me to learn from my mistakes, to grow in resilience, and to trust in Your unending grace. I declare that I can do all things through Christ who strengthens me (Philippians 4:13). May Your grace be my source of strength. In Jesus' name, I pray. Amen.

June 26
Continually Rising

"For you have need of endurance, so that when you have done the will of God you may receive what is promised."

Hebrews 10:36 ESV

Dear Heavenly Father, I bless You today. I magnify Your Holy Name. I exalt You. I come before You with a heart that yearns for change and transformation. I take comfort in knowing that giving up sugar and other unhealthy foods is not defined by a single failure but by my persistence and willingness to rise again. Help me to learn from each relapse and grow stronger in my resolve. Your Word says that, "For though the righteous fall seven times, they rise again." (Proverbs 24:16a). I commit to rising up each time I fall.

In moments of weakness, when I feel tempted to deviate from my path, remind me of the lessons I have learned from my past experiences. Allow me to draw upon the knowledge and wisdom I have gained, so that I may make healthier choices and avoid the pitfalls that lie before me.

Help me to approach setbacks with kindness and compassion, recognizing that this journey is not linear but a process of continual growth. Thank You for the lessons learned, the growth experienced, and the strength You give me. I am evolving. I am growing in grace. I decree that my victory is at hand and I will keep getting back up each time I fall (Galatians 6:9) In Your divine name, I pray. Amen.

June 27
From Entitlement to Gratitude

"Gracious words are a honeycomb, sweet to the soul and healing to the bones."

Proverbs 16:24 NIV

Dear Just and Righteous God, I bless You today and invite You in as Lord over my life today. I confess that I have fallen into the trap of believing that I deserve sugary treats, disregarding the negative impact they have on my health and overall well-being.

Open my heart to understand that what I truly deserve is based on the immeasurable blessings and grace You have bestowed upon me (Hebrews 4:16) and not on fleeting pleasures.

Transform my perspective and align it with Your will. Help me discern what is good, pleasing, and perfect in Your eyes (Proverbs 3:7), rather than succumbing to the worldly notion that indulging in sweet treats is a deserved reward. Teach me to find true satisfaction in seeking and doing Your will.

Father, I desire to prioritize Your kingdom and Your righteousness above all else (Matthew 6:33). I decree that my heart desires Your presence and Your ways above the temporary pleasures of this world. True fulfillment comes from living in alignment with Your perfect plan. In Jesus' name, I pray. Amen.

June 28
From Comparison to Contentment

"But clothe yourselves with the Lord Jesus Christ, and make no provision for [nor even think about gratifying] the flesh in regard to its improper desires."
Romans 13:14 AMP

Dear Abba Father, You are a God of comfort and contentment. I come before You today with the feeling that life is unfair because I cannot eat whatever I want, while others seem to enjoy that privilege without consequences. I confess that this comparison has caused me to struggle with discontentment and bitterness. Today, I seek Your divine intervention to help me overcome these feelings and find true contentment in You.

Lord, You are the giver of every good and perfect gift (James 1:17). Help me to shift my perspective and count my blessings. Teach me to find my satisfaction in You alone, knowing that You have a unique and purposeful plan for my life.

Teach me how to celebrate others without harboring envy, resentment, or bitterness (Luke 12:15). Enable me to support and encourage those around me on their own paths, rejoicing with them in their victories (Romans 12:15).

I am happy with my progress, no matter how small, knowing that it is a step towards the abundant life You desire for me. I speak contentment over my life. In the name of Jesus, who overcame all temptations, I pray. Amen.

June 29
Enduring Victory

"But thanks be to God, who gives us the victory through our Lord Jesus Christ."

1 Corinthians 15:57 ESV

Dear Faithful God, I thank You for Your transformative power. You are so worthy to be praised. I refuse to go back to my old patterns and habits that once held me captive (Galatians 5:1). I will continue to walk in the freedom and transformation You have brought into my life.

Strengthen my resolve, Lord, and remind me of the reasons why I embarked on this journey in the first place. When I am tempted, remind me that I can endure through it (1 Corinthians 10:13). Help me to remember this truth and rely on Your faithfulness in moments of temptation. Provide a way of escape so that I can endure and overcome any allure of sugar that may come my way. Father, I seek Your wisdom and discernment as I navigate a world filled with sugary temptations. Guide me in making wise choices, both in what I eat and in how I approach my relationship with food.

Fill me with Your Holy Spirit, empowering me to embrace a lifestyle of self-control and moderation. Thank You, for the progress made and the transformation experienced as a result of spending time with You. I trust that You will continue to equip me for the journey ahead. May my testimony be a reflection of Your goodness, grace, and faithfulness. In Jesus' mighty name, I pray. Amen.

June 30
Triumph in Transformation

"Oh give thanks to the Lord, for he is good; for his steadfast love endures forever! "

Psalm 107:1 ESV

Dear Gracious God! I thank You for the renewing work You have done in my life, changing my taste buds and renewing my perspective. Your faithfulness and grace have brought me this far, and I trust that You will continue to guide me in the path of victory.

Thank You for the healing and renewed mindset. You have and will continue to wash away my cravings and desires for unhealthy sugars, replacing them with a hunger for Your righteousness (Matthew 5:6) and a passion for honoring my body as Your temple. Continue to purify my heart (James 4:8) and strengthen my resolve as I press forward on this journey.

I will continue to guard my heart (Proverbs 4:23) and mind against any lies or temptations that may seek to ensnare me. I walk in the fullness of freedom, making choices that honor You and bring forth abundant life. I thank You, Heavenly Father, for Your faithfulness. May Your name be glorified as I continue to walk in the freedom You have provided In the mighty name of Jesus, I pray. Amen.

July

STAY STEADFAST

This month's prayers are focused on providing you with the encouragement, strength, and perseverance you need to navigate your health journey when you hit a roadblock.

Life is filled with challenges, and the path to improved well-being can often be arduous and filled with obstacles. However, through the power of prayer, you can find guidance, and renewed determination to press on.

This month, you will pray boldly to stay steadfast. You will pray your way through your "messy middles" — those moments in your health journey where progress may feel stagnant, doubts may arise, and the temptation to give up can loom large. It is precisely during these times that you need to remain steadfast in God's unwavering promises.

May these prayers encourage you to rise above the challenges, to tap into the wellspring of God's strength within you, and to embrace the journey, messy as it may be. Remember, the road to lasting health and well-being is not without its bumps, detours, and moments of uncertainty. However, with prayer, perseverance, and the assurance that quitting is not an option, you can stay steadfast and emerge victorious.

Allow the words in this month's prayers to breathe life into your goals and desires. Believe that with each prayer, you will inch closer to your desires for better health.

May these prayers guide you, uplift you, and remind you to remain steadfast as you surrender everything to God in prayer.

July 1
Endurance to Run the Race

*"Do you not know that in a race all the runners run,
but only one gets the prize? Run in such a way as to
get the prize."*

1 Corinthians 9:24-25 NIV

Dear LORD my Rock, who trains my hands for war, thank You for strengthening me and teaching me how to show up for myself each day ready and equipped (Ephesians 6:10-18). I am clothed in Your strength. In the past, my M-O was to not lose, so I lived each day on the defensive, never experiencing Your peace, joy, and freedom. Now I'm committed to win! I am pressing forward each day toward the mark for the prize of the high calling (Philippians 3:14).

Every time I want to run ahead without You, remind me to slow down so I can hear how You're leading and guiding me. I thank You for being with me every step of the way and guiding me in the way I should go. I know this is a marathon, not a sprint, so I need endurance to maintain a steady pace without constantly starting and stopping. Your Word says that as I wait for You, I will run and not grow weary (Isaiah 40:31). What assurance! I thank You for the grace to run my race without worrying about anyone else around me. I fix my eyes on You and move forward one step at a time. I will run to get the prize, in Jesus' name. Amen!

July 2
God's Perspective on Adversity

"Consider it pure joy, my brothers and sisters, whenever you face trials of many kinds,"

James 1:2 NIV

Dear Lord, who helps and comforts me in times of trials. I come to You today to help me move through the adversities I face. Although I know that change is an ongoing lifelong process, there are things in my health journey that have held me back for too long and I'm ready to give them up. I'm tired of going around the same mountain over and over again, so I'm ready to do a new thing in You (Isaiah 43:19).

Help me to reframe adversity, and see all trials as an opportunity to draw closer to You (Matthew 11:29). Instead of asking 'why is this happening to me,' let me seek, "What are You teaching me in this situation." This new posture will strengthen and mature me.

Forgetting what is behind me, I press on, committed to moving forward each day in faith. I realize that I have this expectation that my life should be easy and then I get frustrated when things get hard. I let go of this belief and now see challenges as opportunities to grow. Keep showing me what the resistance is and keep helping me to cross the finish line (1 Corinthians 9:24). I will be victorious this time. In Jesus' name, I pray. Amen.

July 3
Crossing My Jordan

"When you see the ark of the covenant of the LORD, follow it. Keep a distance of about two thousand cubits to know the way to go, for you have not passed this way before... Sanctify yourselves, for tomorrow the LORD will do wonders among you."

Joshua 3:3-5 NASB

Dear Lord, God of wonder, thank You for always going before me and guiding me. Wherever You lead me, I will follow You (Proverbs 3:6). I am committed to moving forward in my health journey, knowing that victory belongs to You. I trust in Your strength to overcome every setback and challenge I face.

Like the Israelites crossing the Jordan, I'm entering new territory. Instead of rushing ahead in my own strength, I will let You go before me, calming the waters so I can cross in victory.

I acknowledge that this is a new way of being for me, so instead of saying that "it's too hard" or "I can't do it", I'll simply acknowledge that it's just new and like a stumbling baby learning to walk, I will eventually learn to walk, then run (Hebrews 12:1). It will take time for me to learn how to develop new health habits and that's okay. I don't have to be afraid because I know that You are with me leading and guiding me (Isaiah 48:17). In Jesus's victorious name, I pray. Amen!

July 4
Preparing My Mind for Victory

"Therefore, preparing your minds for action, and being sober-minded, set your hope fully on the grace that will be brought to you at the revelation of Jesus Christ."
1 Peter 1:13 ESV

Dear Omnipotent God, You know everything about me. You know my thoughts before I even think them (Psalm 139:2). Today, I come to You seeking renewal of my mind. When I feel frustrated or trapped in negative thinking, I will call on You to help me change my perspective. Thank You for literally transforming my neural pathways so I can cultivate healthy thoughts that lead to freedom.

I recognize that this battle is as much mental as it is spiritual. The enemy may try to control my thoughts, but I will not give him access! You are rewiring my brain to align with the mind of Christ (1 Corinthians 2:16). The world no longer holds my mind captive (Romans 12:2). I have the power to think new thoughts, seeing myself as You see me and taking every thought captive to obey You (2 Corinthians 10:5).

I choose to focus on whatever is true, noble, right, pure, admirable, lovely, excellent, and praiseworthy (Philippians 4:8). In Your Son's name, I pray. Amen.

July 5
Cultivating Contentment

"I have learned the secret of being content in any and every situation… I can do all this through him who gives me strength."

Philippians 4:12,13 NIV

Dear Lord, God of refuge and strength. You are my ever-present help in times of trouble. You strengthen me with Your righteous right hand (Isaiah 41:10). Help me to accept the things I can not change today. There's so much about myself, my body, my habits, and my behaviors that I don't want to accept. Sometimes the truth is too painful or shameful to face so I would rather just bury my head in the sand, but I know that it only prolongs the pain.

I humble myself before You. Gently and lovingly bring to the surface everything that I've been unwilling to face and have repressed or suppressed. Search me and know those hidden parts of me (Psalm 139:23) and clean them up so that they no longer keep me bound. I'm tired of using food and other temporal and fleeting things to pacify me, Lord. I just want You.

I decree that I possess a spirit of contentment that accepts what is and lets go of what I can not control. I declare that I can do all things in You (Philippians 4:13). I am free and content. In Jesus' name, I pray. Amen!

July 6
Cultivating Clarity

"But we all, with unveiled face, beholding as in a mirror the glory of the Lord, are being transformed into the same image from glory to glory,"
2 Corinthians 3:18 NASB

Heavenly Father, I thank You for transforming me from glory to glory. Little by little, step by step, day by day, I am making progress. I come before You today seeking a clear path forward. Your Word reminds me that as I behold Your glory, I am being transformed into Your image by the power of Your Spirit. What a relief that I don't have to do this by myself.

I trust that You will illuminate my path as I take small steps of faith each day. I bind the spirit of confusion and overwhelm. It will no longer keep me stuck. Cultivate clarity in me so that I will keep moving forward and produce good fruit in my life. May I reflect Your love, joy, peace, patience, kindness, goodness, faithfulness, gentleness, and self-control in all that I do (Galatians 5:22).

I thank You for giving me clarity in the midst of the difficulties, trials, and temptations. You are a light unto my feet and You keep showing me which way I should go (Psalm 119:105). My assignment is to keep my eyes and my mind fixed on You (Isaiah 26:3) and it is there that I will find focus, strength, clarity, and peace for this journey. In Jesus' name. Amen.

July 7
Shekinah Glory

"Moses said, 'Please show me your glory.'"
Exodus 33:18 ESV

D ear Lord, God of glory. You uphold the universe by the Power of Your Word (Hebrews 1:3). Like Moses, I too desire to see Your glory in my life, especially when it comes to my health. Sometimes I feel stuck. It feels like I'm forever in this cha-cha dance taking one step forward and two steps back and I'm so over it. Fill me with Your glory today.

You've already given me a vision of what is to come, so I cling to that. My hope is in You and that's why I will never give up. Each day I will continue to get up and put one foot in front of the other and take baby steps even when my flesh wants to quit. As Your shekinah glory fills me, let me reciprocate by giving You glory in all I do (1 Corinthians 10:31). I thank You that although I'm not where I want to be, I'm not where I used to be. For this, I give You praise. I commit my life to You. Show me Your power, Your love, and Your mercy as You heal my body, soul, and spirit and restore me to full health. May my testimony of Your glory and healing power be a witness to others who see You in me. In Jesus' name, I pray. Amen.

July 8
Getting Unstuck

"You've been going around in circles in these hills long enough; go north."

Deuteronomy 2:3 MSG

Heavenly Father, You are a good God who loves to guide and direct Your children. You promise to lead me in the right path (Proverbs 4:5), but I keep going in circles like the Israelites in the desert. Forgive me for choosing the safety and security of my comfort zone more than I choose You. Although it feels safe doing things my own way, it keeps me in a constant state of anxiety and disappointment; like I'm always starting over yet I'm not sure I know how to live any other way. I desperately want to make forward progress without always back-sliding.

Help me to break free from any unhealthy cycles that may be hindering my well-being. I declare that I am moving forward each day toward better health, healing, and wholeness.

Take my knowledge of You from my head to my heart (Romans 10:2). I want more than just reading about You every day. I want to experience Your peace and presence in my life. Open my eyes so I can see a new direction (Psalm 119:19). I will look up and fix my eyes on You (Psalm 141:8). I surrender my habits, my proclivities, my will, and my ways to You, Lord because this is how I get unstuck. I declare forward momentum only; in Jesus' name. Amen.

July 9
Slow Down to Speed Up

"Be still, and know that I am God; I will be exalted among the nations, I will be exalted in the earth."
Psalm 46:10 ESV

Dear Jehovah Shalom, You are my prince of peace. You are my comfort in the storm and my quiet resting place (Psalm 23:2). Yet, I often move through my day so fast that I rarely take the time to experience that peace and rest that I desperately seek. My flesh does not want to be still. I'm not even sure I know how to slow down. My mind is always racing and I'm always moving so fast, yet not really making progress. I feel like a hamster on a wheel, going nowhere fast.

But intuitively, I know that it is in stillness where I can seek and find You. It's in this quiet place that You speak to me and give me Your assurance (1 John 5:13) that You've got me. As I move throughout my day, let me feel Your presence. I know You are with me. When I sit still, I'm sometimes overcome with fear and emotion, but I will sit in my feelings and let Your gift of peace wash over me. Today, I will take moments to connect with You and allow You to center my thoughts on You.

I will let Your Holy Spirit lead me. I will slow down to walk in step with Your pace and unforced rhythm for my life. That's the only way to make forward progress. I love You, Lord, and I give You this day in quietness and trust (Isaiah 30:15). In the mighty name of Jesus. Amen.

July 10
Stay the Course

"And Joseph dreamed a dream …"
"Joseph was thirty years old when he entered the service
of Pharaoh king of Egypt."
           Genesis 37:5 KJV / Genesis 41:46 NIV

Dear Lord, God of the promise. You spoke a word over me and promised to give me a hope and future (Jeremiah 29:11). Teach me how to live out Your plans and purposes for my life each day with determination, grit, and perseverance. Despite how hard it gets, regardless of whether anyone is watching, I will walk in integrity because I know that You are always watching and that's what's most important. Yes, there will be setbacks and the enemy will try to take me off course but You are faithful. I thank You that whatever the enemy meant for evil, You can turn it around and use it for Your glory (Genesis 50:20). All Your promises are "yes" and "amen" (2 Corinthians 1:20).

Like Joseph's testimony in the bible from the pit to the palace, my life has taken so many twists and turns, but through it all, I keep my eyes fixed on You. I recognize that my health journey is also one of trust and obedience. Thank You for the lessons You are teaching me along the way. Regardless of whatever's going on around me, and no matter how long it takes, I will stay the course. In Jesus' name. Amen.

July 11
My Steps are Ordered

"The steps of a man are established by the Lord, when he delights in his way;"

Psalm 37:23 ESV

Dear Lord, God of order, You order my steps and show me the right direction I should travel in. I confess all too often that I let life's distractions get in the way and take me off track and then I beat myself up for finding myself back in the very place I despise.

Thank You for Your forgiveness, grace, and mercy in the midst of my mess! You promise to never leave me no matter how lost or hopeless I feel (Deuteronomy 31:6). Continue to speak Your truth to me. It encourages me and gives me hope. Let me delight in Your Word and meditate on it day and night (Psalm 1:2) because I know that is the secret to living in victory. Your ways are higher than my ways (Isaiah 55:9). so forgive me every time I want to run ahead and do things my way.

Today I run back into Your loving arms and find refuge in them when I want to run ahead of You. Like a child on Christmas morning, let me never lose the awe and wonder of Your Word that leads me and guides me. It is a light unto my feet and a lamp unto my path (Psalm 119:105). Thank You for ordering my steps today. I will follow You as You lead me. In Jesus' name. Amen!

July 12
Managing My Expectations

"... 'Are You the Expected One, or shall we look for someone else?'"

Matthew 11:3 NASB 1995

Dear Omniscient God, You are the alpha and the omega. You know the end from the beginning (Isaiah 46:10). I thank You that You may not always show up when I expect or how I expect, but You are always on time. Thank You for teaching me how to manage my expectations. When I hold on to them too tightly, I always get disappointed, so teach me to set goals, but then trust You to deliver the best outcome. When my goals and plans are in line with Your best for me (Proverbs 3:5-6), I will always be happy with the outcome.

Lord, You know me better than I know myself (Psalm 139:1-4) and I acknowledge that if I keep doing what I'm doing, I'll keep getting what I've always got. So I surrender to Your will today, Lord. I thank You for keeping me during the times when I wanted to do things my way. I will never grow weary of running back to You when I miss the mark.

Your thoughts are higher than my thoughts and Your ways are higher than my ways. Keep me mindful of that when I forget. I love You, Lord, and give You all my expectations and desires. Amen!

July 13
Maximizing My Energy

"But David pursued, he and four hundred men, for two hundred who were too exhausted to cross the brook Besor remained behind."

1 Samuel 30:10 NASB

D ear Lord, God of strength, I thank You for strengthening me during the tough days when I lack energy and discipline. Sometimes I get so tired. I just want to throw my hands in the air and give up. I question if it's worth it or if I have what it takes to go on. But then I hear Your voice encouraging me telling me that I can do it because You're strengthening me (Philippians 4:13).

Help me to maximize my energy so I don't quit before the finish line. I need Your strength to run this race with endurance (Hebrews 12:1). Fill me with Your encouragement each and every day so I can keep making progress—step by step, little by little, one habit at a time. Keep reminding me that this is a marathon and not a sprint and that the race is not given to the swift or to the strong but to the one who endures to the end (Ecclesiastes 9:11). I thank You for reviving my energy (Psalm 85:6) and preparing me spiritually, mentally, and physically to live in victory. I declare that I am energetic and full of vigor. In Your Holy Name, I pray. Amen!

July 14
Thankful in the Trials

"Rejoice always, pray without ceasing, give thanks in all circumstances; for this is the will of God in Christ Jesus for you."

1 Thessalonians 5:16–18 ESV

Dear most compassionate and gracious God, I thank You today for walking with me during the hard times that I go through (Psalm 23:4). Sometimes, I feel so alone, like no one else knows what I'm going through, but I stand on Your promise that You will never leave me or forsake me (Deuteronomy 31:6).

I admit that I want a life free of challenge, but I know that is not realistic, nor is it helpful. It's in the trials that I grow stronger in You. So I thank You for Your gift of peace during the challenges I face. I take heart because You see me (John 16:33), You see my pain and struggles.

Help me to develop a consistent habit of rejoicing, praying, and giving thanks in all circumstances. Teach me contentment in every situation, trusting that You have a purpose and a plan for my life. I will rejoice in You, my God who sees and hears my cries and gives me comfort. May my heart always be filled with thanksgiving and praise for You, my God and my Redeemer. In Jesus name, I pray. Amen.

July 15
Finding Strength in Humility

"For those who exalt themselves will be humbled, and those who humble themselves will be exalted."
Matthew 23:12 NIV

Dear Lord, who makes the impossible possible (Luke 18:27). You create a way when there seems to be no way. You are my way-maker so I thank You for always going before me and clearing a path for me. In my own strength, it feels like I'll forever be circling the same mountain. And sometimes, Help me to reframe my perspective and remind me that in Your kingdom everything is flipped upside down. The first shall be last and the last shall be first. The weak are made strong (2 Corinthians 12:10) and humility is rewarded.

In Your kingdom structure, I don't need to be the best, look the best, make the most money, or have the happiest life. In fact, You are calling me to humble myself under Your almighty hand. You're calling me to cease striving and surrender my will to You. Admittedly, I've been doing it my way for so long that I'm not even sure I know how to cast my cares (1 Peter 5:7) on You so teach me, Lord.

Guide me in the path of humility by reminding me that it's all about You. Let me follow Your example of humility and selflessness. May I always remember that it is through Your grace and not my own merit that I am saved, and may I strive every day to become more like You in all that I do. In Jesus name, I pray. Amen.

July 16
Calming My Nervous System

"The Spirit of God has made me, and the breath of the Almighty gives me life."

Job 33:4 ESV

Dear Lord, breath of life. Thank You for Your life-giving breath that sustains me each and every day. In the messy middles of life, You sustain me. When I feel stressed or anxious, remind me to pause and take a deep breath.

Let nothing separate me from Your love (Romans 8:35). I trust that with each breath I take, I am drawing closer to You and becoming more like the person You created me to be (Genesis 1:27). Your power in me literally decreases my heart rate, blood pressure, and muscle tension, and I feel so much more calm and relaxed. Thank You for calming my nervous system and reminding me that You are always with me (Psalm 16:8).

May Your breath be the anchor that keeps me rooted and grounded in Your love, and may I never forget the power that comes from relying on You. And so I pause right now Lord, and feel Your breath fill my lungs with air; my mind and spirit are at ease, and I recognize that there is nothing to worry about when You are in control. In the mighty name of Jesus. Amen.

July 17
Growing Through Discipline

"… but I discipline my body and make it my slave, so that, after I have preached to others, I myself will not be disqualified."

1 Corinthians 9:27 NASB

Dear Abba Father. Holy is Your name. You always give good gifts to Your children (Matthew 7:11). Thank You for Your constant presence in my life and for Your gifts of guidance and discipline when I need it. Your correction is always done in love (Hebrews 12:5-6) and with the intention of conforming me into Your image. I trust that You know what is best for me, and I surrender myself to Your will today.

I want discipline to prioritize my health each day. I know that it's what will help me grow and move from victim to victory, from trying, to triumph, and from struggle to success. Help me to discipline my body so that it's not always betraying me. It feels like it has a mind of its own and I know that when I learn from Your discipline, then I can bring my body under subjection. I will grow through discipline instead of running from it.

Father, I ask that You help me to always remember that Your discipline is not a punishment but a means to guide me toward the right path. May I always have a teachable spirit and a humble heart (Proverbs 12:1), willing to accept Your correction and learn from it. In Jesus name, I pray. Amen.

July 18
Walking in Wisdom

"Those who trust in themselves are fools, but those
who walk in wisdom are kept safe."
Proverbs 28:26 NIV

Dear Lord, God of infinite wisdom and authority, You give understanding to minds and vision to eyes (Deuteronomy 29:4). I thank You for dispensing Your wisdom so generously whenever I ask. It is more precious and valuable to me than gold (Proverbs 16:16).

Too often, I don't know which way to turn. There are so many alternatives and I'm never sure if I'm doing the right thing. I see what others are doing and wonder if I should be doing it too. Sometimes it's all so overwhelming.

That's why I'm so grateful for Your wisdom that leads and guides me. I have the power under Your authority to take every thought captive (2 Corinthians 10:5) and keep my mind free of thoughts that pull me into sin.

I thank You for Your wisdom today which helps me to make good decisions. Be my rational, sound mind amid my irrational responses, and help me to abide in You. In You, I find wisdom, serenity, calm, and peace. You are my refuge and my strong tower (Proverbs 18:10). In the precious name of Jesus. Amen.

July 19
Developing a Servant's Heart

"Humble yourselves, therefore, under God's mighty hand, that he may lift you up in due time."

1 Peter 5:6 NIV

Dear Gentle and Humble Lord (Matthew 11:29), Thank You for sending Your son Jesus to model what a heart of lowliness and service looks like. That's how I want to live too.

Jesus humbled himself and took on the nature of a servant even though by nature He was God (Philippians 2:5-7). I desire to live like that even though right now, that is a far cry from how I live. Please save me from me. Give me a heart to serve others instead of always thinking about my own needs and wants (Mark 10:45). Let me get to a place where I'm so busy helping others that I feel fulfilled and satisfied and am no longer focused on what I lack or fixated on all the ways I come up short.

Today I count it a privilege to serve and to be Your hands and feet. Show me where You need me to serve and I will go. It is the secret to true contentment and peace in my spirit, soul, and body. I thank You for leading by example. I surrender my will to You today so use me, Lord. In Jesus name, I pray. Amen!

July 20
Faith Through the Fire

"But he must ask in faith without any doubting, for the one who doubts is like the surf of the sea, driven and tossed by the wind. For that man ought not to expect that he will receive anything from the Lord, being a double-minded man, unstable in all his ways."
James 1:6-8 NASB

Dear God, the Rock of my Salvation (Psalm 62:2), You are so faithful. You never change. You are a firm foundation that can never be shaken.

I bring my flimsy and fickle faith to You today and ask You to strengthen it. I want mustard seed faith to move mountains (Matthew 17:20-21). I want faith to believe the impossible (Luke 18:27). Speak to my heart and remove all the self-doubt and faulty beliefs that keep me from fully trusting and believing that You are who I read about in Your Word and that You can do what Your Word says You can do. Upgrade my expectation to want all of Your promises so that I can move forward, no longer feeling I should not expect anything from You, others, or even myself.

I come to You today in bold faith and confidence, believing in all of the hopes and dreams that You've laid on my heart. Continue to lead me away from self-sabotage or anything that will keep me from believing the enemy's lies. I declare unwavering and unshakable faith especially as I walk through the fires and flames of life. In Your Holy Name, I pray! Amen.

July 21
Safe in His Arms

"He will cover you with his feathers, and under his wings you will find refuge; his faithfulness will be your shield and rampart."

Psalm 91:4 NIV

Dear God of protection, You are my strength and shield. You are my refuge (Psalm 91:4) that I can run to when it feels like the world is swallowing me up. My reaction has been to do whatever I can to protect myself, but my strategies have not been successful.

Today, I pray for Your protection as I begin this day. I will come out of self-protection mode today as I stand on Your Word that tells me that I don't have to worry about anything (Philippians 4:6). No matter where I am, I will look to You as my Protector, the one who goes before me and fights for me every day. You are my hiding place, and under Your wings, I can always find refuge when I feel afraid. Protect me from trouble wherever I go, and keep evil far from me (Psalm 140:1). I bind the spirit of fear.

As I do my part by eating healthy, managing my stress levels, getting adequate amounts of sleep, and moving my body each day, I ask for Your protection from illness, diseases, and injuries. I thank You for satisfying me with long life (Psalm 91:16), I will live to the fullest and give You glory in all I do. In Jesus Name. Amen.

July 22
Strength in Numbers

"Again I say to you, if two of you agree on earth about anything they ask, it will be done for them by my Father in heaven. For where two or three are gathered in my name, there am I among them."

Matthew 18:19-20 ESV

Dear Lord who calls me friend (James 2:23), I'm in awe that You are mindful of me (Psalm 116:12). It's amazing to think that I am on Your mind. Just as You love me, You have also wired me for relationships and collaboration with others.

Admittedly, it's so hard to ask for help. It makes me feel weak or like I've failed in some way. Help me to get over this. I know that Godly relationships with others are one of the spiritual weapons (Proverbs 27:7) that You have given me to help and strengthen me, but I don't like feeling vulnerable, and hate when others disappoint me. Help me to put away my self-consciousness of what people think, and be open to the gifts of friendships and the support and accountability they provide. I know I was not created to do life on my own.

I recognize that it's sometimes easier for me to be the one helping than the one asking for help, but I recognize that I will be better equipped to help others when I am transparent, covered, and fortified by my fellow believers. Thank You for strengthening me. There is power in numbers! In the powerful name of Jesus. Amen.

July 23
Come of Out Hiding

"Better is a poor person who walks in his integrity than one who is crooked in speech and is a fool."
Proverbs 19:1 ESV

Dear Lord, promise keeper, You are faithful to ALL Your promises, and loving toward ALL You have made (Psalm 145:13). You never waiver from who You are.

I humble myself before You today, Lord. I'm so tired of hiding. I'm so tired of living a life of mediocrity succumbing to everyone else's expectations of me and my false expectations of myself. I'm ready to live a life of truth. A life that truly reflects who I am as Your daughter. I want a life of integrity where I can walk in confidence with who I am because I know that You live in me. Forgive me for trying to be who I'm not. It's exhausting and keeps me feeling frustrated and empty. Thank You for giving me the unconditional love (Romans 6:8) to live my best life—the life You designed me to live. Help me to Fully express my strengths, passions, personality, and even my idiosyncrasies and quirks.

Thank You for setting me free from my own (2 Corinthians 3:16) self-consciousness and insecurities. Today, I come out of hiding and walk out Your promises in boldness and sureness. In the precious name of Jesus, I pray. Amen.

July 24
Speaking Truth and Life

… but no human being can tame the tongue."
James 3:8 NIV

Dear God of power and authority, You spoke and the earth was created. Since I am created in Your image, You have also given me the power to create through my words. You have authorized me with power to speak life and death (Proverbs 18:21). Lord help me to speak life and blessings. Help me to take control of my mouth so that every word that I utter lines up with Your Word. As I renew my mind in You, I know that my words will follow and my actions will fall in line. I speak only blessings over my life. I call on You to help me to change the narrative.

Let my new story be one of health, wellness, joy, and freedom. Bridle my tongue (Psalms 39:1) so that it only affirms, builds up, encourages, and exhorts. I walk in the newness of who You called me to be, meditating on Your Word all day long (Psalm 119:97).

It is then out of the abundance of my heart filled with love for You that I will speak (Luke 6:45). Thank You for guiding my tongue when words escape me. In the Holy Name of Jesus, I pray. Amen.

July 25
Remaining Steadfast

"And let steadfastness have its full effect, that you may be perfect and complete, lacking in nothing."

James 1:4 ESV

Dear Good and loving Father, Your goodness is always running after me. You have loved me with an everlasting love. You're always pursuing me (John 6:44) and I know You'll never stop. I want to model Your consistency in all areas of my life, especially in my faith and health. I'm so inconsistent in my routines. Some days, I feel so accomplished and others it takes everything I've got just to get out of bed.

I will continue to seek Your best for me every day. In the highs and lows, I will never stop pursuing You; I will never stop making time for You; I will never stop submitting my plans and purposes to You.

Help me to keep the zeal. Help me to remain steadfast. I rebuke the spirits of boredom, laziness, and complacency. I find my strength and momentum in You so that I can continue on each day. You are my north star—my guiding light (Psalm 23:8) that keeps me motivated. If I ever lose momentum or motivation, that's my cue to come back in alignment with You. Thank You for loving me so much (Jeremiah 31:3) that You will never let me wander away from You. In Jesus' name. Amen.

July 26
Staying Full

"And the LORD will guide you continually and satis-fy your desire in scorched places and make your bones strong; and you shall be like a watered garden, like a spring of water, whose waters do not fail."
Isaiah 58:11 ESV

Dear Lord, my portion and my cup, I thank You for filling me completely with everything I need. I trust You to meet all of my needs—emotionally and spiritually. I will continue to feast on Your word so that I will never allow myself to run on empty.

Help me to stay consistent and spend time on Your word each day because that's what keeps me full. Let me never experience spiritual malnourishment because that's when I make unhealthy choices and unwise decisions.

When the insatiable hunger builds in the pit of my stomach, remind me that it's not really food I'm craving. It's You. Let me crave You instead of food. You give me just what I need. You are my daily bread (Luke 11:3). I will hide Your Word in my heart (Psalm 119:11). It is like a lamp that guides me in the darkness. When I'm feeling stuck, it's Your Word that will see me through. Thank You for satisfying me with good things (Psalms 103:5). In Your Son's Holy and precious name, I pray. Amen.

July 27
Just One Bite

"But put on the Lord Jesus Christ, and make no provision for the flesh, to gratify its desires."
Romans 13:14 ESV

Dear Lord, Your name is a strong tower where I can run and be safe (Proverbs 18:10). I thank You for Your strength that helps me to overcome my cravings and desires. Sometimes I feel like a spoiled brat—I want what I want, when I want it, although I know that it will only hurt me in the long run.

Help me to stop deceiving myself with lies like, "I'll just have one bite." The truth is, one bite will never be enough for my insatiable appetite for more (Proverbs 30:15). Thank You for helping me resist temptation and establish firm boundaries. I know not to trust my carnal desires (Philippians 3:3) because they've always led me astray. Help me to keep the door shut firmly on my appetites, which will drag me down roads that are difficult to find my way back from.

I will only seek Your best for me. I declare I have the strength to resist the enemy when he tries to tempt me. Thank You for always providing a way of escape (2 Corinthians 10:13). In Jesus' Name, I pray! Amen.

July 28
Bless the Mess

"But one thing is needful: and Mary hath chosen that good part, which shall not be taken away from her."
Luke 10:42 KJV

Dear Righteous God, Splendid and majestic are Your works. Your righteousness endures forever (Psalm 111:3). You look beyond all my faults and see me just as I am. You see all the anxiety I have around getting things done and You give me peace in the midst of the chaos.

Help me to recognize the beauty and majesty of each day instead of focusing on what I did not do or what I did poorly. Each day so many decisions have to be made and errands need to be taken care of and people are pulling at me from all directions. And then there's my health, which sometimes does not even make the priority list. But in all the mess, remind me of what's important.

Help me to reframe life from Your perspective. Let me see opportunities where I now see burdens and stress. I thank You for the blessings in all the lessons of life. I thank You for the ability to move my body. What a privilege! I thank You for an abundance of food to eat. Today I will sit at Your feet (Luke 10:39) and see Your faithfulness, grace, and loving-kindness in my life every day instead of focusing on all the work that needs to be done, all I lack, and all the hardships I face. Thank You for reminding me to prioritize my life around You (Matthew 6:33). In Jesus' Name I pray, Amen.

July 29
Use My Weapons

"The weapons we fight with are not the weapons of the world. On the contrary, they have divine power to demolish strongholds."

2 Cor 10:4 NIV

Dear strong and mighty God, You are mighty in battle (Psalm 24:8). I thank You for always going before me and fighting for me. You have given me spiritual weapons and taught me how to fight my battles on my knees.

I find myself constantly worrying about my health, my life and the uncertainty of my future. I don't know what lies ahead and it scares me sometimes. But as I spend time with You, You remind me that if worrying is the whisper of my fears, then prayer is the roar of faith and if I can worry then I possess in me the power to unleash a mighty force through prayer. Prayer is just worry turned upside down and surrendered to You.

Thank You for reminding me that I have spiritual weapons that are mighty enough to pull down the strongholds in my life (2 Corinthians 10:4). I recognize that prayer might not be the answer to every problem I face but I can take every problem I face to You in prayer (Philippians 4:6). The next time I feel like I'm about to throw in the towel, remind me that You're always with me so I don't have to worry about anything. I cast all my cares on You right now and leave them there. I declare that I've got the victory in Jesus' name, I pray. Amen.

July 30
It's Messy in the Middle

"I am the Alpha and the Omega, the first and the last, the beginning and the end."

Revelation 22:13 ESV

Dear Omnipotent God, Sovereign Lord, You transcend all space and time. You are a limitless God. I thank You for the privilege of spending time with You and allowing Your word to calm my anxious mind and help me to keep on persevering.

Thank You for reminding me that regardless of what's happening around me, You are sovereign. You know the end from the beginning and everything in between. You know everything about me (Psalm 139:1-6) and every mess that I'm about to make. Yet You walk with me through my messy middles, always holding my hand and reassuring me that I am not alone. What blessed assurance.

Despite all my mess, You still love with an everlasting love (Jeremiah 31:3) You never give up on me even when I want to give up on myself. Thank You for Your steadfast love, Your grace, and Your tender mercy towards me. Thank You for reminding me that I can endure every challenge I experience because I have You on my side. I stand on Your promise that You will never leave me or forsake me (Heb 13:5-6) and that I will reap a harvest if I don't quit (Gal. 6:9). In Jesus' name I pray. Amen.

July 31
Stay Steadfast, God's Way

"Know therefore that the Lord your God is God; he is the faithful God, keeping his covenant of love to a thousand generations of those who love him and keep his commandments."

Deuteronomy 7:9 NIV

Dear Faithful God, as I close out this season of surrendering my messy middles to You, I want to thank You for all You've revealed to me as I've spent time with You. Your strength and guidance have been my anchor, and I am deeply grateful for Your unwavering support.

Your Word encourages me to remain steadfast, knowing that my labor is not in vain (1 Corinthians 15:58). When obstacles arise and progress seems slow, I find comfort in Your promise to be with me through every trial (Isaiah 43:2). Help me to persevere, trusting that each challenge is an opportunity to grow stronger and align more closely with Your will.

In difficult moments, may I always remember that You guide and sustain me. Teach me to remain faithful, finding hope and encouragement in Your presence. As I move forward, fill me with perseverance and hope, and help me to stay steadfast in Your ways. Thank You for Your constant presence and for leading me through each trial. I trust in Your continued guidance and support. In Jesus' name, Amen.

August

REST IN THE LORD

This month's prayers are dedicated to seeking God for rest, restoration, and rejuvenation in the Lord. In a world that often pulls you in countless directions, where the demands of daily life can leave you feeling drained and overwhelmed, finding peace in the gentle embrace of the Almighty is essential.

Throughout this month, you will receive the healing power of rest, find refuge in the Lord, and learn to let go of the stress and anxiety that weigh heavily upon your heart and mind. Daily stress threatens to steal your peace, often leaving you caught in the clutches of anxiety. Remember, you are not meant to bear the burdens of this world alone. In the stillness of prayer, you will uncover a divine invitation to surrender your stress and lay down your worries at the feet of the One who holds the universe together.

The Lord, in His infinite wisdom, longs to grant you the gift of rest—a respite from the noise and busyness of your daily life. As you learn to rest in Him, you will witness the restorative power of divine rejuvenation, not only in your spiritual life but also in your overall health and well-being.

May this month of prayers be a time of renewal as you open your heart to the restorative grace of the Almighty. You will be guided towards a life characterized by peace, contentment, and unspeakable joy as you commit to casting your cares on the Lord.

August 1
Embracing Rest

"This I declare about the LORD: He alone is my refuge, my place of safety; he is my God, and I trust him."

Psalm 91:1-2 NLT

God of peace, You are the Lord almighty and You are on my side, so I don't have to worry. Thank You for inviting me to cast my anxiety on You (1 Peter 5:7). This month, teach me how to seek refuge and safety in You instead of in food and other things that don't satisfy me.

I acknowledge the relentless pace of life and the demands that often consume my days. I find myself caught in the whirlwind of responsibilities, deadlines, and expectations, leaving little room for rest and restoration. But today, I surrender everything and everyone to You. Help me to be still and know that You are God (Psalm 46:10) and to develop a lifestyle anchored by a heart at rest.

Today, I confess that I have the mind of Christ (1 Corinthians 2:16). This month, and always, grant me the courage to let go of everything that weighs me down. May the gift of rest pervade my life, grounding me in the present, nourishing my soul, and guiding me toward a healthier life. In Jesus' name I pray. Amen.

August 2
Benefits of Rest

"Six days you shall labor, and do all your work, but the seventh day is a sabbath to the Lord your God."
Exodus 20:9–10 NIV

Dear God of Wisdom, I thank You for waking me up this morning and for this new day. Guide me to see Your wonder-working power (Psalm 96:3)in all things.

You, Lord, set the example of rest during the creation of the world. After six days of magnificent work, You rested on the seventh day. You sanctified it and blessed it, reminding me of the importance of rest. You designed me with limitations and knew that rest would be essential for my overall good health

When I neglect rest, my body becomes weary, my mind becomes overwhelmed, and my spirit becomes restless. I lose sight of the joy and peace that come from spending time with You and allowing myself to recharge. It is in rest that I find restoration, rejuvenation, and a deep connection with You.

Help me to remember that You give sleep to those You love and that rest is a gift of Your grace (Psalm 127:2). Grant me the wisdom to prioritize rest in my life and to let go of my worries, placing them in Your loving hands. Teach me to trust that You will guide and support me on my journey (Proverbs 3:5), even when I take moments of rest. Thank You for the precious gift of rest that allows me to maximize my energy each day. In Jesus' mighty name, I pray. Amen.

August 3
Surrendering to Jehovah Shalom's Peaceful Oasis

"Are you weary, carrying a heavy burden? Then come to me. I will refresh your life, for I am your oasis."
Matthew 11:28 TPT

Jehovah Shalom, my Lord of Peace, I thank You for loving me and wanting me restored. I say yes to Your beautiful invitation to roll my heavy burdens onto You and I invite Your loving conviction now to show me any yoke I have taken that is not Yours.

Lord, I surrender to You every part of me. You are my oasis! I will settle beside You, Father, on the warm sun-kissed beach (Psalm 23:2), resting my head on Your shoulder, hearing Your heart beat for me as Your words wash upon my spirit—gentle and reassuring. There, in my time with You, I find peace beyond any I can imagine!

Help me recognize and release any lingering doubts or fears that hinder my journey towards true rest. Grant me the wisdom to discern between the world's fleeting standards and Your eternal truth (Matthew 7:13). Help me embrace the beauty and worth that come from being Your beloved child, knowing that my value is not defined by societal expectations but by the depth of Your love. I surrender right now to Your gift of peace. In Jesus' restorative name. Amen!

August 4
Embracing Divine Priorities

"Teach us to number our days, that we may gain a heart of wisdom."

Psalm 90:12 NIV

Dear Sovereign God, You reign over all things, including time. You, the Creator of the universe, have ordained time as a gift for me to steward wisely (Ephesians 5:16). I confess that at times, I have not fully understood the importance of managing Your time and have allowed busyness and distractions to consume my days. As a result, I often feel anxious, rushed and stressed.

Help me to understand that true rest is found in You and that by managing Your time well, I can experience a deeper sense of peace. Allow me to see that rest is not merely a physical break from activities but a necessary requirement that nourishes my soul and strengthens my relationship with You.

In the midst of my day help me to create intentional moments where I can commune with You, listening for Your still, small voice (1 Kings 19:12) and receive Your guidance. As I surrender my time to You, I trust that You will guide my steps, leading me to the paths of peace. Thank You, Heavenly Father, for the gift of time. As I seek to manage Your time well (Psalm 31:15), I will find true rest and peace in Your presence. In Jesus' name, I pray. Amen.

August 5
Reject Lies Embrace God's Peace

"You will know the truth, and the truth will set you free."

John 8:32 CSB

Dear God of Truth, I bless You today. I give You all glory, honor, and praise that is due to You. Your Word has the power to liberate me from the chains that bind me. Grant me the discernment to recognize the lies that have entangled my thoughts and actions. Lead me in all truth (John 16:13) and dispel every darkness that hinders me from experiencing Your peace.

Loving Shepherd, I recognize that true rest and peace can only be found in You. Lead me to green pastures (Psalm 23:2) of spiritual nourishment, where my soul can be rejuvenated. Guide me beside still waters (Psalm 23:2b), where my restless heart can find serenity. ,

I renounce every lie and deceitful agreement I have made with the enemy that has kept me from experiencing Your rest. I choose to align my thoughts, words, and actions with Your truth. Fill me with Your Holy Spirit, who empowers me to resist deception and embrace the fullness of Your rest and peace. May Your truth guide my steps, illuminate my path, and bring transformation to every area of my life. In Jesus' mighty name, I pray. Amen.

August 6
Surrendering Guilt, Finding Rest

"Jesus said to them, 'The Sabbath was made for man, not man for the Sabbath.'"

Mark 2:27 AMP

Dear God of Rest, I come before You with a weary heart, burdened by guilt and the weight of my mistakes. But in this moment, I surrender it all to You. I long to find rest in Your loving embrace and be freed from the chains of guilt that bind me (Psalm 55:22).

Help me to truly believe in Your unconditional love, to let go of the guilt that seeps into my thoughts and steals my peace. Fill my mind with Your truth and assurance, that I may find safety and comfort in Your arms (Deuteronomy 33:27).

Lord Jesus, I ask for Your restoration in my life. Heal the wounds of guilt that I carry and restore my soul from the weariness that lingers within me. As I open my hands and surrender all to You, pour out Your boundless love and wholeness into the depths of my being. Let Your grace wash over me and cleanse me from the stains of guilt, leaving me refreshed and renewed (1 John 1:9). May I radiate Your love and grace to those around me, being a vessel of Your rest and peace. In Jesus's holy name, I pray. Amen.

August 7
Resting in God's Presence

*"Repent therefore and be converted, that your sins may
be blotted out, so that times of refreshing may come
from the presence of the Lord."*

Acts 3:19 NKJV

Dear Emmanuel, God with me, thank You for Your constant presence. I would rather spend one day with You than a thousand elsewhere (Psalm 84:10). Though You have given me so much, I seek Your face above all.

As I move away from striving, especially concerning my physical health, I choose today to relax and receive Your presence. I embrace Your promise of rest and recall the atonement of the cross, where my sins were removed as far as the east is from the west (Psalm 103:12). The old is gone and the new has come (2 Corinthians 5:17).

In this moment of surrender, I lay down my burdens and worries at Your feet. I find rest in Your unfailing love and perfect peace. In Your presence, there is fullness of joy and everlasting comfort.

May my heart be replenished, my mind renewed, and my soul refreshed. Help me to dwell in Your presence continually and trust in Your perfect timing. Thank You for being my refuge and sanctuary. In Jesus' name, Amen.

August 8
Surrendering Self-Sufficiency

"Unless the Lord builds the house, those who build it labor in vain. Unless the Lord guards the city, the guard keeps watch in vain."

Psalm 127:1 NRSV

Heavenly Father, Master Builder, today I pour out my heart to You, acknowledging the futility of attempting to do life on my own without You. I confess that at times I have been enticed by the allure of self-sufficiency, thinking that I could find fulfillment and peace in my own strength and abilities. But I realize that this path leads only to emptiness and leaves me feeling robbed of the abundant peace You long to bestow upon me.

It's only through Your grace and mercy that I can find true fulfillment and peace. Teach me to rely on Your strength, wisdom, and guidance in all that I do, so that I can rebuild your temple according to your blueprint.

Replace my self-sufficiency with a humble heart that seeks Your will above all else (Matthew 6:33). I cease striving (Psalm 46:10) and entrust everything to You. Guide me in aligning my goals, plans, ambitions, and desires with Your perfect plan for my life, so that I may labor not in vain, but in the abundant life You have promised (John 10:10). Today and always, I embrace Your purpose and live fully in Your grace. In Jesus' name, I pray. Amen.

August 9
Psalm 23

"The LORD is my Shepherd; I shall not want."
Psalm 23:1 KJV

Dear Jehovah Jireh who provides for all my needs (Philippians 4:19). Just as a shepherd leads his sheep to lie down in lush green pastures, You guide me to places of rest and tranquility. In those serene moments, my weary soul finds comfort, and my heart is at peace.

Beside the still waters, You gently lead me, soothing my spirit and quenching the thirst of my soul (Revelation 22:17). In Your presence, there is a deep and abiding calmness that refreshes and restores me. My weary and burdened soul finds rest in the oasis of Your love and grace.

Even in the darkest valleys, where the shadow of death looms, I will fear no evil. Your presence is my comfort and my refuge. Your unwavering love and faithful guidance give me the strength to persevere. Your rod protects me from harm, and Your staff gently corrects and guides me on the right path. I am secure in Your arms, knowing that You will never forsake me (Psalm 23:4). As I rest in You, O God, I find true beauty and serenity. In the embrace of Your love, I discover the peace that surpasses all understanding (Philippians 4:7). In the name of Jesus, I pray. Amen.

August 10
Breathing in God's Presence

*"... then the Lord God formed the man of dust from the
ground and breathed into his nostrils the breath of life,
and the man became a living creature."*

Genesis 2:7 ESV

Lord, You are my Creator and Maker, designing me with
purpose. You formed me from dust and breathed life
into me (Genesis 2:7). I rest in being exactly who I am, the
crown of Your creation (Psalm 8:5), perfectly fathered by You.
Every breath I take reminds me of Your presence and wonder,
filling me with life (Job 33:4). In these breaths, I find peace,
connecting with the rhythm of Your creation.

As the air enters my lungs, it carries away my stress and fears.
With each exhale, I release my burdens to You, knowing You
are always with me, guiding and carrying them. In the stillness,
I feel Your gentle touch, reassuring me that I am not alone.
Your breath sustains and nourishes my soul, calming my restless
spirit.

In this moment, I pause and inhale deeply, receiving Your
peace, love, and grace. My mind and spirit are at ease, trusting
in Your control (Proverbs 19:21). I surrender my worries to
You and find communion with Your divine presence. Thank
You for this practice that reminds me of Your infinite care. In
Jesus' name, Amen.

August 11
Overcoming the Spirit of Overwhelm

"O God, hear my prayer. Listen to my heart's cry."
Psalms 61:1 TPT

Dear Lord, I thank you for creating me in your image (Genesis 1:27) and giving me everything I need to live a godly life (2 Peter 1:3). Today, I surrender my spirit of overwhelm to you. It is robbing me of so much joy and peace, overshadowing my desire to rest in Your presence.

I acknowledge that this overwhelm comes from believing I must constantly do more, give more, and be more. It weighs heavily on my soul and causes me to doubt my worth and forget Your unconditional love. Help me remember that my value is not defined by my achievements but by Your grace. Teach me to find balance, allowing myself to rest in Your peace and trust in Your provision. Guide me to let go of control and embrace the freedom that comes from relying on Your strength.

Fill me with tranquility, making Your presence my refuge in distress. As I face today's challenges, remind me of Your promises and renew my spirit with hope. Lead me to serenity and trust, where I am safe and sheltered. In Jesus' name, I pray. Amen.

August 12
The Physiology of Rest

"Hear this, O Job; stop and consider the wondrous works of God."

Job 37:14 ESV

Dear Jehovah Shalom, I come before You today with a humble heart, seeking Your guidance and wisdom. I acknowledge Your boundless love and infinite knowledge, knowing that You are the source of all understanding.

Lord, in this chaotic world, where 'grinding' and 'burning the midnight oil' are praised and rewarded, remind me of the importance of rest. I am constantly, pushing myself to the limits without realizing the consequences it has on my physical body

In your infinite wisdom, you created my body to naturally replenish, heal, and rebuild during moments of stillness (Psalm 127:2). Teach me to recognize the importance of sleep, meditation, and relaxation, as they nurture my cognitive abilities, enhance my creativity, and sharpen my focus (Proverbs 3:24).

During periods of rest, especially sleep repairs and rebuild damaged tissues. I pray that You would transform this knowledge into practical wisdom in my life. Grant me the discipline to prioritize rest and the courage to embrace the stillness that You offer (Psalm 46:10). May my pursuit of rest be an act of faith, trusting that You are the ultimate source of restoration and renewal (Isaiah 40:31). In Jesus' name I pray. Amen.

August 13
Emotional and Mental Benefits of Rest

"We destroy arguments and every lofty opinion raised against the knowledge of God, and take every thought captive to obey Christ."

2 Corinthians 10:5 ESV

Dear Heavenly Father, I come before You, humbled by the magnificence of Your creation. Thank You for the gift of my mind, an anointed wonder of creativity and understanding. I confess my thoughts swirling in my mind are often consumed with worries and anxieties, leaving me in turmoil. Yet, You are the God of peace, inviting me to find rest for my weary soul (Jeremiah 31:25).

Grant me the ability to recognize that rest is not a luxury but a necessity for my well-being. Teach me to prioritize rest for my physical, emotional, and mental health. Show me how moments of quiet can bring clarity amidst noise and still the storms of life.

Help me surrender my worries to You, for Your peace surpasses all understanding (Philippians 4:7). Guide me to activities that refresh my soul, whether it's spending time in nature, reading Your Word, or simply being still in Your presence (Psalm 46:10). In Jesus' name, I pray. Amen.

August 14
Sleep Well

"In peace I will lie down and sleep, for you alone, LORD, make me dwell in safety.."

Psalm 4:8 NIV

Dear God of Peace, you are the one who leads me beside peaceful streams (Psalm 23:2) and makes true rest available to me. Thank You so much for always making a way and for providing everything I need to live a godly life (2 Peter 1:3), including sleep and rest.

I confess that I often struggle to allow myself the deep, soul rest and sweet sleep You have provided. As I work toward being a healthier me, help me understand that it is Your will for me to live from Your rest, rather than frantically trying to accomplish everything on my own.

Grant me the discipline to prioritize sleep, to establish healthy sleep patterns, and to create an environment conducive to rest. Remind me that "in peace I will lie down and sleep, for You alone, LORD, make me dwell in safety" (Psalm 4:8 NIV). Teach me to value and prioritize this gift, knowing that in doing so, I honor the body and life You have given me. I declare that as I lay down to sleep tonight, my sleep will be sweet and restorative. In Jesus' name I pray. Amen.

August 15
Sabbath Rest and Renewal

"Remember the sabbath day, to keep it holy. Six days shalt thou labour, and do all thy work:"
Exodus 20:8-9 KJV

Dear God of wisdom, you've created everything with intention, including the need for Sabbath rest. As Sundays have become workdays, leaving us overworked and overwhelmed, I seek Your guidance to renew Your command for Sabbath rest (Exodus 20:8-9). Help me honor this sacred time.

The world pressures me to be constantly active and striving. Yet, in Your wisdom, You designed Sabbath rest as essential for my well-being. Teach me to view rest as an act of faith, believing that by setting aside my work, I will actually enhance my productivity. In the stillness of Sabbath, help me reconnect with You, listen to Your gentle whispers, and seek Your guidance. Open my eyes to the wonders of nature that reflect Your majesty (Psalm 145:5). Grant me strength and courage to resist worldly demands that steal my peace (John 10:10).

Enable me to establish boundaries and protect my Sabbath time (Hebrews 4:9). Through this practice, may I experience renewal, strength, and a deeper connection with You. I thank You for the wisdom and benefits of Sabbath rest. Guide me as I strive to honor this sacred time and find the fullness of life You desire for me. In Jesus' name, I pray. Amen.

August 16
Embracing God's Timing and Transformation

"But we all, with unveiled face, beholding as in a mirror the glory of the Lord, are being transformed into the same image from glory to glory, just as from the Lord, the Spirit."

2 Corinthians 3:18 NASB 1995

Dear God of Patience and Peace, I come before You with a humble heart, seeking Your divine guidance and strength. I am grateful for the transformation You have worked in my life, moving me from glory to glory (2 Corinthians 3:18). I surrender my desire to rush the process and confess my impatience. Help me trust in Your perfect timing and embrace the growth that comes from following You (2 Peter 3:9).

I often long for immediate results and struggle with instant gratification. Today, I choose to align my will with Yours and trust that You see me as a beloved child, securely held in Your hand. I know rushing this process will not bring lasting freedom or healing. So, I choose to see myself through Your loving eyes and allow You to mold me into the person You designed me to be.

I surrender my stress, anxiety, and need for control, placing my faith in You, knowing that You are working all things together for my good (Romans 8:28). Thank You for Your faithfulness and perfect timing. May Your will be done in me as I grow closer to You. In Jesus' name, I pray. Amen.

August 17
Carving Out Time For God

"Draw near to God, and he will draw near to you."
James 4:8 ESV

Dear good, good Father, I am honored that You call me 'friend' and desire to spend time with me. Amid my busy life, I confess I've neglected to prioritize time with You. My soul yearns for nourishment and restoration, so I ask for Your help in carving out moments for our connection.

You understand the demands and responsibilities I face. My schedule often feels overwhelming, and there never seems to be enough time. Yet, I seek solace in Your presence and wish to be refueled by Your grace and love. Help me set aside distractions and dedicate quality time to commune with You.

Grant me wisdom to discern what truly matters and the courage to adjust my routine. Teach me to prioritize my spiritual well-being over trivial pursuits and to simplify, delegate, or let go of unnecessary tasks. Show me how to seek Your face (Psalm 27:8), meditate on Your Word (Psalm 119:15), and pray sincerely. As I make You the center of my life, strengthen me to overcome distractions and guard this sacred time. Renew my mind and spirit, so I can face challenges with Your wisdom and strength (1 Samuel 10:6). Thank You for Your constant love and patience. In Jesus' name, I pray. Amen.

August 18
Peace, Generosity and Service

"In all things I have shown you that by working hard in this way we must help the weak and remember the words of the Lord Jesus, how he himself said, 'It is more blessed to give than to receive.'"

Acts 20:35 ESV

Dear Heavenly Father, I come before You with a humble heart, recognizing how easily I can become consumed by my own desires. I confess that chasing after personal goals often leaves me stressed and spinning my wheels, disconnected from the true joy You offer.

Your Word reminds me that "it is more blessed to give than to receive" (Acts 20:35). Help me shift my focus from selfish pursuits to serving others with a heart of compassion. Teach me to find fulfillment not in what I can accumulate for myself, but in how I can support and uplift those around me.

Guide me to channel my efforts towards helping and being a blessing to others (Philippians 2:4). Let my life reflect Your love and grace through my actions, as I strive to serve others (Galatians 5:13).

Thank You for Your guidance and the opportunity to make a difference in the lives of others. In Jesus' name, I pray. Amen.

August 19
Resting at Jesus' Feet

"Martha, Martha," the Lord answered, "you are wor-
ried and upset about many things, … Mary has chosen
what is better,"

Luke 10:41-42 NIV

Dear God of Wisdom, you promise to give wisdom generously to those who ask (James 1:5). I long to understand
the importance of resting at Jesus' feet, like Mary did. Help
me to be more like Mary, who chose to be still and listen to
Your words, rather than being consumed by life's demands like
Martha. Teach me to find fulfillment not in constant activity
but in the stillness of Your presence.

Lord Jesus, remind me that only one thing is truly necessary,
as You gently taught Martha. Help me to prioritize my time
with You and cherish moments of silence where Your voice
can be heard and Your peace felt. Forgive me for letting distractions pull me away from these sacred moments. Grant me the
courage to say no to demands that interfere with my time for
prayer, meditation, and reflection. Strengthen my resolve to set
aside time for You, knowing that it brings rest and rejuvenation
to my soul.

Instill in me a spirit of contentment (1 Timothy 6:6-8) and
fill my heart with Your peace that surpasses all understanding
(Philippians 4:7). May I find grounding and grace at Your feet.
In Jesus' name, I pray. Amen.

August 20
Releasing Worry

"Do not be anxious about anything, but in every situation, by prayer and petition, with thanksgiving, present your requests to God."

Philippians 4:6 NIV

Hello, Lord Jehovah-Jireh, Thank You for this new day with You (Psalm 84:10). You are my supplier and provider. While I know in my mind that I should not worry, the habits of anxiety have become deeply ingrained in me, creating an atmosphere of worry and stress.

I need Your help to change the strongholds of worry in my mind. I agree with Your Word that You have overcome the world (John 16:33). Understanding that surrender is a daily practice, I give myself completely to You today, with thanksgiving, rolling my burdens over to You. I surrender everything and everyone to You, Lord, releasing the spirit of worry that robs me of peace, health, joy, and my relationship with You.

I call on Your supernatural power to uproot these lies, rewire my mind, and create new pathways based on Your Truth. Guide me in how I think about my body and health, drawing me closer to You (James 4:8). Take my hand as I let go of my worries and find rest in Your power through prayer. Thank You for carrying these burdens for me. In Jesus' name, I pray. Amen.

August 21
It Is What It Is

"For freedom Christ has set us free; stand firm there-fore, and do not submit again to a yoke of slavery."
Galatians 5:1 ESV

Dear God of the Universe, I thank You for this day and I will rejoice and be glad in it. In the glory of Your presence (Psalm 145:5), I admit my struggle to let go of control, which brings anxiety and stress. I recognize that my need to control outcomes hinders my peace and prevents me from fully living in the present.

Grant me wisdom to understand that I cannot control every-thing and that sometimes the best action is to let things be. Teach me to trust in Your perfect plan, believing that You will work all things together for my good (Romans 8:28).

In moments of uncertainty, remind me to accept circumstances as they are, and declare "It is what it is" which will help me to accept my circumstances and help me find peace. Grant me serenity to accept what I cannot change, courage to change what I can, and wisdom to know the difference. May Your peace dwells within me now and always. In Jesus' name, I pray. Amen.

August 22
Embracing God's Gift of Sleep

*"In vain you rise early and stay up late, toiling for food
to eat—for he grants sleep to those he loves."*
Psalm 127:2 NIV

D ear Lord, I am amazed that You call me Your beloved.
Thank You for Your promises, including the gift of rest-
ful sleep (2 Corinthians 1:20). I accept this gift with gratitude.

You created me to live a surrendered life in union with You,
not for endless toil or anxiety. As I strive to live from a place of
rest (Matthew 11:28), I invite Your Spirit to calm my fears and
replace them with trust (Isaiah 26:3). I declare that sleep will
come easily when I lay my head down each night.

Grant me wisdom to distinguish between activities that nourish
my soul and those that drain my energy. Help me prioritize
what truly matters and resist the temptation to stay up late on
unproductive tasks. Remind me of the purpose You've set for
me and guide me to align my actions with Your will.

I purpose to wake up each morning giving You glory, spend
the day being thankful for all that You have enabled me to
do, and go to bed each night with a 'good tired,' feeling
knowing that I've completed my assignment for the day. In
Your gracious name of Jesus, I pray. Amen.

August 23
Rest Equals Trust

"In repentance and rest is your salvation, in quietness and trust is your strength."

Isaiah 30:15 NIV

Heavenly Father, I surrender everything and everyone to You today. I trust in You Lord (Isaiah 12:2) Help me to grasp the profound truth that rest is an expression of trust in You. When I struggle with taking a break, remind me that finding rest is not a sign of weakness or laziness, but an act of faith in Your loving provision and sovereignty.

In times of rest, may Your peace wash over me and grant me the strength and clarity I need for the journey ahead (Philippians 4:6-7). As I embrace the truth that rest equals trust, may it deepen my faith and reliance on You. Help me to continually surrender to Your loving care, finding rest in the assurance that You are with me every step of the way.

Thank You, heavenly Father, for Your boundless grace and faithfulness. May my life be a testimony of trust in Your provision, and may rest become a sacred space where I experience the fullness of Your peace and restoration. In Your son's name, I pray. Amen.

August 24
Surrendering Unrealistic Expectations

""Are you the one who is to come, or should we expect someone else?""

Matthew 11:3 NIV

Dear God of Truth, Lord, sometimes I find myself seeking You in self-serving ways, expecting specific outcomes or answers to my prayers. I forget that Your ways are higher than my ways and that Your plans for me may differ from what I anticipate (Isaiah 55:8-9).

Father, I confess that these expectations hinder my ability to fully trust in Your perfect will. They cloud my vision and create barriers in my relationship with You. Help me to surrender my own expectations and desires to You, knowing that Your ways are perfect and Your timing is impeccable. I pray for a spirit of contentment and gratitude to fill my heart (Philippians 4:11-12). May I find joy in the present moment, knowing that You are with me every step of the way.

Lord, I ask for the strength to surrender my will to Yours, to release my expectations into Your capable hands. Grant me the faith to trust in Your divine plan, even when it's different from what I envision. Help me to walk in faith, knowing that You are the Expected One and that You will lead me according to Your perfect will and purpose (Luke 22:42). In Jesus' name, I pray. Amen.

August 25
Trusting God's Promise of Refreshment

"I will refresh the weary and satisfy the faint."
Jeremiah 31:25 NIV

Abba Father, thank You for Your boundless love and for sending Your Son to die for my sins. I praise You that You never leave me nor forsake me (Deuteronomy 31:6). Life's burdens have left me feeling weary and faint. Yet, in the midst of it all, I draw confidence in Your Word and Your unfailing love.

Today, I ask for Your divine refreshment. Revive my spirit when it feels weak and weary. Infuse me with Your strength to face each day with hope and courage. Pour out Your peace that surpasses all understanding (Philippians 4:7), calming the storms within my heart and mind.

Guide me with Your wisdom. Help me see the path You have set before me and direct my steps according to Your will. Show me what drains my energy and give me the courage to let go of burdens that are not mine to carry.

Satisfy my weary soul with Your love, grace, and provision. Quench my thirst with Your living water (Isaiah 55:1), and fill me with Your Holy Spirit. Thank You, Lord, for Your promise to refresh and satisfy me. I pray this in the name of Jesus. Amen.

August 26
Self Care is Not Selfish

"Then, because so many people were coming and going that they did not even have a chance to eat, he said to them, 'Come with me by yourselves to a quiet place and get some rest.'"

Mark 6:31 NIV

Dear God of Love, thank You for loving me with an everlasting love (Jeremiah 31:3). As I face life's challenges, I often forget the importance of self-care. Caught up in others' demands, I neglect my need for rest and rejuvenation. Today, I am reminded that self-care is not selfish; it is essential for my well-being and faith.

Help me release guilt or shame when I prioritize self-care. Just as Jesus withdrew to quiet places to pray and replenish (Mark 6:31), teach me to carve out moments for myself. By nourishing my body, mind, and soul, I can serve You and others better with renewed spirit. In these moments, let me find peace in Your presence. As I engage in activities that bring joy and peace, help me see Your hand in the beauty of creation and Your blessings. Guard me from distractions that pull me away from self-care (Psalm 23:2-3), and give me wisdom to prioritize my needs.

Thank You, Heavenly Father, for Your grace and unconditional love. May my self-care practices be acts of worship and reminders of Your abundant grace. In Jesus' name, Amen.

August 27
God's Rest Amidst Distractions

"Turn my eyes from looking at worthless things; and give me life in your ways."

Psalm 119:37 ESV

Heavenly Father, I acknowledge that my heart and mind are often consumed by distractions like social media and TV. These diversions pull me away from Your presence and the rest You offer (Romans 12:2). I confess that I sometimes prioritize these distractions over seeking Your peace. Today, I surrender them to You, longing to be anchored in Your presence.

Help me manage the allure of social media and TV. Help me set boundaries and use my time purposefully to be still in Your presence.

Lord, as I commit to reducing these distractions and embracing Your rest, I ask for Your strength and perseverance. Fill my heart with a deep desire to seek You daily, to rest in Your presence, and to find true satisfaction in the depths of Your love. Help me to cultivate a disciplined mind and heart that are firmly anchored in Your truth, enabling me to discern what truly matters (Colossians 3:2)and to invest my time and energy in endeavors that align with Your will. I pray all these things in the name of Jesus, who provides us with the ultimate example of surrendering earthly distractions and finding rest in Your presence. Amen.

August 28
Reframing Stress, Embracing Peace

*"I have told you these things so that in me you may
have peace. In this world you will have trouble. But
take heart! I have overcome the world."*
John 16:33 NIV

Dear Jehovah Shalom, I seek Your divine help to reframe the stress and worries that overshadow my days. Grant me the wisdom to see these challenges as opportunities for growth and to enter Your rest, where true peace resides.

Lord, help me shift my perspective on stress and view it as a chance to deepen my faith and character (James 1:2-3). Remind me that through You, I can overcome any obstacle (Psalm 18:29). When anxiety clouds my mind, fill me with Your light and replace worry with trust in Your plan. Teach me to surrender my anxieties, knowing You hold all things in Your hands.

Grant me peace that surpasses understanding and let me rest amidst the chaos (Matthew 11:28). Help me anchor my soul in Your promises and find calm in Your presence. May I see trials as growth opportunities, stress as a call to depend on You, and worry as a reminder to cast my cares upon You.

Thank You for Your unwavering love. I surrender my burdens and trust in Your guidance. In Jesus' name, Amen.

August 29
Sacred Pauses

"But Jesus often withdrew to lonely places and prayed."
Luke 5:16 NIV

Dear God of Stillness and Rest, I seek moments of calm amidst the chaos to pause and acknowledge Your presence. Grant me grace to take frequent pauses throughout my day, allowing me to slow down and feel Your divine presence.

In the morning, before the day begins, help me pause, breathe deeply, and center myself in Your peace. Let this moment ground me in Your love and prepare me for the challenges ahead. Throughout the day, remind me to pause and focus on You. Help me appreciate the beauty around me and recognize Your blessings. Give me wisdom to prioritize moments of reflection, seek Your guidance, and express gratitude.

In times of stress or uncertainty, grant me the courage to pause and surrender my anxieties. Let me find rest in the stillness, knowing You are my refuge and strength (Psalm 46:1). Fill me with peace that surpasses understanding, restoring my weary soul.

In the evening, guide me to pause and reflect on the day's journey. Help me see growth and release regrets, knowing Your grace is abundant and Your forgiveness boundless. May Your grace accompany me in each pause, and may Your divine presence permeate every moment of my life. In Jesus' holy name, I pray. Amen.

August 30
The Rhythm of Rest

"The LORD will fight for you; you need only to be still."

Exodus 14:14 NIV

Dear Sovereign God, my ever-present Helper, and Counselor, I seek Your divine presence and guidance today. You are the source of all peace and rest, and I long to experience the stillness You provide (Exodus 14:14). Amidst daily stress, grant me the wisdom and strength to pause, pray, and realign my spirit, soul, and body.

I acknowledge that my reactive nature often distracts me from Your love and care. Teach me to pause, quiet my racing thoughts, and focus on You (Proverbs 4:20-21). Help me let go of control and surrender my burdens into Your hands. In these pauses, instill in me the wisdom to recognize the power of prayer (Mark 11:24). Let my prayers be heartfelt conversations where I release my fears and anxieties, trusting that You will replace them with peace.

Remind me that rest is an intentional act of trust, not laziness. Guide me in setting healthy boundaries, prioritizing self-care, and nurturing meaningful relationships. May embracing this rhythm of rest remind me of Your constant presence and unfailing love. In Jesus' name, I pray. Amen.

August 31
Continued Rest

"So don't worry about these things, saying, 'What will we eat? What will we drink? What will we wear?' ... Seek the Kingdom of God above all else and live righteously, and he will give you everything you need."
Matthew 6:31-32 NLT

D ear Faithful Father, I am deeply grateful for this month of prayer, which has led me to rest, restoration, and renewal in Your presence. I am humbled by Your faithfulness and the transformative power of communing with You. Throughout this month, You have drawn me closer, guiding me to find comfort and peace in Your arms (Deuteronomy 33:27). In my weariness, You have been my refuge and source of peace. You have heard my cries and responded with unwavering love and grace, soothing my soul and replenishing my spirit.

Thank You for the countless moments of connection during these prayers. You have taught me to cast my burdens upon You, knowing that You care for me (1 Peter 5:7). Your understanding and compassion have shown me that I am never alone. Your words have brought healing and ignited a flame of faith within me.

As this month of focused prayer ends, engrave these lessons in my heart. Help me seek You fervently in prayer, not just during this time but throughout my life (Ephesians 6:18). May the rest I have found in You continue to shape my journey of faith. In Jesus' name, I pray. Amen.

September

FIT & FEARLESS

Welcome to this month of learning how to pray so you can live fearlessly in the Lord.

Fear, in its many forms—whether fear of failure, rejection, the unknown, or the future—can subtly undermine your confidence and impede your progress. It often lurks in the shadows, whispering doubts that paralyze your actions and obstruct your path to wholeness.

As you pray these bold prayers, you will grow in the knowledge that fear will not dominate you, for you are a child of a loving and omnipotent God. In Him, you'll find courage and strength. Through prayer, reflection, and surrender, you will face your fears with courage, knowing you do not walk this path alone. The Lord is your refuge and rock, offering the support you need to release the fears that hold you captive.

This month, you will gain confidence in surrendering your fears to God, trusting in His divine plan. Cultivate a fearless spirit rooted in faith and nurtured by His grace. Let your prayers be fervent, your heart open, and your soul receptive to God's healing touch.

May this month bring you grace, courage, and a deep connection with the Father. As you surrender your fears, may God's perfect love cast out all fear and lead you to vibrant health and well-being. In His name, you pray. Amen.

September 1
Search Me O God

"I the Lord search the heart and test the mind, to give every man according to his ways, according to the fruit of his deeds."

Jeremiah 17:10 ESV

Dear Omnipotent and Everlasting God, it amazes me that You know everything about me, even the number of hairs on my head (Luke 12:7). Because of Your intimate knowledge of me, I feel safe bringing all my fears to You. I acknowledge that these fears have held me back from becoming my best self, but I am ready to surrender them this month. I trust that You will transform me into a fearless daughter of Yours.

Today, I open myself to Your examination. Test me and search my heart (Psalm 139:23). Reveal the fears that hold me back, and remove every lie and obstacle that keeps me from seeing myself as You see me and from fully enjoying fellowship with You. Help me understand why these hidden fears have made my health journey feel challenging and grant me endurance to remain committed despite them. I am grateful for the truth and wisdom You will reveal, knowing it will set me free (John 8:31).

I am committed to staying the course and prioritizing You in my life. I surrender all my fears to You, both those I am aware of and those yet to be uncovered. Guide me in identifying any ways that offend You and lead me on the path of everlasting life (Psalm 139:24). In Jesus' name, Amen.

September 2
My Future Inheritance

"So Jacob was left alone, and a man wrestled with him till daybreak. When the man saw that he could not overpower him, he touched the socket of Jacob's hip so that his hip was wrenched as he wrestled with the man."
Genesis 32:24-25 NIV

Dear Lord, You are a chain-breaker and burden-bearer. Just as you changed Jacob's name to Israel, you also call me by a new name. I often label myself by my limitations like lazy, overweight, procrastinator, or quitter. But you look beyond my faults and you call me your child (John 1:12); redeemed (Romans 3:24) and an heir (Romans 8:17).

Like Jacob, I will fight for my freedom. I will fight to break free from debilitating fears, limiting beliefs, and generational curses. Struggle and hardship will not define my future. As You changed the name Jacob (meaning deceiver) to Israel (meaning overcomer), I will walk also in who You say I am and not what the past, the evil one, or the world says I am.

Thank God, for the generous inheritance waiting for me. Thank You for showing me that my past does not need to be our future as I confront it, overpower it, and reclaim my identity in You. As You did for Jacob, You will do that for me too. I declare that I am created to be in good health, I am healthy in spirit, soul, and body. In Jesus' name, Amen!

September 3
Limitless God

I have appeared to you to appoint you as a servant and
as a witness of what you have seen and will see of me."
Acts 26:16 ESV

Dear Limitless God. You transcend all space and time. You know the end from the beginning (Isaiah 46:10) and are not bound by anything. Today, I lift up my limited and narrow-minded thinking to You. Help me to believe beyond what I can see with my eyes. My desire is to see life from Your perspective instead of my narrow, myopic view. There are so many fears and wrong beliefs that I've held on to because I can't see beyond my own limitations but You transcend them all.

Give me the courage to believe in limitless possibilities. You know the end from the beginning. Only You know what's around the corner, so today, I let go of all the limits. I let go of the word 'never' and believe that change is possible (Mark 9:23) when I put my trust in You.

I was blind but now I see as You remove the scales from my eyes (John 9:25) . I am limitless, I am unstoppable. I can and will do all You say I can do. I have the victory. In Jesus' name! Amen.

September 4
Overcoming Overthinking

"I pray that the eyes of your heart may be enlightened in order that you may know the hope to which he has called you, the riches of his glorious inheritance in his holy people,."

Ephesians 1:18 NIV

Dear Lord, light of the world, Your light overcomes all darkness (John 1:5). I thank You for this truth, as I sometimes become overwhelmed by the multitude of programs and strategies for my challenges, feeling paralyzed by indecision. Today, I choose to take small steps in faith, moving in the right direction despite my tendency toward analysis paralysis (Matthew 6:25).

I decree that my mind is at peace. I will focus on one thought at a time, refusing to be overwhelmed by a flood of ideas. As You fill my mind with Your light, my thoughts realign with Yours, bringing calm and clarity. I accept helpful thoughts and let go of the rest, embracing the empowering truth that I don't need to overthink everything.

Help me to take every dark thought captive (2 Corinthians 10:5). Your light shines brightly within me, realigning my thoughts and guiding me to act in obedience. I release the spirit of overthinking and decree that I have the mind of Christ. With this truth, I anticipate breakthrough! In Jesus' name, Amen.

September 5
Weathering The Storms of Life

"Blessed is the man who trusts in the Lord, whose trust is the Lord. He is like a tree planted by water, that sends out its roots by the stream, and does not fear when heat comes, for its leaves remain green, and is not anxious in the year of drought, for it does not cease to bear fruit."
Jeremiah 17:7-8 ESV

Dear Abba Father, You are my shield, my glory, and the lifter of my head (Psalm 3:1-3). You are my strength, sustainer, and provider, promising never to leave or forsake me. Yet I often try to avoid fear rather than trusting You. Your Word assures me that in placing my trust in You, I need not fear; I can face the future with confidence (Proverbs 31:25).

Thank You that as I progress in my health journey, I need not fear backsliding. Surrendering to You means I am always moving forward, even if I stumble. I can learn from my mistakes without letting guilt or shame hold me back. I am growing and learning, never failing.

Like a tree planted by streams of water, I will bear good fruit in season—fruit of self-control, peace, love, joy, and patience (Psalm 1:3). Life's storms make me more resilient and adaptable. I declare that whatever I do prospers because my trust is in You. I plead the blood of Jesus over my health today, declaring that every muscle, tendon, organ, joint, and tissue functions as it should. In Your precious Holy Name, I pray. Amen.

September 6
Will I Ever Change?

*"I do not understand what I do. For what I want to do
I do not do, but what I hate I do."*
Romans 7:15 NIV

Dear Jehovah Shalom, God of peace (John 14:27), You bring calm to my restless mind and tame my unruly flesh. Like Paul, I struggle with doing what I don't want to do and failing to do what I intend. It feels as though my mind is hijacked, and I fear I'll never change.

Show me that true change starts with You, not my own efforts. I've been trying to change on my own, which only leads to frustration. Help me understand that change comes through surrendering my will to Yours (Luke 22:42). You alone can meet my needs (Philippians 4:19), satisfy me (John 6:35), and control my appetites. Thank You for renewing my mind and transforming me from within. Even when I can't see it, I trust that change is happening.

Today, I lay aside my will, ways, and wants, aligning them with Yours. I trust that this alignment will make a difference. Only You can rescue me from this struggle, and I am grateful. I decree transformation and breakthrough, declaring that I am changing day by day, one habit at a time. In Your Name, I pray, Amen.

September 7
FearLESS

*"But now, this is what the Lord says … Fear not, for
I have redeemed you; I have summoned you by name;
you are mine."*

Isaiah 43:1 ESV

"Dear Lord, my Teacher and Mentor. You show me great and mighty things that I did not know (Jeremiah 33:3) thank You for guiding me to live a life with less fear through faith in You. Right now, I admit I'm not feeling fearless; I'm anxious about facing my emotions without food as a crutch. I worry about being overwhelmed and about my new normal.

I've relied on food and other strategies to manage my fears, so confronting them head-on feels daunting. Grant me the courage to face and uproot these fears, trusting that You will heal them. Remind me that my strength is in You (Psalm 59:9) and that You will never leave me (Deuteronomy 31:8).

You teach me that fear, when directed to You, can be a guide and a reminder of my dependence on You. Fear becomes a tool when I trust in Your power to overcome it. Thank You for redeeming me from fear's chains. Help me to fear less and trust more. I declare today, Fear, who cares? In Jesus' name, Amen.

September 8
Overcoming Health Fears With God's Help

"I sought the LORD, and he heard me, and delivered me from all my fears"

Psalm 34:4 NIV

Dear God, my Deliverer, you promise that when I seek You with my whole heart, I will find You (Jeremiah 29:13). As I embark on my health journey, I seek Your guidance and protection. You deliver me from all my fears and redeem my life from the grip of anxiety and limiting beliefs.

I never realized how deeply fear was intertwined with my health struggles. As I confront the consequences of my past habits, I see how fear of surrendering control, fear of judgment, fear of being left behind, and fear of failure have hindered my progress. These fears have stolen my joy, peace, and freedom, leaving me feeling trapped.

Today, I lift the shield of faith, trusting that it will extinguish all the fiery darts of fear that threaten to keep me bound (1 Peter 5:7). I believe that You have called me to this journey because You know I am ready. I cast all my fears upon You, knowing You are with me. I declare faith over fear, confident that I am equipped to face any challenge that arises. With Your strength, I will overcome and move forward. Thank You for Your unwavering support and deliverance. In Jesus' Name, Amen.

September 9
Overcoming Fear of Illness or Injury

"You will not fear the terror of night nor the arrow that flies by day, nor the pestilence that stalks in the darkness, nor the plague that destroys at midday."
Psalm 91:5-6 NIV

"Dear Jehovah Jireh, You provide for my every need. You bring health and healing to my body and keep me from injury. Reflecting on past injuries, I realize I've been avoiding growth due to fear. Yet, staying in my comfort zone hinders my progress.

Help me overcome my fear of illness or injury. You've kept me safe until now, and I'm grateful. Remind me that focusing on these fears only attracts them. Instead, let me view illness and injury as signs of misalignment, guiding me to listen to Your direction.

I stand on Your word that, "if I make the Most High Your dwelling, no harm will overtake You, no disaster will come near me" (Psalm 91:10). I will move my body without fear of injury. I will put it within healthy limits, knowing that, like a diamond, pressure is needed to produce anything of value or quality. My body is Your temple, created in Your image therefore it functions optimally without illness or injury. I declare this in the mighty name of Jesus! Amen.

September 10
Standing on Your Promises

"I will make you a great nation; I will bless you and make your name great, and you shall be a blessing."
Genesis 12:2 NIV

Dear Promise-Keeping God, You have given us precious promises that will never fail (2 Peter 1:4). Each time I read Your Word, I'm reassured by Your unwavering faithfulness. Yet, I sometimes fear that Your promises won't come to pass because I feel like I keep getting in my own way. Remind me that if You said it, it will come to pass (Isaiah 46:8–11).

You have promised me hope and a future (Jeremiah 29:11). My role is to keep my focus on You, trusting that You will perfect everything concerning me, including my health and how to care for it. Help me to look forward in faith rather than dwelling on past disappointments and regrets.

Today, I embrace the truth that I am a new creation in You, and the old has passed away (2 Corinthians 5:17). I stand firm on Your promises: You will meet all my needs (Philippians 4:19), restore my health and heal my wounds (Jeremiah 30:17), keep me from every disease (Deuteronomy 7:15), and Your Word will bring life and health to my body (Proverbs 4:22). I come into agreement with every promise You have made. In Your Name, I pray. Amen.

September 11
I Have Dominion

"God blessed them and said to them, "Be fruitful and increase in number; fill the earth and subdue it."
Genesis 1:28 NIV

Dear God of Creation, You formed the heavens and the earth and granted us dominion over it all, including dominion over sin (Romans 6:14). Today, I remind myself of the authority You have given me over my fears, anxieties, emotions, and cravings. Though it often feels like these things control me, I know that my true authority comes through You.

I thank You for the power You've given me. I choose to exercise this dominion according to Your will. I boldly declare victory over sickness, lack, fear, and every hindrance. You've given me authority to overcome all the power of the enemy (Luke 10:19).

I declare that I have dominion over my thoughts and emotions. You have not given me a spirit of fear, but of power, love, and a sound mind (2 Timothy 1:7). I embrace this truth and reject fear and anxiety, focusing instead on Your promises.

Thank You for the victory I have in Christ Jesus. I renounce all doubt and fear and embrace the truth that I am more than a conqueror through Him who loves me. May my life reflect Your goodness, grace, and dominion. Amen.

September 12
Overcoming Fear of Success

"Where can I go from your Spirit? Where can I flee from your presence?"

Psalm 139:7 NIV

Dear Omniscient God, You know everything about me—my every action and thought. You are not surprised when I stray from the path You've set for me. Despite my deep desire to achieve my health goals, anxiety grips me. I worry about maintaining success, losing too much of myself, or facing negative attention. So many questions fill my mind, Lord.

Remind me that true success honors You and gives You glory. As long as this journey focuses on You rather than myself, I need not fear success. Today, I release the lies and limiting beliefs I've held onto and choose to trust that I can achieve what You have promised, without fear of future outcomes. Help me avoid getting caught up in "what ifs" and remind me not to worry about tomorrow (Matthew 6:33). You will supply all my needs today and in the future (Philippians 4:19), so there is no need for fear.

I agree with Your promises and plans for me (Jeremiah 29:11). I move towards success and victory with confidence. I want to live my life to the fullest! In Your name, I pray. Amen.

September 13
Overcoming Stinkin' Thinkin'

"Finally, brothers, whatever is true, honorable, just, pure, lovely, commendable, excellent, if there is anything worthy of praise, think about these things."
Philippians 4:8 ESV

Dear Sovereign Lord, You know my thoughts even before I think them and have given me Your mind (1 Corinthians 2:16). I come before You with a humble heart, seeking Your intervention in the battle within my mind. My thoughts are filled with doubts and fears that hinder my journey toward health and success. I lift my voice to You, knowing You are my ultimate source of strength and guidance.

Lord, I surrender these thoughts to You. Help me recognize their deceptive nature and reject their power over me. Fill my mind with Your truth and light so I may rise above negativity and embrace the path of health and well-being You have set before me. I declare that I am fearfully and wonderfully made (Psalm 139:14), and I ask that my mind align with Your original intent for me.

Grant me Your peace that surpasses all understanding (Philippians 4:7). Quiet my thoughts and give me clarity and focus as I pursue a healthy lifestyle. I place my health and success in Your loving hands, trusting You to align my thoughts with Yours. In Jesus' name, Amen.

September 14
Exchanging Lies for Truth

"They exchanged the truth about God for a lie, and worshiped and served created things rather than the Creator—who is forever praised. Amen."

Romans 1:25 NIV

Dear Lord, God of truth, guide me into complete truth today. Speak into my future and reveal what is to come (John 16:13). Lead me in Your truth and teach me, for You are my salvation (Psalm 25:5). I thank You for showing me the lies and limiting beliefs that hold me back. Getting healthy physically, spiritually, and emotionally is challenging but worth it!

I've been lying to myself with thoughts like, 'I'll start tomorrow' or 'This bite won't hurt,' even though I know they're false. Help me to reject these lies and recognize Your truth. Give me the strength to follow Your instructions faithfully and cling to Your laws (Psalm 119:29-31).

Today, I speak Your truth over my health and hold myself accountable for false beliefs. Bring subconscious lies to the surface and root them out. Let me walk in Your spirit of truth, rejecting every lie that hinders my unity with You. In Jesus' name, I pray. Amen.

September 15
Flowing in My Gifts

"Each of you should use whatever gift you have received to serve others, as faithful stewards of God's grace in its various forms."

1 Peter 4:10 NIV

Dear Father, I thank You for anointing me with natural and spiritual gifts. You bless me with good gifts (Matthew 7:11) and do not withhold anything when I walk uprightly (Psalm 84:11). Yet, I often hide or downplay my gifts out of fear of alienating others or feeling undeserving of Your favor.

Today, remind me that I am Your friend, called to let my light shine brightly so that You are glorified (Matthew 5:16). When I use my gifts, I feel energized and healthy. Help me find balance—walking confidently in my gifts without letting them define me. I am complete in You, so my gifts are meant to bless others and bring glory to You.

Thank You for Your grace and anointing as I operate in my gifts today. I release the fear of shining too bright, knowing it's all for Your glory. I am the light of the world and will let my gifts shine brightly for You (Matthew 5:14). In Your name, I pray. Amen.

September 16
Overcoming the Need for Approval

"Who satisfies your mouth with good things, So that your youth is renewed like the eagle's."
Psalm 103:5 NKJV

Dear Lord, You fill me with contentment and satisfaction. When I seek approval or acceptance from others, remind me that everything I need is found in You alone. I tend to overgive and sometimes do more for others than they do for themselves. Help me balance serving others with avoiding people-pleasing. Your Word says that if I try to please others, I cannot be a servant of Christ (Galatians 1:10).

My need for approval often stems from fear of rejection and feeling inadequate. Remind me that Your Spirit fills me completely, so I don't need validation from others, food, or anything else that offers only temporary pleasure. Guide me in surrendering my crutches of temporary fulfillment, like seeking approval from others. Help me cultivate compassion and understanding to be a source of love and support without losing myself in the process.

As I pursue better health, remind me that You meet all my needs and fears. You satisfy me with good things and are my sustainer and provider. It is a privilege to serve, and I will do so with gladness, bringing glory to You alone. In Your name, I pray. Amen.

September 17
Overcoming the Spirit of Perfectionism

"Then Daniel became distinguished above all the other presidents and satraps because an excellent spirit was in him."

Daniel 6:3 NIV

Dear Lord, How majestic is Your name in all the earth! (Psalm 8:9) You have done excellent things, and I'm grateful for the spirit of excellence You've given me. Let this spirit guide me to steward my body in a way that honors You and brings You glory.

Sometimes, I become obsessed with every detail of my health journey and think, "If it can't be perfect, why bother?" I recognize that this drive for perfection is rooted in fear, not in Your will. You've given me a spirit of love, power, and a sound mind.

Help me understand that I don't need to be the best; I simply need to be the best version of myself according to Your standards. When I accept myself as You created me, I'll find contentment and joy in the journey rather than fixating on the end result.

Guide me to cease striving and trust You more (Psalm 46:10). I'm fearfully and wonderfully made (Psalm 139:14), and I embrace all parts of myself. Thank You for the great work You're doing in me. In Your name, I pray. Amen.

September 18
Overcoming Worry

"Anxiety in a man's heart weighs him down, but a good word makes him glad."

Proverbs 12:25 ESV

Dear Jehovah Shalom, I thank You for the gift of peace that surpasses all understanding and guards my heart and mind. Despite this precious gift, I struggle to experience it fully. I find myself consumed by worry, especially regarding my health. I worry about achieving my goals and the possibility of relapsing and regaining the weight I've lost. This anxiety drains my time and energy.

Your Word assures me, "Peace I leave with You; my peace I give You. I do not give as the world gives. Do not let Your hearts be troubled and do not be afraid" (John 14:27). When I focus on You, my worries begin to fade. Help me quickly recognize and replace the spirit of worry with worship.

Teach me to concentrate on today and not be anxious about tomorrow (Matt 6:33). Worrying about the future is futile, as I cannot control it. My concerns are grounded in fear of the unknown and feelings of powerlessness. Yet, You are in control, and that is enough. Transform my worry into prayer, as praying is the roar of faith against fear. I reject worry and rest in Your presence. In Jesus' name, I pray. Amen.

September 19
Practicing Self Care

"Then, because so many people were coming and going that they did not even have a chance to eat, he said to them, "Come with me by yourselves to a quiet place and get some rest."

Mark 6:31 NIV

Dear Lord, I thank You for the gift of self-care and for Jesus' example of balancing service with rest. Help me follow His lead by taking time to rest and be still in Your presence. I often push myself to exhaustion, which leads me to break my health boundaries and sabotage my efforts. Remind me that my body is Your temple (1 Corinthians 6:19) and that caring for myself is an act of worship.

In the midst of life's demands, I sometimes neglect my physical, emotional, and spiritual needs. Help me remember that I cannot pour from an empty cup. By taking care of myself, I am better equipped to serve others (1 Peter 4:10) and fulfill Your purpose for my life.

Keep reminding me that self-care is not selfish, but a vital part of being able to serve others effectively. Grant me wisdom and discipline to prioritize self-care, set healthy boundaries, and make time for activities that bring joy and peace. Thank You for Your love and grace that sustains me and for the rest found in Your presence (Exodus 33:14). In Jesus' name, I pray. Amen.

September 20
Developing a Spirit of Self-Control

"Then God said, "Let us make mankind in our image,"
Genesis 1:26 NIV

Almighty God, Creator of all, I come before You with a humble heart, acknowledging Your sovereignty and power. You made me in Your image, designed me fearfully and wonderfully, and authorized me to have dominion over all things, including my own body.

I recognize that self-control is vital for maintaining my health and well-being, and I need Your help to cultivate it. Reveal to me the fears and temptations that lead me to overindulge and act against my best interests. You are a God of discipline and order (Proverbs 25:28), and I desire that same spirit within me. Through Your Holy Spirit, empower me to resist harmful behaviors and embrace a balanced, disciplined lifestyle.

Thank You for the intricate design of my body, which knows to eat when hungry and stop when full. Help me restore this natural balance and embrace self-control as a path to good health and overall well-being. May my journey in self-control reflect Your grace and inspire others to seek a disciplined life. I declare that I will not be enslaved by anything (1 Corinthians 6:12). In Jesus' name, Amen.

September 21
Overcoming Doubt and Indecision

"But when you ask, you must believe and not doubt, because the one who doubts is like a wave of the sea, blown and tossed by the wind."

James 1:6 NIV

Dear God of Strength, You are unwavering and eternal, and Your spirit within me is steadfast. I confess that doubt and indecision have consumed me, leaving me paralyzed and unproductive. I often waste time researching but fail to act. Yet, with You, all things are possible (Matthew 19:26), and I trust in Your infinite wisdom and love.

Thank You for reminding me to trust in You with all my heart and not rely on my own understanding (Proverbs 3:5-6). I surrender my fears and uncertainties to You, knowing that You understand the desires of my heart and will guide me to better health in a way that honors You.

Your strength is made perfect in my weakness (2 Corinthians 12:9), so grant me the confidence and courage to act even when I don't have all the answers. Fill me with determination and perseverance to make healthy choices for my body, mind, and spirit. I reject analysis paralysis and embrace Your guidance. I trust You to lead me in the right direction. In Jesus' name, Amen.

September 22
Avoiding the Comparison Trap

"…when they measure themselves by one another and compare themselves with one another, they are without understanding."

2 Corinthians 10:12 ESV

Lord God of Creation, You crafted me with a unique and intentional design, a masterpiece in Your eyes. I confess that I often fall into the trap of comparing myself to others, letting their progress overshadow my own. I fear being left behind and worry that others are judging the pace of my journey.

Today, I surrender this habit of comparison to You. Help me embrace the uniqueness of my own path and focus on my progress rather than measuring it against others. Your Word teaches me not to conform to worldly standards (Romans 12:2) and reminds me to test my own actions, finding pride in my own journey (Galatians 6:4-5).

Father, teach me to appreciate my individual journey and celebrate the beauty of my own progress. Let me not be swayed by external standards or the achievements of others, but find contentment in knowing that I am fearfully and wonderfully made. I trust in Your plan and have faith that You will guide me every step of the way. In Jesus' name, Amen.

September 23
Asking My Way to Success

"Ask and it will be given to you; seek and you will find; knock and the door will be opened to you. "
Matthew 7:7-8 NIV

Dear Jehovah Jireh, thank You for Your boundless love and for inviting me to come to You. I confess I often turn to the internet or friends for help instead of seeking You first. I feel like my struggles are my fault, and I worry that asking You feels like a bother. But I know that's a lie, and You welcome me with open arms (Matthew 11:28-30).

Today, I come to You with humility and trust, seeking Your wisdom and guidance to steward my life and bring my body into health and balance. Thank You for the gift of the Holy Spirit, my constant companion. You promise to be my ever-present help (Psalm 46:1), and I lean on Your strength when my willpower wanes, when temptations arise, and when discouragement sets in.

I will no longer hesitate to ask for help, no matter how many times I need to. You never tire of answering me, and Your guidance leads me toward great health and a deeper relationship with You. I ask for the Holy Spirit's energy and strength today, trusting in Your grace to guide me. In the holy name of Jesus, I pray, Amen.

September 24
Keep Showing Up Each Day

"Let us not become weary in doing good, for at the proper time we will reap a harvest if we do not give up."

Galatians 6:9 NIV

Dear Everpresent God, You are always vigilant, never sleeping or slumbering, and You are my keeper and shade (Psalm 121:3-6). I come to You today seeking to mirror Your consistency. Some days, I feel discouraged and tempted to quit. I recognize that the journey to wellness is challenging, and setbacks are inevitable.

Grant me the grace to embrace patience and compassion for myself, especially when the path is tough. Help me to see setbacks not as failures but as chances for growth. Remind me that progress isn't always linear and that through difficulty, I build the strength and resilience to overcome.

Fill me with unwavering commitment to my health, even when the road is difficult. Give me the wisdom to make choices that benefit my mind, body, and soul. Let me find joy in every step I take towards well-being, and may my efforts lead to positive results. I commit to showing up today and taking small steps in faith. I will not grow weary but develop perseverance, knowing You walk with me every day. In Jesus' name, Amen.

September 25
Overcoming Stagnation

"Whatever you have learned or received or heard from me, or seen in me—put it into practice. And the God of peace will be with you."

Philippians 4:9 NIV

Dear Teacher and Master, Your word became flesh and dwelt among us, revealing Your glory (John 1:14). I thank You for setting an example for me to follow. Help me understand that progress, not perfection, is what matters. I fear making progress only to become stuck or backslide. Remind me that every small step forward brings me closer to the person You created me to be.

Grant me the courage to move forward even when doubts and emotions arise. Strengthen my resolve to practice Your principles consistently, knowing that perseverance leads to progress. Align me with Your divine guidance and wisdom each day.

Lord, I believe my breakthrough is on the way. I won't be disheartened by stagnation or setbacks. Let me view setbacks as setups for a victorious comeback. With Your grace, I will press forward, knowing You are with me every step of the way. Empower me to stay focused and determined, trusting in Your promises and knowing that as I practice Your principles, transformation, and victory in health will follow. I trust that the good work You've begun in me will be carried to completion (Philippians 1:6). In Jesus' name, Amen.

September 26
Come Out of Hiding

"Therefore, I remind you to stir up the gift of God, which is in you…"

2 Timothy 1:6 NKJV

Dear Lord, my strength and comforter, You are my refuge (Psalm 46:1). I come before You, standing exposed and vulnerable. You know the fears that make me hide from the truth about my weight and health, preventing me from fully embracing the life You've given me. I confess that sometimes my beliefs about my weight have held me hostage, preventing me from stepping into the light of Your truth and grace.

Yet, You call me out of hiding. You remind me that I am safe with You, and when I feel exposed, You cover me with Your feathers (Psalm 91:4). You created me in Your image and called me to a purpose. Your love for me is boundless, so today I come out of hiding and trust that I am safe with You. I can come to You uncovered, and You accept me without judgment.

Help me to show up in the world boldly, without shame or reservation. Strengthen me to face challenges head-on, knowing that I can do all things through Christ who strengthens me (Philippians 4:13). Remind me that I am not alone; You are with me (Isaiah 46:10). Grant me the courage to step out of the shadows and live a life of purpose and joy. In Jesus' name, Amen.

September 27
I am Supported

"It is the Lord who goes before you. He will be with you; he will not leave you or forsake you. Do not fear or be dismayed."

Deuteronomy 31:8 NIV

Dear Lord, my Comforter and Friend, You are my ever-present help in times of trouble, upholding me with Your righteous right hand (Isaiah 41:10). Today I confess that I often worry that others may no longer relate to me as I make changes to my health. This fear has led to anxiety, guilt, and self-punishment. Even if others may forsake me, You never will (Psalm 27:10). I trust that You will bring the right people into my life who will support my new healthy lifestyle.

Anchor my heart in the truth that nothing can separate me from Your love (Romans 8:38-39). Let this truth dispel my fears and give me the courage to move forward without anxiety or the temptation to revert to old habits just to please others. Help me embrace this journey toward better health with confidence and self-compassion, knowing that the opinions of others do not define my worth. Grant me the grace to extend the same understanding to others, recognizing that their responses are not a reflection of my value.

May Your peace, which surpasses all understanding, guard my heart and mind as I navigate this health journey. In Jesus' name, I pray. Amen.

September 28
Little by Little

"Little by little I will drive them out before you, until you have increased enough to take possession of the land."

Exodus 23:3 NIV

Dear God of Glory and Majesty, You create everything in its perfect time (Ecclesiastes 3:11), and Your ways are always flawless. I am learning that small, incremental achievements pave the way to success. Although I desire rapid, significant changes, I trust that Your timing is perfect (Jeremiah 29:11). By focusing on manageable tasks, the overwhelming burden diminishes, and Your guiding presence brings comfort and reassurance.

Help me to recognize and celebrate the small wins each day. Teach me that these minor victories, accumulated over time, lead to ultimate triumph. Grant me the wisdom to view challenges as opportunities for growth and resilience (James 1:2-3).

Lord, assist me in making each day an opportunity for spiritual growth and deepening our connection. Strengthen me to move away from anything that hinders this divine union. I look forward to the end of this month, knowing that with Your guidance, I will emerge stronger and closer to You. I commit to embracing every small step, trusting that with You, all things are possible (Matthew 19:26). In Jesus' name, I pray. Amen.

September 29
Valuing Each Day

"And o"God finished his work that he had done, and he rested on the seventh day."

Genesis 2:2 ESV

Dear Mighty God, You set the sun to shine by day and the moon by night (Jerimiah 31:35). I thank You for the precious gift of today's 24 hours. Help me value each moment in relation to my health and well-being, and use my time wisely.

Lord, I recognize that time is a precious commodity, and I ask for Your guidance to use it wisely. I've wasted time saying I'll get healthier without acting on it. Teach me to number my days and gain wisdom (Psalm 90:12). Guide me in prioritizing my time to align with Your purpose for my life. Help me invest in activities that promote physical, mental, and spiritual health.

As I plan my days, help me put first things first and align my priorities with Your will (Proverbs 16:3). I surrender my schedule to You, seeking Your guidance to balance work, health, and rest. Remind me that true fulfillment comes from seeking Your presence (Luke 10:38). May each day be filled with health, purpose, joy, and a deep appreciation for Your gift of time. In Jesus' name, I pray. Amen.

September 30
Fear, Who Cares

"The fear of man lays a snare, but whoever trusts in the Lord is safe."

Proverbs 29:25 ESV

Dear Lord, You are my shield and protector, guarding me from all danger. This month, I have learned that I don't need to retreat when fear grips my heart. Instead, I can trust in You, knowing You go before me (Psalm 54:3).

I've realized that courage is not the absence of fear but the ability to move forward despite it. Thank You for transforming my fears into stepping stones of faith that draw me closer to You. You've encouraged me to be strong and courageous, not just in my health journey but in all areas of my life (Joshua 1:9).

Lord, You fight on my behalf, pushing back the fears that try to derail me. I will cast my cares upon You, knowing You care for me deeply. Whenever fear attempts to overtake me, I will reject it boldly in the name of Your Son, Jesus.

Today, I declare that fear will no longer dominate my life or hinder my path to a healthy weight and purposeful living. I am confident in Your power to overcome every obstacle. Help me remember that Your Spirit within me is one of courage and strength. May I grow in faith, knowing You are with me every step of the way. In Jesus' name, Amen.

October

REBUILD YOUR TEMPLE

W elcome to this month of prayer dedicated to rebuilding your temple—God's way. As you pray each day,
surrender your broken walls to Jesus. Call out to Him and let
Him speak to you and guide your temple reconstruction.

As you pray each day, you will not only focus on physical
restoration but also on the emotional and spiritual aspects of
your well-being. Your temple is a reflection of the life God has
called you to live, and by nurturing it, you embrace the fullness
of His purpose.

As you navigate through this month, you'll be guided to reflect
on the areas of your life that need healing and revitalization.
Allow this time to be one of introspection, inviting the Holy
Spirit to illuminate your path toward transformation.

May this month be a time of renewal and growth, where you
continue to revitalize your health and faith. Let your prayers

rise as a sweet offering, inviting divine grace and blessings into your life.

Be strengthened as you rebuild your temple with purpose and dedication, walking in alignment with God's will. Embrace the prayer, knowing that with each effort, you are moving closer to the vibrant health and spiritual fullness that God desires for you. Trust in His promises and the power of prayer to transform your life and restore your temple to its intended glory.

October 1
Reestablishing My Health Boundaries

"The wall of Jerusalem is broken down, and its gates have been burned with fire."

Nehemiah 1:3b NIV

D ear Lord, You are my Redeemer, rescuing me from despair and crowning me with love and compassion. (Psalm 103:4) As I commit to rebuilding my temple, I recognize my struggles with maintaining strong boundaries. Despite progress, it feels like I've barely started. "How could I have let things get so out of hand?", I sometimes think to myself. Please help me set boundaries that can withstand any setback.

Put a watch over my mouth to prevent me from sinning against You. Set a guard over my lips and keep watch over what I say and eat. (Psalm 141:3) My goal is to change both my words and my eating habits, ensuring nothing harmful crosses my lips.

Help me re-establish and protect these boundaries, Lord. I'm tired of them being compromised. Let them be firmly rooted in You so nothing can break them down as this year ends. Cultivate the fruits of the Spirit in me to maintain these boundaries and grant me strength to stand firm. I declare my strength in You (Psalm 31:24) and commit to finishing this year with strong health boundaries. In Your name, I pray. Amen.

October 2
Praying and Fasting My Way Through

"Is not this the fast that I choose: to loose the bonds of wickedness, to undo the straps of the yoke, to let the oppressed go free, and to break every yoke?"

Isaiah 58:6 NIV

Dear God of Heaven, Your mercy endures forever. I give thanks to You today (Psalm 136:26). You are faithful and will teach me to persevere as I seek to strengthen my faith through prayer and fasting. You have given me the gift of prayer, and today I add fasting to it. As I commit to rebuilding my temple and approaching the final part of this year, I realize I'm still not fully committed to You. Help me finish strong, with passion and desire to fulfill Your call.

Your Word says certain strongholds are overcome only by prayer and fasting (Matthew 17:21). Teach me how to fast and pray to know You intimately and trust You with all areas of my life, including my health. I am anxious about going without food, so remind me that You will satisfy me (Isaiah 58:11) more than any food ever could.

I surrender my desires, comforts, and will to You. Grant me discipline and self-control to focus on You, removing impurities, doubts, and fears. Help me detach from worldly pleasures and seek Your face with sincerity and devotion. Open my eyes to what truly matters. In Jesus' name, Amen.

October 3
When God Whispers

*"After the earthquake came a fire, but the LORD was
not in the fire. And after the fire came a gentle whisper."*
1 Kings 19:12 NIV

Lord, You are my Rock and Strong Tower, my refuge in times of need. I am grateful for Your presence as I persevere in my health journey. When I feel stuck and uncertain, and can't seem to hear from You, I trust that You are always with me and will never abandon me (Hebrews 13:5).

In moments of silence, my anxieties often increase, and I long for Your comforting words. I understand that You work in mysterious ways so I will continue to seek You, even when I can't hear You. Help me trust in Your unfailing love and believe that You are working behind the scenes (Daniel 10:13).

Grant me patience to endure seasons of silence, knowing Your timing is always perfect (Habakkuk 2:3). Remind me that challenges are opportunities for growth and transformation. Strengthen my faith so I may not waver when I feel stuck. Help me stand firm, knowing You are my rock and fortress.

Teach me to listen to the stillness and discern Your presence in the gentle whispers, the beauty of creation, and the love of those around me. Open my eyes to see Your hand at work. Thank You for Your constant presence. In Jesus' name, Amen.

October 4
Repentance

"I confess the sins we Israelites, including myself and my father's family, have committed against you. ... We have not obeyed the commands, decrees, and laws you gave your servant Moses."

Nehemiah 1:6 NIV

Dear Gracious Father, You are faithful, and Your mercy endures forever. I come to You today with a heart of confession and repentance, knowing it is essential for my journey toward healing and wholeness. Your Word says that if I confess my sins, You are faithful to forgive and purify me (1 John 1:9). Forgive me for prioritizing my flesh over my faith, turning to food instead of seeking You, and for moments when I acted as though I knew better than You.

I repent for focusing on myself rather than seeking Your kingdom first. In my repentance, I accept responsibility for my health. I acknowledge the power of Your transforming grace and ask for strength and guidance to overcome behaviors that hinder my spiritual and physical well-being.

Grant me wisdom to make choices that honor the temple You have given me. Empower me to walk in obedience and perseverance, knowing that through You, I find true healing and restoration. I commit to actively restoring my temple and aligning my heart with Yours. As I walk in the light, I am made new by Your cleansing power (1 John 1:7). In Jesus' name, I pray. Amen.

October 5
Persevering Through Your Promises

"Through these he has given us his very great and precious promises, so that through them you may participate in the divine nature, having escaped the corruption in the world caused by evil desires."

2 Peter 1:4 NIV

Dear Lord, Sovereign God, You are a promise-keeper and a burden-bearer. Your promises are "yes" and "amen" (2 Corinthians 1:20), and standing on them ensures I cannot fail. I'm grateful for Your Word hidden in my heart (Psalm 119:11) and for the reminder of Your promises, not because You need reminding, but because I do.

As I persevere on my health journey, I commit to living by Your Word (Psalm 119:9). My body is a temple, and through obedience, I honor You by making choices aligned with Your will. Give me discipline to nourish my body, exercise regularly, and rest as needed.

Help me trust in Your guidance and follow Your commands faithfully. Strengthen my resolve to persevere through challenges and setbacks. Grant patience and courage to rely on Your promises. I also ask for Your grace and mercy for others on their health journeys, so that we may support and uplift one another. In Jesus' name, I pray. Amen.

October 6

Persevering Through the Emotional Rollercoasters

"A hot-tempered man stirs up strife, but he who is slow to anger quiets contention."

Proverbs 15:18 ESV

Dear God of Strength and Authority, You have created me in Your image and entrusted me with the task of rebuilding my temple, both physically and spiritually. Thank You for the gift of emotions, which allow me to connect deeply with You. Today, I lift up my prayer, asking for strength to persevere through the emotional highs and lows that accompany this journey of renewal.

I surrender my emotions to You, recognizing that they are not meant to control me but to guide me closer to You. Teach me to use them wisely as I work on restoring and strengthening my temple. Remind me of Jesus, who experienced a range of emotions during His ministry (John 11:35). Help me trust that You can transform even the most tumultuous emotions into opportunities for growth and Your glory.

Guide me to feel my emotions without letting them lead me to unhealthy choices. May my emotional experiences shape my character, deepen my faith, and support the rebuilding of my temple. Grant me wisdom, discernment, and resilience as I align my emotions with Your will. In Jesus' name, I pray. Amen.

October 7
It Takes a Village

"When Moses' hands grew tired, they took a stone and put it under him and he sat on it. Aaron and Hur held his hands up—one on one side, one on the other—so that his hands remained steady till sunset."

Exodus 17:12 NIV

"Dear Lord, You are my strength and shield. You have designed us to be in relationship with each other, recognizing that it is not good for us to be alone. As I focus on rebuilding my temple, help me understand the importance of community and accountability in this journey.

I know that I am responsible for the stewardship of my health, but I struggle with asking for help due to fear of rejection or pride. Your Word says, 'As iron sharpens iron, so one person sharpens another' (Proverbs 27:17). Surround me with people who will hold me accountable, encourage me, and support me as I work to restore and strengthen my temple.

Give me the courage to seek their counsel and be open to their loving correction. I surrender my health journey to You, knowing that true accountability comes from seeking Your will above all else (Matthew 6:33). Grant me strength, wisdom, and humility as I rebuild my temple with the support of a community that will uplift and challenge me. Help me bear others' burdens (Galatians 6:2) while staying aligned with Your purpose for my life. In Jesus' name, I pray. Amen."

October 8
Time to Retool

"For we are God's handiwork, created in Christ Jesus to do good works, which God prepared in advance for us to do."

Ephesians 2:10 NIV

Dear Lord, You are the master builder, guiding me in the reconstruction of my temple. Just as one must estimate the cost before building a tower (Luke 14:28), help me to continually check in with You, lean on Your wisdom, and reassess my choices as I rebuild and strengthen my temple.

As I go about my daily life, it's easy to lose sight of Your will. I long to remain connected to You, my Heavenly Guide, for You hold the key to my true purpose and fulfillment. Help me prioritize my relationship with You above all else, finding clarity, peace, and strength in Your presence.

Your Word reminds me to trust in You with all my heart (Proverbs 3:5-6). I surrender my plans and desires for rebuilding my temple to You, seeking wisdom and courage to follow where You lead. When doubt arises, remind me to trust You wholly, knowing You will direct my steps.

Search my heart, reveal any hidden motives, and lead me in Your way everlasting (Psalm 139:23-24). You hold my future securely (Jeremiah 29:11). In Jesus' name, I pray. Amen.

October 9
Benevolent Detachment

"Are you tired? Worn out? Burned out on religion? Come to me. Get away with me and you'll recover your life. I'll show you how to take a real rest."
Matthew 11:28–29 The Message

Dear Benevolent Father, I come to You today seeking to practice benevolent detachment as I rebuild my temple. I release my worries and burdens, trusting that in letting go, I create space for Your peace and guidance (1 Peter 5:7).

Father, I long to experience the fullness of Your love and the restoration it brings (Philippians 4:7). May my act of releasing be rooted in faith and trust, allowing Your grace to flow through me and bring healing to my body, mind, and spirit. Mold me into an instrument of Your peace, so that I may radiate Your love and compassion to others on their own health journeys.

In surrendering to You, I find comfort and hope, knowing You are orchestrating healing and wholeness in my life. Teach me to find peace in Your stillness and to let go of distractions that hinder my well-being. As I practice benevolent detachment, may Your presence fill the void and guide me toward complete restoration. In Jesus' precious name, I pray. Amen.

October 10
It's Bigger!

"…the eyes of your heart may be enlightened in order that you may know the hope to which he has called you, the riches of his glorious inheritance in his holy people,"

Ephesians 1:18 NIV

Dear God of Wisdom and Understanding, You are full of wisdom, peace, and mercy (James 3:17). As I recommit to building my temple, remind me that this path is about more than just weight loss. It is about honoring You and reflecting Your love and grace through every aspect of my health.

Guide me to make choices that align with Your will—nourishing my body with wholesome foods and embracing regular exercise. Help me to see these choices are not only about self-improvement but acts of stewardship of the body You have entrusted to me. Let my health journey be a testament to Your promise of abundant life and transformative power (John 10:10).

I commit my health journey to You, seeking to honor and glorify Your name beyond the goal of weight loss. Provide me with courage, wisdom, and faith in Your perfect plan. As I rebuild my temple, help me to inspire others to seek You and find strength in Your presence too. Thank You, Heavenly Father, for the opportunity to glorify You through my health. May this journey be a reflection of Your greater purpose for my life. In Jesus' name, I pray. Amen.

October 11
The Space of Grace

"But he said to me, 'My grace is sufficient for you, for my power is made perfect in weakness."
2 Corinthians 12:9 NIV

Dear Precious Lord, You guide me each day with grace. As I work to rebuild my temple, I recognize there are areas where I feel strong and others where I feel powerless. I turn all my weaknesses and insecurities over to You, knowing Your grace is sufficient. Your Word assures me, "When I am weak, then I am strong" (2 Corinthians 12:10). I surrender all my triggers and struggles to You, trusting that they do not have to control me.

It's Your grace that sustains me daily. I often feel alone in my efforts, trying to fix everything myself. Yet, You offer a different approach, inviting me to find rest in You (Matthew 11:28).

Today, I release my burdens and let go. I receive Your grace and am reminded that Your grace is essential for rebuilding my temple and persevering in victory. Your grace will cover me when I fall short and will restore me to wholeness. My self-criticism has not worked so far, so help me stop and instead embrace Your grace. I declare that I will operate in Your grace today. In Jesus' name, I pray. Amen.

October 12
A Mind to Work

"So we built the wall, and the entire wall was joined together up to half its height, for the people had a mind to work."

Nehemiah 4:6 ESV

Dear Lord, I am grateful for Your unwavering faithfulness and trust in Your higher ways (Isaiah 55:8-9). As I work to rebuild my temple, thank You for giving me a resilient and determined spirit. It was one of the missing pieces in my previous attempts. Help me embrace the hard work and sacrifice involved in this journey without becoming overwhelmed by stress and burdens.

Teach me that through diligent effort, I am shaped and strengthened, and guide me to find joy in the process. Grant me the courage to persevere, even when weariness sets in, and sustain me with Your divine strength. Let my health journey be marked by balance and joy, knowing that I can do all things through You (Philippians 4:13).

Guide me to make choices that honor and nourish my body, mind, and soul. Teach me to work with ease and joy, aligning my actions with Your will. I entrust my health and the rebuilding of my temple to You, confident that You are my ultimate healer and sustainer. Bless the work of my hands (Deuteronomy 28:12) and grant me the perseverance to overcome obstacles. In Jesus' name, Amen.

October 13
Commit to Finishing

"So now finish doing it as well, so that your readiness in desiring it may be matched by your completing it out of what you have."

2 Corinthians 8:11 ESV

Dear Mighty Sustainer, I come before You with gratitude, trusting that You are with me through every trial. As I work to rebuild my temple, I seek Your guidance to finish this year with strength and unwavering commitment. Grant me the wisdom and resilience to face challenges, knowing that with Your support, I can overcome them.

I confess that I sometimes falter and abandon my goals before reaching the finish line. Yet, with Your help, I am determined to remain steadfast. Each day, I commit to working diligently, drawing strength from Your divine presence. Help me to be proactive, fulfilling my responsibilities with faith and perseverance. Your Word assures me that perseverance leads to completion (Matthew 24:13) and that "I can do all things through Christ who strengthens me" (Philippians 4:13). Let this truth guide me as I strive for optimal health and well-being, aligning my efforts with Your will.

Thank You for the lessons and strength You provide. I am resolute in my commitment to rebuild my temple, trusting that You will see me through to the end. In Jesus' name, Amen.

October 14
Developing Mental Resilience

"Set your minds on things that are above, not on things that are on earth."

Colossians 3:2 ESV

Dear Sovereign Lord, I come to You with a heart full of gratitude for the promise You've given me, empowering me to take control of my thoughts. As I work to rebuild and reclaim my temple, Your way, I realize the importance of mental well-being in this journey. My mind is often bombarded by distractions and narratives that stray from Your Word.

Strengthen me more than ever to take every thought captive and align it with Your truth (2 Corinthians 10:5). I desire a mind governed by the Holy Spirit, leading to a transformed life filled with Your peace (Romans 8:6). I understand that total health includes spirit, mind, and body and that mental health is essential for true wellness.

I consecrate my mental life to You. Protect my thoughts and focus. Heal past memories that replay in my mind and surrender my imagination and negativity to You. Help me to fix my mind on whatever is true, pure, right, and worthy of praise (Philippians 4:8). Guide me on the path of mental well-being and spiritual growth. In Jesus' name, I pray. Amen.

October 15
Spiritual Discernment

"But solid food is for the mature, for those who have their powers of discernment trained by constant practice to distinguish good from evil."
Hebrews 5:14 ESV

Dear Divine Shepherd, Your Word assures me that Your sheep hear Your voice (John 10:27). I thank You for the wisdom and discernment to recognize when You are speaking to me. Silence the voices that do not come from You. I'm overwhelmed by the countless programs and contradictory information in the weight-loss industry, often feeling lost and misled.

Grant me the spiritual discernment to choose what's right for my unique needs and body. Help me navigate the abundance of information and guide me toward a path that aligns with Your purpose for me. I recognize that this journey is not just physical but spiritual as well. The enemy may challenge me as I approach my goals, but I stand firm in Your truth, knowing it sets me free (John 8:32).

I find refuge and strength in Your presence (Deuteronomy 33:27). As I work to rebuild my temple using Your blueprint this time, I surrender my worries to You, trusting in Your guidance. Thank You for Your grace and faithfulness. May Your wisdom permeate every aspect of my health journey. In Jesus' name, I pray. Amen.

October 16
No More Backsliding

"Watch yourselves, so that you may not lose what we have worked for, but may win a full reward."
2 John 1:8 ESV

Dear Lord, my Faithful Builder, I am deeply grateful for the breakthroughs You have granted me as You guide me in rebuilding my temple physically, spiritually, and emotionally. Through every test and trial, I've learned that these challenges are opportunities to grow closer to You and deepen my trust in Your unfailing love.

As I continue this journey, I pray for the strength to remain committed to my health—body, soul, and spirit. Keep my mind focused and my heart steadfast, guarding me from old habits that hinder my progress. Grant me wisdom to recognize when I am growing weary or vulnerable to the enemy's attacks (2 John 1:8). May I always feel Your abiding presence, drawing strength from You in every step I take.

Let my obedience to Your will be the driving force behind my actions, inspiring and motivating me to persevere each day. I thank You for being my constant source of strength and protection in the face of adversity. Through Your divine power, I triumph over challenges and rebuild my temple as You intend (Hebrews 12:1-2; Philippians 4:13). In the mighty name of Jesus, I pray. Amen.

October 17
Unleashing the Power of His Word

> "The word of God is alive and active. Sharper than any sword, it penetrates even to dividing soul and spirit, joints and marrow; it judges the thoughts and attitudes of the heart."
>
> Hebrews 4:12 NIV

I come before You, reverent of Your Word, which is a lamp for my feet and a light for my path (Psalm 119:105). I recognize that Your Word is alive, powerful, and sharper than any sword (Hebrews 4:12). I confess that in the past, I haven't valued it as I should. Help me understand its healing power on my spirit, soul and body.

Grant me the perseverance to dive deep into Your Word, uncovering essential truths for my health, life and walk with You. Open my eyes to the wisdom within it (Psalm 119:18). May Your Word penetrate my soul and shape me into who You've called me to be.

Instill in me a hunger for righteousness and help me approach Your Word with reverence. Let it guide my thoughts, words, and actions, aligning them with Your will. I desire to be a light in this world, drawing others to You through Your life-giving truths. May Your Word be my foundation and guide in every decision I make. I pray this in Jesus' name. Amen.

October 18
This is How I Fight My Battles

*"Rejoice in the Lord always: and again I say, Rejoice.
… Be careful for nothing, but in everything by prayer
and supplication with thanksgiving let your requests be
made known unto God."*

Philippians 4:4-6 KJV

Dear God of Mercy and Grace, I come to You acknowledging that my battles are spiritual, not fought with worldly means (2 Corinthians 10:4). As I focus on rebuilding my temple—my body, mind, and spirit—I ask for Your help to fight on my knees rather than through my own efforting and scheming.

True strength and victory come from You alone. You are the Almighty God who fights for Your children and rebuilds us from within. Teach me to rely on Your wisdom as I face the challenges in my health and spiritual journey.

When I feel overwhelmed, help me to bring all my concerns to You in prayer (Philippians 4:6). Strengthen my faith in Your perfect timing (Habakkuk 2:3) and unfailing love.

As I rebuild my temple, renew my mind and spirit. Equip me with the armor of God daily (Ephesians 6:11) to protect me from the enemy's schemes. I trust that Your victory is assured and that I am never alone. In Jesus' name, I pray. Amen.

October 19
I am my Sister's Keeper

"And the things you have heard me say in the presence of many witnesses entrust to reliable people who will also be qualified to teach others."

2 Timothy 2:2 NIV

Dear Lord, what an honor that You call me friend (John 15:15). I come before You with a heart full of gratitude for the privilege of bringing others alongside me on this remarkable journey of health. I realize that it's not just about my own growth; supporting others is a tremendous responsibility. As I rebuild my temple, physically, spiritually, and emotionally, I am humbled by the chance to positively impact others.

As I share my testimony, may others see Your presence within me. Let my actions and words reflect Your love, grace, and mercy, drawing those around me closer to You. Help me to decrease so that You may increase (John 3:30). Remind me that every choice I make, every step I take, has significance not only now but for eternity (Matthew 16:27).

Guide me to view this responsibility not as a burden but as a privilege to lead in Your kingdom. Empower me to pursue better health in all aspects, inspiring others to do the same. May my journey bring glory to Your holy name. In Jesus' name, I pray. Amen.

October 20
Repentance

"Thus I cleansed them from everything foreign... Remember me, O my God, for good."
Nehemiah 13:30-31 NASB

Dear God of Restoration, I come before You humbled and broken, acknowledging my shortcomings on this journey to rebuild my temple, Your Way. I am grateful for the forgiveness and grace offered through Your Son, Jesus Christ, whose sacrifice has redeemed me (John 3:16). I confess that I have strayed from the path of good health and wellness. I ask for Your strength to overcome temptations and resist unhealthy habits.

Help me to turn away from the clutches of evil that hinder my progress and guide me in making choices that honor You. I am burdened by my repeated mistakes, but I find comfort in Luke 15:7, knowing that there is joy in heaven over one sinner who repents. I repent before You, seeking Your forgiveness and guidance to return to the path of righteousness.

Cleanse and purify my thoughts, actions, and desires. Remind me that in my weakness, Your strength is made perfect (2 Corinthians 12:9). I rely on Your presence and unfailing love to sustain me. Grant me the courage to persevere in rebuilding my temple, knowing that through You, all things are possible. In Jesus' name, I pray. Amen.

October 21
It's Now O'Clock

"The LORD has done it this very day; let us rejoice today and be glad."

Psalm 118:24 NIV

Dear Ever-Present God, I come before You with awe, knowing that in Your manifest presence, there is fullness of joy (Psalm 16:11). You are the same today, yesterday, and forever (Matthew 28:20). It is incredible to realize that You are with me right now.

I often focus on past blessings or future hopes, forgetting that this very moment is sacred. It's 'Now O'Clock!' This moment is what matters. It is holy. It's where You speak to me. Now is when You are calling me to take the next step in faith.

Help me make my 'now' holy, knowing that my thoughts and actions today shape my future and reflect my past. Guide me to act with purpose and urgency in this moment, rather than procrastinating.

As I rebuild my temple, Your Way, remind me that each action I take now is crucial. Help me take enlightened and empowered steps, trusting that You have already gone before me and prepared the way (Deuteronomy 31:8). I thank You for this holy 'now' and choose to rejoice in it. In Jesus' name, I pray. Amen.

October 22
Overcoming Distractions

"I am doing a great work, so that I cannot come down."
Nehemiah 6:3 KJV

I approach You with gratitude, recognizing Your unwavering presence (Psalm 121:4) and the responsibilities You have entrusted to me (Luke 19:11-13). Despite my commitment, I confess that my fervor sometimes fades and distractions pull me away from Your divine calling.

Grant me strength to stay focused and engaged in Your work, following the example of Jesus, who was dedicated from a young age (Luke 2:49). Help me to overcome the fear of missing out (FOMO) and remember that true joy and peace come only from You, not from the fleeting pleasures of this world.

This time around, I make a solemn commitment to rebuild my temple with resolute determination. Empower me to persevere daily, keeping my eyes on You and not on the distractions around me. I affirm that I am strengthened by Your love and fortified by Your strength. I am dedicated to this good work and will remain steadfast. In Jesus' mighty name, I pray. Amen.

October 23
Long, Ain't Wrong

"With the Lord a day is like a thousand years, and a thousand years are like a day. The Lord is not slow in keeping his promise... Instead he is patient with you,"
2 Peter 3:8-9 NIV

Dear Patient God, Thank You for Your unwavering faithfulness and for modeling long-suffering. I confess that I can be so impatient, wanting results now. When things aren't moving as quickly as I'd like, I often rush to the next thing. Help me cultivate a spirit of patience and recognize the virtue of endurance. Length of time does not equate to failure. Just as a fruit tree takes years to bear fruit, I trust that as I abide in You, I will also bear much fruit.

Grant me the endurance to keep Your commands and remain faithful to Jesus (Revelation 14:12), regardless of how long the journey may seem. Your timelines are not mine. Your Word reassures me that a day with You is as a thousand years, and a thousand years as one day (2 Peter 3:8). I thank You for the slow and steady progress taking place in my life, even in ways I'm unaware of. I will wait on You and give You glory in the process. In Jesus' name, Amen.

October 24
Ongoing Awareness

"The Lord will guide you continually and satisfy your soul in drought and strengthen your bones; you shall be like a watered garden, and like a spring of water, whose waters do not fail."

Isaiah 58:11 NKJV

Dear Ever-present Lord, You are always with me, protecting and guiding me each day. I ask for Your help to recognize Your presence and to confront any limiting beliefs, harmful habits, and unproductive patterns that hinder my journey toward rebuilding my temple, Your Way.

Please keep my spirit alert to the mental and emotional traps laid by the enemy, aiming to disrupt my path to health and well-being. Your Word says, "For there is nothing covered that shall not be revealed, neither hid that shall not be known" (Luke 12:2). With Your light revealing hidden areas of my life, I surrender these to Your care. Help me remain vigilant and guard my heart (Proverbs 4:23) to avoid falling into deceit.

Thank You for opening the eyes of my heart (Ephesians 1:18) so that I can follow the Holy Spirit's guidance. As I advance in awareness, I seek purification through the blood of Jesus, striving to align my actions with Your will. Help me rebuild my temple in a way that reflects Your glory and grace. I offer my deepest devotion and seek wisdom within Your embrace. In Jesus' name, Amen

October 25
Overcoming Plateaus

"For I, the Lord, do not change; therefore you, O sons of Jacob, are not consumed."
Malachi 3:6 ESV

Dear Ever-present Lord, I hold on to Your unchanging hand, for with You, there is no variation (James 1:17). You are my solid rock, providing stability and solace when everything around me feels uncertain (Psalm 18:2).

At times, it seems I'm making progress, only to hit a plateau—this affects my emotional, mental, and spiritual states, as well as the numbers on the scale. I am exhausted by this cycle and yearn for change.

Lord, I need You. When I hit a plateau, reassure me that You are still working within and through me. Remind me that growth is occurring mentally and emotionally, even if I can't see it yet. Grant me patience and endurance, teaching me that success ebbs and flows (Galatians 6:9). I seek Your guidance, knowing You are faithful and steadfast.

I entrust my struggles and desires to Your loving care, believing You will sustain me throughout this journey. Empower me to overcome obstacles and grow in faith. I declare with unwavering determination that I am resolute, resilient, and consistent, despite the plateaus. I decree victory in Jesus' name. Amen.

October 26
Keep Showing Up

"...for though the righteous fall seven times, they rise again"

Proverbs 24:16 NIV

Dear Gracious and Merciful God. You uphold me with your righteous right hand (Psalm 34:24) Grant me the discipline and motivation to show up for myself every day, even when I feel weary or discouraged. Help me remember that my commitment to my health honors You and the life You have blessed me with.

As I recommit to rebuilding my temple, may I never take this gift for granted, but use it as a vessel to glorify You. You promise that I will reap a harvest if I don't give up (Galatians 6:9). Help me stay focused on my journey, especially when I see others making progress and feel stuck. Remind me to believe in my ability to overcome obstacles and make choices that align with Your plan for my well-being.

Instill in me a renewed reverence for my body as a dwelling place for Your Spirit. May I nourish it with wholesome food, engage in regular activity, and rest when needed, glorifying You each day. I will keep showing up, walking in confidence that You are leading and guiding me. Your grace is sufficient for me (2 Corinthians 12:9). In Jesus' name, I pray. Amen.

October 27
The Wisdom of My Body

"My frame was not hidden from you when I was made in the secret place.

Psalm 139:15 NIV

Dear God of Creation, You know me inside and out; You crafted me from nothing into something (Psalm 139:15-16). I honor You today, recognizing that everything You created is good and perfect (Deuteronomy 32:3-4). Help me to see my body as You see it and to appreciate its design and purpose.

Grant me wisdom to understand and respond to my body's needs. Teach me to nourish it when hungry and to stop when satisfied. Guide me to embrace movement and exercise, valuing restorative sleep while managing stress (1 Corinthians 6:19-20).

Help me avoid complicating matters with unnecessary rules, understanding that Your ways are filled with grace and clarity. I seek a balanced life, trusting Your wisdom to guide me on this wellness journey. May my body reflect Your love and wisdom, dedicated to Your glory both on Earth and in Heaven. I surrender to Your guidance, persevering with steadfastness and dedication. Thank You for this incredible temple that I've recommitted to build for Your glory. In Jesus' name, Amen.

October 28
My Holy 'No'

"Was I fickle when I intended to do this? Or do I make my plans in a worldly manner so that in the same breath I say both "Yes, yes" and "No, no"?"
2 Corinthians 1:17 NIV

Dear Faithful God, In the past, it's been so hard for me to say "no". The fear of disappointing others and the fear of depriving myself often lead me to say yes even though I know it's not in my best interest.

Help me to no longer overextend myself by doing more than You've called me to. Remind me that "No" is a complete sentence. When the enemy tries to seduce me and tell me that I'm being too rigid, help me to dismiss his taunts and temptations (Matthew 6:13) Let my speech *be* always with grace, seasoned with salt, so that I may know how to respond to others (Colossians 4:6). And help me to no longer give in to the peer pressure of this world that makes me feel like I'm missing out.

My desire is to serve You and You alone as I persevere on my health journey. Help me to develop a 'holy NO.' This means that I'm saying 'yes' to Your will and Your ways above all else. My holy 'no' means that I am clear on my health boundaries every day and am confident to live them out boldly and unashamedly so that I may glorify You. I declare that I am firm in my decisions and I respect my 'holy no.' In Jesus' name, I pray. Amen.

October 29
Emotional Resilience

"The righteous cry out, and the Lord hears them; he delivers them from all their troubles. The Lord is close to the brokenhearted and saves those who are crushed in spirit."

Psalm 34:17–18 NIV

Dear Compassionate God, Your grace helps me to rebuild my physical and emotional health as I recognize that it's my emotions that often lead my body astray. Today, I pray for Your divine guidance and strength to develop emotional resilience.

You will uphold me with Your righteous right hand when my emotions threaten to swallow me (Isaiah 41:10). As I spend time with You and allow You to feed my hungry soul then my unruly emotions will reflect that healing. Help me to feel my feelings instead of feeding them with food. Remind me that my emotions are a gauge that alerts me to deeper needs that are found in You.

As I rebuild my temple, teach me emotional resilience by focusing on your truth, gratitude, and a surrendered heart. You work all things together for the good of those who love You (Romans 8:28). Father, I commit myself to developing emotional resilience, knowing that through Your power, I can experience a range of emotions and respond appropriately. Mold me into a vessel of strength and perseverance, so that I may persevere in my health. In Jesus' name, I pray. Amen

October 30
The Shift

"But the Lord said to Samuel, "Do not consider his appearance or his height, for I have rejected him. The Lord does not look at the things people look at. People look at the outward appearance, but the Lord looks at the heart."

1 Samuel 16:7 NIV

Dear Gracious Father, Let Your transforming power fill me today to change the way I've approached my health and my body. Instead of viewing exercise as a punishment or a necessary evil, guide me to see it as a form of worship,

Transform my taste buds so that I can develop a genuine craving for nourishing and healthy foods. Let the flavors and textures of wholesome foods become a delight to my senses. Reframe my thinking so I see that investing in my well-being is not selfish but rather an act of stewardship, enabling me to better serve others with renewed energy and strength.

Lord, change my perspective on this health journey. In the past, it has felt burdensome and overwhelming, but I know that Your ways are not burdensome (1 John 5:3). Teach me to approach my pursuit of health with ease and fun. I thank You, dear Father, for the shift that is taking place within me. As I commit to rebuilding my temple, I cast my cares upon You (Matthew 11:28) I trust in Your guidance and grace, knowing that with You, all things are possible (Matthew 11:26). In Jesus' name, I pray. Amen.

October 31
Christ's Perseverance

"May the Lord direct your hearts into God's love and Christ's perseverance."
2 Thessalonians 3:5 NIV

Dear Faithful God, I worship and magnify Your name with a grateful heart, honoring You for guiding me through another month of rebuilding my temple, Your way. I realize now that honoring my body is not about clinging to rigid plans or forcing change but about surrendering to Your divine guidance. As I reflect on this journey, I understand that rebuilding my temple involves aligning my heart with Your love and allowing Christ's perseverance to guide me. His life serves as the most perfect example of endurance, as He faithfully finished the race set before Him (Hebrews 12:2-3).

Thank You for teaching me that true transformation comes through Your strength, not my own efforts (Philippians 4:13). You are the one who works within me to will and to act according to Your good purpose (Philippians 2:13). Help me to continuously receive Your grace, trusting that Your guidance is leading me toward a healthier and more fulfilling life.

In every step of this journey, may I embody Christ's perseverance, embracing each moment with patience and faith. I surrender my plans to You and trust in Your perfect timing and wisdom. Thank You for Your unwavering support and for helping me rebuild my temple with grace and purpose. In Jesus' name, I pray. Amen.

November

THANKFUL HEART, HEALTHY BODY

This sacred month of prayers is dedicated to expressing gratitude to the Almighty for the blessings bestowed upon you in your health journey. In a world where busyness and distractions often consume your attention, it is even more essential to pause, reflect, and offer heartfelt appreciation to the One who guides and sustains you. This month, you will cultivate a heart of thanksgiving, recognizing the countless blessings and miracles that have unfolded in your life.

Health is undoubtedly one of the greatest treasures gifted to you. The intricate workings of your body, the resilience to overcome challenges, and the opportunity to experience the beauty of life are all manifestations of divine grace. You are invited to acknowledge the gift of your health and well-being, however imperfect it may be, understanding that every breath you take is a reminder of God's unwavering love.

Through these prayers, you will celebrate the strength you've discovered in your health journey—the battles fought, the lessons learned, and the triumphs achieved. You will embrace vulnerability and acknowledge the times when your health may have faltered, recognizing that even in those moments, there were valuable insights and opportunities for growth.

May this sacred time of gratitude touch your life and graciously humble you, and may you emerge from it with a heart filled with love, compassion, and thankfulness for your Father's love and care. I pray that this month of prayers will encourage and inspire you to embrace the power of thankfulness and rejoice in the miracles of your health.

November 1
Cultivating a Heart of Thankfulness

"For although they knew God, they neither glorified him as God nor gave thanks to him, but their thinking became futile and their foolish hearts were darkened."

Romans 1:21 NIV

Dear Lord God of Glory, how excellent is Your name in all the earth (Psalm 8:1). You are worthy of all glory, honor, and praise. I ascribe greatness to You (Deuteronomy 32:3-4). I confess that I don't reverence You as You deserve. My "thank yous" are often shallow and rote, but as I go back to Your Word, I see that You are to be praised, adored, admired, and worshiped.

I want to know You in a way that transcends my intellectual knowledge. Let my daily actions reflect the depth of love and thankfulness I have for You. I want to glorify You and give You thanks in everything I do. Renew a right spirit in me (Psalm 51:10-13) so I can fix my focus on who You are instead of always looking to You like a magic genie who grants my wishes.

My desire this month is to know You better and develop a heart of praise and thanksgiving. I want to cultivate a heart of thanksgiving that flows from my adoration and deep love for who You are (Psalm 63:1-4). In Your name, I praise You and give You thanks. Amen!

November 2
Raise a Hallelujah

"Jesus asked, 'Were not all ten cleansed? Where are the other nine? Has no one returned to give praise to God except this foreigner?' Then he said to him, 'Rise and go; your faith has made you well.'"

Luke 17:17-19 NIV

Dear Lord, Today, I thank You for Your grace and for the renewal of mercy each day (Lamentations 3:22-23). I am grateful for another day and for the countless times I have been showered with Your goodness. Forgive me for the times I have neglected to express my gratitude and overlooked the blessings You have poured into my life.

Like the foreigner who returned to glorify Your name, I stand in awe of Your boundless love and healing touch. You are the God of all, extending Your grace to heal my body and renew my spirit. Your divine touch has made me well, and I am eternally grateful.

As I move into this day, help me to maintain a heart of worship and gratitude. Let today be a testament to Your faithfulness, as I strive to give You praise and glory in my body (1 Corinthians 6:19). I pray that You would open my eyes to see the wonder of my physical body and to appreciate the gift of health I often take for granted. May I recognize Your hand at work in both the big and small things that my body can do. It is a wonder and I'm so thankful. In Jesus name, I pray. Amen.

November 3
Unburdened

"Thanks be to God, who delivers me through Jesus Christ our Lord! So then, I myself in my mind am a slave to God's law, but in my sinful nature a slave to the law of sin."

Romans 7:25 NIV

Dear Lord, You are my shield, the horn of my salvation, and my stronghold. I call on You today, knowing You are worthy of praise (Psalm 18:3). Thank You for rescuing me from the burden of sin and for Your deliverance. I confess that I often operate in my fleshly desires, focusing on my needs and agenda, and fail to give You the thanks and praise You deserve. I admit that there are areas of my life not fully submitted to You.

As this month unfolds, I yearn to cultivate a heart of thanksgiving (1 Thessalonians 5:18), shifting from fleshly ways to being led by Your Spirit (Romans 8:6). Teach me to find the answers to life's challenges in You alone. I am grateful for Your unwavering presence and guidance.

Today, I surrender my will and ways to You, knowing that Your grace frees me from the weight of sin. Thank You for unburdening me from the chains that hold me captive. Strengthen me daily to walk in the freedom and joy that come from following You. I release my heart from worries that hinder my praise. In Jesus' name, I pray. Amen.

November 4
The End of Murmuring

"For it is God who works in you to will and to act in order to fulfill his good purpose."
                                        Philippians 2:13 NIV

Dear God of Peace, Today I lift my voice in praise, exalting You above all. Your peace surpasses understanding (Philippians 4:7), and I exchange it for my tendency to murmur and complain. While venting my frustrations may offer temporary relief, it ultimately drives a wedge between us. Transform my heart to complain less and grow in gratitude for who You are.

Help me to see Your guiding hand in every circumstance (Romans 8:28). Remind me that all things work together for good and that my life is meant to glorify You, not center on my own needs. Teach me that not every thought needs to be spoken, guiding my words away from grumbling (Philippians 2:14).

I acknowledge that You work within me to fulfill Your purpose (Philippians 2:13). I offer heartfelt praise, willingly dethroning my worries and restoring You as my Lord and King. Thank You for Your continual presence in my life. May my words reflect Your goodness and grace. In Jesus' name, Amen.

November 5
Overcoming Complacency

"Therefore we must give the more earnest heed to the things we have heard, lest we drift away."
Hebrews 2:1 KJV

Dear Precious Lord, I thank You for Your mercy and compassion that never fail. Today, I come with a humble heart, seeking forgiveness for the times my gratitude has grown cold and I've become complacent in my health journey. I regret taking Your blessings for granted. Open my eyes to the countless gifts You bestow each day, and help me recognize and appreciate both big and small miracles in my life (Hebrews 2:1-3).

Fill my heart with renewed wonder, gratitude, and praise. Teach me to be truly thankful for Your ever-present help (Psalm 46:1). Let me not expect or take Your blessings for granted but treasure and acknowledge them with heartfelt gratitude. In moments of weakness and complacency, remind me that You will never abandon me (Deuteronomy 31:6). Give me strength to accept and work through shortcomings and motivation to pursue a healthier lifestyle with diligence. Grant me wisdom to make choices that honor and glorify Your name.

May my actions reflect my gratitude and my words honor Your holy name. May Your love and grace be my constant companions. In Jesus' name, Amen.

November 6
Thank You, Lord

"Let all that I am praise the Lord; may I never
forget the good things he does for me."
Psalm 103:2 NLT

Dear Gracious Lord, Today, I come before You, reflecting on the importance of gratitude in my life. How often do I rush through my days, consumed by my to-do lists, and overlook the countless blessings You pour into my life? Help me recognize the grace and mercy that surround me each day (Psalm 46:1).

When I forget to express my gratitude, I risk falling into a cycle of discontent and self-centeredness. Remind me that true contentment comes from acknowledging Your faithfulness. As I consider all that You have done—healing my spirit, providing for my needs, and guiding my steps—I choose to cultivate a heart of thankfulness (Philippians 4:19).

Lord, instill in me the importance of pausing to thank You. In moments of anxiety or frustration, help me remember Your unwavering presence. May I never forget the goodness You have shown, and may my life reflect Your love and grace to those around me. I give You all honor and praise, in Jesus' name. Amen.

November 7
A Heart of Contentment

"... I have learned to be content whatever the circumstances."

Philippians 4:11 NIV

Dear God of peace and contentment, I confess that I have often fallen into the trap of never feeling satisfied, despite the abundant gifts You shower upon me each day. Forgive me, Father, for my lack of contentment. Help me to trust in You completely and to cast away all anxiety from my heart (1 Peter 5:7).

Remind me, dear Lord, that You are the ultimate provider (Genesis 22:14). You supply all my needs, and whatever I require, You will graciously provide (Philippians 4:19). When discontentment creeps into my soul, gently nudge me to remember that my fulfillment lies in You alone. Grant me the wisdom to strike a balance between patiently waiting upon You and taking action in accordance with Your guidance.

Help me cultivate a heart that seeks You above all else. From this moment forward, I choose to live with gratitude and embrace a spirit of contentment in every situation. I surrender my health journey into Your loving hands, knowing You are the author of my life. Guide me to make wise choices, care for my body, and find peace that surpasses all understanding. In the precious name of Jesus, I pray. Amen.

November 8
Thankfulness as a Path to Joy

"You make known to me the path of life; you will fill me with joy in your presence, with eternal pleasures at your right hand."

Psalm 16:11 NIV

Dear Lord, Thank You for the true joy that comes from knowing You and recognizing Your blessings in my life. Help me to focus on the good things You have provided, and let gratitude lead me to this deep-seated joy, one that isn't dependent on my circumstances.

Remind me that "every good and perfect gift is from above" (James 1:17) and that true joy transcends fleeting moments of happiness. In times of struggle, help me remember that "in everything, by prayer and supplication with thanksgiving, let my requests be made known to You" (Philippians 4:6). As I embrace a spirit of thankfulness, may I find strength in the knowledge that "the joy of the Lord is my strength" (Nehemiah 8:10).

Guide me to seek Your presence, knowing that lasting joy is found in a relationship with You, regardless of my circumstances and regardless of my weight. Let my gratitude be a reflection of Your love and grace, leading me down the path of enduring joy. In Jesus' name, Amen.

November 9
Unashamed Praise

"One of them, when he saw he was healed, came back, praising God in a loud voice. He threw himself at Jesus' feet and thanked him—and he was a Samaritan."
Luke 17:15-16 NIV

Dear God of Glory, You are worthy of all praise and honor. I come before You with a humble and contrite heart, seeking forgiveness for the times I have failed to express genuine gratitude. Often, I forget that every good thing in my life is a gift from You (James 2:7). Forgive me for my lack of humility in these moments.

I want to be like the Samaritan who returned to give thanks. You have blessed me with eternity in my heart (Ecclesiastes 3:11) and showered me with Your Spirit, peace, presence, and grace. How can I withhold my thanks from You? Help me to cherish every moment with You and to praise You freely.

Remove any inhibitions or fears that keep me from expressing my praise fully. Grant me the freedom to prostrate myself before You in worship, unhindered by pride or concerns about how others perceive me. I long to openly and wholeheartedly express my gratitude and praise to You, allowing the depth of my emotions to overflow from the depths of my heart. May my words and actions be a reflection of a heart filled with genuine appreciation and love for You. In Jesus' name, I pray. Amen.

November 10
Thankful in The Trials

*"Not only so, but we also glory in our sufferings,
because we know that suffering produces perseverance"*
Romans 5:3 NIV

Dear Comforter, You are my ever-present help in times of need. You are my rock, fortress, and deliverer; my strength, in whom I trust (Psalm 18:2). I praise You in both good and hard times. Let praise fill my heart, especially during trials. Help me to run to You first instead of seeking answers elsewhere.

Reframe my thinking, shifting from asking why this is happening to recognizing Your sovereignty and asking, "What are You teaching me?" Let this curiosity lead me to a more peaceful, victorious life. Help me embrace trials as opportunities for growth and maturity (James 1:2-3). I refuse to see myself as a victim. Life is not inherently good or bad; it is a teacher about who You are. I choose to rejoice in this day (Psalm 118:24), regardless of what comes my way.

Grant me the strength to persevere and the wisdom to discern Your purpose. Increase my faith to trust in Your divine plan, even when I cannot see the bigger picture. May my life reflect Your grace and mercy, extending love and forgiveness to those around me. With gratitude, I offer this prayer in Jesus' name. Amen.

November 11
A Living Sacrifice

"And they brought in the ark of God … and they offered burnt offerings and peace offerings before God."
1 Chronicles 16:1 ESV

Dear Comforter, You are my rock, fortress, and deliverer (Psalm 18:2). Help me praise You in both good times and trials. May praise fill my heart, especially during difficult seasons. Let me turn to You first for answers rather than seeking help elsewhere.

Reframe my thinking so that I view trials as opportunities for growth (James 1:2-3). Instead of asking why this is happening, guide me to ask what You are teaching me through these challenges. I choose to rejoice in this day (Psalm 118:24), regardless of the circumstances.

Grant me strength to persevere and wisdom to discern Your purpose. Increase my faith to trust in Your divine plan, even when I cannot see it. Help me surrender control and follow Your guidance through the darkest valleys.

May my life reflect Your grace, love, and compassion. Use me as an instrument of Your peace, and let Your peace guard my heart and mind in Christ Jesus (Philippians 4:7). In Jesus' name, Amen.

November 12
Intentional Praise

"Repent, all of you who forget me, or I will tear you apart, and no one will help you."
Psalm 50:22 NLT

Dear God of Grace and Mercy, I thank You for Your unwavering love, mercy, and grace that You pour out daily. I am humbled by Your presence and goodness. Forgive me for the times I forget to give You thanks and praise.

When my life gets busy and overwhelming, I often lose sight of Your eternal presence and blessings. I pause now to express my gratitude. Help me cultivate a heart of constant thankfulness, recognizing that every breath, step, and heartbeat is a gift from You. May I never take these blessings for granted but see them as evidence of Your love and faithfulness.

Teach me to give thanks in all circumstances, knowing You are working for my good (Romans 8:28). Help me find beauty in simplicity, lessons in challenges, and growth in trials. Remind me that even in the darkest nights (John 1:5), Your light shines through, guiding my path. Grant me a heart of worship, so my words and actions reflect gratitude and surrender to Your will. I will magnify Your name (Psalm 34:3-5) in everything I do, for You alone are worthy of all honor, glory, and praise. In Jesus' name, Amen.

November 13
Thankful for The New Covenant

"And when He had taken some bread … saying, "This cup which is poured out for you is the new covenant in My blood."
Luke 22:19-20 NASB

Dear Covenant Keeping God, I am overwhelmed with gratitude for Your love and sacrifice. Thank You for sending Jesus to lay down His life on the cross so I could be redeemed (Colossians 1:13-14). Through Him, I am saved, forgiven, and granted eternal life.

Christ's resurrection shattered the power of sin and death, offering me hope and comfort (Isaiah 1:18). This new covenant is built on love, allowing me to experience a relationship with You rooted in freedom. Thank You for revealing that this covenant is about heart transformation rather than external rituals (Mark 12:28-31). I embrace the freedom from legalism and judgment, welcoming love, compassion, and forgiveness. Through Jesus' sacrifice, I am no longer bound by sin, and I am eternally grateful for Your unconditional love.

Help me live out this covenant daily in all areas of my life including my health as I reflect Your love and freedom in my actions. May my words and thoughts honor You and fulfill Your purpose for my life. In Jesus' name, Amen.

November 14
Thanksgiving Brings Peace

"Be anxious for nothing, but in everything by prayer …
with thanksgiving let your requests be made known to
God."

Philippians 4:6 NASB

D ear Jehovah Shalom, Your peace envelops me, guiding my steps beside still waters and restoring my weary soul (Psalm 23:2). In life's storms and daily temptations, You faithfully guard my heart and mind with Your unwavering peace.

Thank You for teaching me the power of a thankful heart. When doubt and anxiety arise, You remind me to approach everything with gratitude. Surrendering my worries to You brings a peace that surpasses all understanding, calming my troubled heart. I am humbled by Your ceaseless provision, O Jehovah Shalom. With a grateful heart, I trust that You supply all my needs abundantly (Zechariah 4:6). You are the source of every blessing. In scarcity, You provide abundance; in weakness, You offer strength.

Reflecting on Your gift of peace today, my heart swells with thanks. Your presence assures me not to be anxious about whether or not I will achieve my health goals. It will happen as I rest in You. May my life be a testament to Your faithfulness, as I trust in Your perfect peace. In Jesus' name, Amen.

November 15
Counting My Blessings

"Bless the Lord, O my soul, and forget not all his benefits, …"

Psalm 103:2 ESV

Dear Jehovah Jireh, You are the merciful God who forgives all our sins and heals all our diseases (Psalm 103:3-5). Your grace knows no bounds, redeeming my life and crowning me with love and compassion. Even in difficult situations, You provide a way out and escape from temptation (1 Corinthians 10:13). Your blessings are too numerous to count.

As I consider my imperfect body, I see Your magnificent creation. Each part, including these humble legs, supports me daily, carrying me from place to place with unwavering strength. Fill my heart with gratitude for my shelter, food, clean water, and clothes. Help me never to forget these daily blessings and use them to bless others in return.

Open my eyes to the opportunities You've given me (Revelation 3:7), the talents I possess, and the possibilities ahead. Grant me the courage to seize these opportunities with gratitude and make a positive impact. I commit to counting my blessings daily, acknowledging Your goodness and faithfulness. Thank You for the countless blessings You've showered upon me. May my gratitude reflect Your love and grace. In Jesus' name, Amen.

November 16
Thank You for Daily Strength

"The Lord is my strength and my song, and he has become my salvation, and I will praise him."
Exodus 15:2 ESV

Dear Mighty God, You are my daily strength, my rock, and my refuge. In life's challenges and uncertainties, Your unwavering love and grace sustain me. I am grateful for the strength You provide, enabling me to face each day with hope and courage.

You promise that those who wait on You will renew their strength (Isaiah 40:31). I've seen this truth in my life, finding that when I trust in You, I am empowered to soar on wings like eagles, run and not grow weary, walk, and not faint. I know I can do all things through Christ when I surrender to You (Philippians 4:13). Your limitless power works within me, equipping me to overcome every obstacle. My strength comes not from my own abilities but from Your mighty hand guiding me.

You are my strength and shield; my heart trusts and finds help in You (Psalm 28:7). Your strength surrounds me, guarding me and assuring me that I am never alone. Today, I thank You for the strength You provide each day. Help me rely on Your power, knowing that through You, I am more than a conqueror. In Jesus' name, Amen.

November 17
A Thankful and Peaceful Heart

"Let the peace of Christ rule in your hearts, since as members of one body you were called to peace. And be thankful."

Colossians 3:15 NIV

Dear Jehovah Shalom, I pray that Your peace rules in my heart today, filling it with praise and thanksgiving. If there's anything hindering Your peace from guarding my heart, please reveal it to me.

I desire to approach my health journey with calm and peace, though I often feel anxious. Lead me as I grow into Your image and likeness (2 Corinthians 3:18), so Your peace may guard and guide my heart. I acknowledge that anxiety will sometimes overtake me, and peace may feel distant. Yet, I trust that Your peace is always within reach, and for this, I am grateful! Lord, grant me grace and strength to release anxiety, embrace self-compassion, and let go of resentments. Teach me to cultivate a heart of gratitude for Your abundant blessings and the gift of salvation through Christ.

I recognize that peace involves living in harmony with others. As I give grace to myself, help me be a peacemaker, seeking reconciliation and understanding in my relationships. May the peace of Christ in my heart (Ephesians 5:20-21) extend to those around me, fostering unity and love. In Jesus' name, Amen.

November 18
You Hear Me

"... And Jesus lifted up his eyes, and said, Father, I thank thee that thou hast heard me."

John 11:41 KJV

Dear Ever-present Father, I am humbled by Your unwavering presence in my life and I thank You today for hearing and answering my prayers.

You have shown me time and time again that You are the God who listens. When my words failed me (Romans 8:26) and I found myself at a loss for what to say, Your Spirit interceded on my behalf, translating the depths of my heart to the language of heaven. In moments of despair, You heard my silent cries, and in moments of confusion and overwhelm, You provided clarity. Your gentle touch has been evident in the way You have guided my steps and granted me the desires of my heart (Proverbs 3:5-6).

I am astounded by Your faithfulness, Lord. You have answered my prayers in ways I never could have imagined. You have granted me strength when I was weak, hope when I was despondent, and peace when I was engulfed in turmoil. As I reflect on Your goodness, I am reminded that my faith in You is not in vain. You are a God who hears, a God who answers, and a God who delights in blessing Your children. Thank You, gracious God, for hearing my prayers and for answering me in ways that exceed my expectations. May Your name be forever praised. In Jesus' name, I pray. Amen.

November 19
Continual Praise

"I will bless the Lord at all times; his praise shall continually be in my mouth."

Psalm 34:1 ESV

Dear Almighty God, Creator of all things and source of every blessing, You alone are worthy of all honor and glory. I declare that Your praise will continually be on my lips. Through every season—joy, frustration, anxiety, and triumph—I will lift my voice in praise to You. You are the rock on which I stand (Matthew 7:25) and the constant presence guiding me.

As long as I have breath, I will proclaim Your mighty works and declare Your name. I will honor You with every note and melody, offering my body as a living sacrifice (1 Corinthians 6:20; Romans 12:1). In times of plenty and lack (Philippians 4:12), certainty and doubt, I will praise You. You are my strength in weakness, peace in chaos, and hope in despair. Your promises are true, and Your Word guides me.

Grant me the strength to remain steadfast in praising You. Help me recognize Your blessings in every circumstance and cultivate a heart filled with gratitude and awe. Today and always, I surrender my life to You. I will never stop praising You, for You alone are worthy of all honor, glory, and praise. In Jesus' name, Amen.

November 20
Creation Sings Your Praise

"Let the sea and everything in it shout his praise! Let the earth and all living things join in. ..."
Psalm 98:7-9 NLT

Dear God of Creation, thank You for the beauty of all that Your hand has made. From forests to skies, fragrant plants to animals, every part of creation sings Your praises. Thank You for the rain that nourishes the earth, the morning sun, and the night moon. Your invisible nature is revealed in the majesty of it all (Isaiah 55:12).

As I spend time outside getting fresh air, I am blessed to be the recipient of all the beauty that surrounds me, and it testifies to Your awesome love and care. In the vastness of nature (Psalm 96:11-12), I find rest and peace (Psalm 145:5). The whispering trees and winding paths remind us of the intricate balance You have established in creation. I am grateful for the opportunity to walk amidst this natural splendor and find respite from the busyness of life.

Help me to spend more time outside, appreciating and protecting the beauty around me. Teach me to be a good steward of Your creation, cherishing it for future generations. With a grateful heart, I offer my praises to You and commit to living in harmony with Your creation. In Jesus' name, Amen.

November 21
Temple Worship and Praise

"Thank you for making me so wonderfully complex!
Your workmanship is marvelous."

Psalm 139:14 NLT

Dear God of Creation, I humbly bow before You, deeply grateful for the intricate masterpiece of creation that I am. In Your infinite wisdom, You have fearfully and wonderfully made me (Ecclesiastes 3:11), reflecting Your beauty, intelligence, and health. I recognize that my worth and value come from bearing Your divine image (Genesis 1:27).

As Your precious workmanship, molded by Your loving hands, I am devoted to bringing glory to Your name through my physical being. Guide me, Lord, in the path of healthy eating and exercise, so I may honor You with how I care for this temple You've entrusted to me. Grant me the strategies and strength to nourish and maintain my body, knowing that my movements and my very existence are found in You (Acts 17:28).

With unwavering faith, I declare Your power over my health. I pray for complete wholeness, healing, and vitality in every aspect of my being. Thank You for this moment of reflection and connection with You. I treasure this time and present my prayers and praises, trusting in Your divine will for my health and life. May Your will be done, Lord. In Jesus' name, Amen.

November 22
You Kept Me

"Surely he will save you from the fowler's snare ... He will cover you with his feathers, and under his wings you will find refuge."

Psalm 91:3-4 NIV

Dear Almighty Protector, I'm so grateful for Your constant love and protection. Thank You for keeping me safe from dangers I can't even see—the things that could harm me physically, emotionally, and spiritually. You've guided me through challenges and shielded me from pitfalls that could have derailed my health journey.

When uncertainty weighs heavy on my heart—whether it's fear of illness, struggles with cravings, or discouragement over slow progress—I know You are there, steady and faithful. Your presence gives me strength, and Your hand keeps me on the path of wellness. I trust that You're working even when I don't understand what's ahead (Isaiah 55:8-9).

You've dismantled traps that could have led me astray, and Your wisdom has helped me make better choices for my body and mind (1 Peter 5:8-9). I surrender my health, fears, and uncertainties to You, knowing You are my shield and refuge. Thank You for walking this journey with me and for keeping me safe as I strive to honor You with my body, mind, and spirit (1 Corinthians 6:19-20). In Jesus' name, Amen

November 23
Daily Sustenance

"Give us this day our daily Bread."
Matthew 6:11 ESV

Dear God, my provider and sustainer, Thank You for Your constant provision. You meet my needs each day—physically, emotionally, and spiritually. I am grateful for the nourishment You give me, not just in food but in every aspect of my health and life. You are the source of my strength, and I trust in Your daily provision.

Lord, You remind me that I do not need to worry about tomorrow (Matthew 6:34). When I focus on today and the blessings You've provided, I am filled with peace. Help me to stay present and trust that You will provide all I need in each moment. Whether in times of abundance or lack, help me to remember that You will always sustain me (Philippians 4:19).

Thank You for guiding me on this health journey. I surrender my fears and uncertainties to You, knowing that Your provision is enough. I don't have to worry about the future, for You will provide what I need in Your perfect timing (Isaiah 55:8-9). Let me rest in Your faithfulness today. In Jesus' name, Amen.

November 24
Thanks For Daily Movement

"For in him we live and move and have our being."
Acts 17:28 NIV

Dear Gracious Creator, I come before You with deep gratitude for the gift of movement each day, even when motivation falters. This ability to move is a precious privilege, allowing me to embrace life and my physical potential. Thank You for granting me strength in my arms and legs, enabling me to explore and serve others. May my actions bring joy and healing to those in need.

Thank You for the intricate workings of my heart and lungs, tirelessly sustaining my life. In each heartbeat, I see a reflection of Your divine wisdom and design. I am fearfully and wonderfully made (Psalm 139:14)!

As I engage in my holy movement today, I humbly offer this time as an act of worship and prayer (Romans 12:1). May each step, each lift, and each movement be a testament to Your love. Grant me the strength to push through moments of resistance and the discipline to make exercise a consistent part of my life. With a grateful heart, I thank You, O Lord, for the ability to exercise and move my body freely. May this gift be a constant reminder of Your abundant grace and an invitation to honor and care for the temple You have entrusted to me (1 Corinthians 6:20). In Jesus' name I pray. Amen!

November 25
Thank You For The Air I Breathe

"The Spirit of God has made me; the breath of the Almighty gives me life."

Job 33:4 NIV

Dear Breath of Life, You are my sustainer and source of vitality. Every breath I take is a gift of Your grace, yet I often overlook this miracle that happens 25,000 times a day. You silently fill my lungs with energy, allowing me to explore, love, and experience life.

Today, I bow in humility, acknowledging the magnitude of Your divine orchestration. With each inhale, You provide life-giving oxygen, revitalizing my body. With each exhale, You carry away waste and impurities. Help me to be more mindful of Your constant presence (James 4:8). Let every breath remind me of Your love and provision, and let each exhale be a release of gratitude.

As I exercise and move my body, let my heart and lungs be strengthened and revitalized. As I go about my day, let me breathe in the wisdom (James 1:5) and guidance that You offer, filling my spirit with clarity and purpose. May I exhale any burdens or worries, trusting that You will provide, sustain, and protect. May I never again take for granted this sacred exchange that gives me life. In Jesus' name, I pray. Amen!

November 26
Thankful for The Gift of Health

"Beloved, I pray that you may prosper in all things and be in health, just as your soul prospers."
3 John 1:2 NKJV

Thank You for the strength and vitality that allows me to fulfill my daily tasks and responsibilities. I am grateful for freedom from pain and illness, enabling me to enjoy Your creation and serve others joyfully. Help me to cherish this gift of health as a precious blessing from You.

I commit to caring for the temple You have given me (3 John 1:2). Guide me to make wise choices in my lifestyle, nourishing my body and mind with wholesome food, exercise, and rest. Grant me wisdom to prioritize self-care and seek balance in all areas of my life. Use my good health as a way to glorify Your name, and empower me to be a vessel of love, compassion, and encouragement to those around me.

Thank You for the energy to serve, explore, and find joy. In moments of illness and weakness, You have been my healer (Psalm 30:2) and refuge (Psalm 23:4). Your presence has comforted me and Your healing touch has restored me. I commit my health to Your loving hands and pray that my physical well-being aligns with the prosperity of my soul. In Jesus' name, I pray. Amen.

November 27
Thankful in The Little Things

"Catch for us the foxes, the little foxes that ruin the vineyards, our vineyards that are in bloom."
                                    Song of Solomon 2:15 NIV

Dear Great God, I thank You that Your mercies are new every morning (Lamentations 3:22-23). Today, I am grateful for the small blessings that make up each day. You are the giver of all good things James 1:17), and I recognize that even the tiniest gifts are signs of Your love and provision.

It's easy to be consumed by the desire for big changes and victories. Help me focus on the small daily wins and develop a heart that appreciates the seemingly insignificant moments that bring joy and progress. Let me not overlook these small victories in my health journey, knowing that each step forward is important. I understand that life's larger tapestry is woven from these small moments. Each day is a gift from You (Psalm 118:24), and I want to be thankful for every breath, heartbeat, and opportunity to experience life fully. Help me see that lasting change often starts with small choices and victories.

Grant me the wisdom to trust in Your perfect timing and embrace the journey with patience. In these daily wins, I find the strength to persevere and the motivation to continue. In Jesus' name, I pray. Amen.

November 28
Thank You For Food

"As they sat down to eat, he took the bread and blessed it."

Luke 24:30 NLT

Dear Bread of Heaven, I thank You for meeting my daily needs (Philippians 4:19) and providing the food that sustains me. I come before You with a grateful heart, recognizing Your presence at my table and the abundance of blessings in my life.

Just as You blessed the meals shared with the disciples, I thank You for Your divine provision and the reminder of Your love through the breaking of bread. I am also mindful of those involved in bringing food to my table—farmers, workers, and those who prepare and cook the food. Their labor is a testament to Your grace. Help me appreciate every morsel and cultivate a heart of gratitude and generosity. I pray for those who lack access to enough food (Matthew 6:11) and ask that You use me to provide for their needs. Increase my compassion and guide me to share my resources to support others.

As I eat today, may it nourish my body and strengthen my spirit to fulfill Your purpose for my life. Let my gratitude extend beyond this prayer, inspiring me to live a life of service and generosity. In Jesus' name, I pray. Amen.

November 29
Thank You For Creating Me

"So God created man in His own image, in the image and likeness of God He created him; male and female He created them."

Genesis 1:27 NIV

Dear God of Creation, I am in awe of Your magnificent handiwork. You, in Your infinite wisdom, created the world and intricately fashioned me (Hebrews 11:3; Psalm 139:13). Yet, I confess that I sometimes fail to appreciate the masterpiece You made. Negative thoughts and self-doubt have led me to undervalue Your work in me. Forgive me for this and help me to see myself as You do.

In light of Your incredible craftsmanship, I commit myself to offer each day as a living sacrifice of thankfulness, praise, and gratitude. I acknowledge that You created me with a specific purpose, a role to fulfill in this world. May I constantly seek to align my thoughts, words, and actions with Your will. Strengthen me, Lord, to honor and cherish the work of Your hands and to walk confidently in the path You have set before me.

Like the stars, mountains, oceans, and everything else You created, I live to worship and reverence You. Let me lift Your name on high all the days of my life by living my life in purpose and thankfulness. In Jesus' name, I pray. Amen.

November 30
Thankful For a Willing Spirit

*"Watch and pray that you may not enter into tempta-
tion. The spirit indeed is willing, but the flesh is weak."*
Matthew 26:41 ESV

Awesome, Almighty God of the Whole Universe, I declare Your Lordship over me and my desire to submit myself fully to Your caring control. Lord, some days it's not so hard to make myself Play-Doh in Your hands, but other days I need Your help! Give me a willing spirit to put my life in Your loving hands today, especially the corner of it that I like to keep in my control—my health journey. As I close out this month focused on thankfulness, help me to continue putting into practice what You have shown me (Philippians 4:9). Let me see life from Your perspective as my loving Father, my Shepherd, my Protector, the only One who truly knows and desires what is best for me. Conform my will to Your will, especially when it comes to the guardrails I place in my life.

Continue to change my 'stinkin' thinkin'' and perspectives as You conform my life to Yours. Restore to me the joy of Your salvation, and uphold me with a willing spirit (Psalm 51:12). When I want to quit or self-sabotage, make me willing to be willing! Thank You that You did not give me a spirit of fear, but of power, of love, and of self-discipline (2 Timothy 1:7)! In Jesus' holy name. Amen.

December

RECEIVING GOD'S LOVE

Welcome to this month of prayers dedicated to experiencing God's love. Over the next few weeks, you'll embrace God's love and allow it to saturate every fiber of your being. As the world pursues never-ending self-improvement, you will recognize that true healing and lasting change come from a place deeper than mere physicality. While exercise, proper nutrition, and medical care are undoubtedly valuable, you mustn't overlook the incredible impact that God's love can have on your life.

God's divine love has the power to touch every aspect of your being. It reaches into the depths of your soul, where your self-esteem and self-worth reside. As you embrace God's love, you open yourself up to a beautiful journey—one that helps you see yourself, your body, and your role in the world in a whole new light.

When you recognize that you are fearfully and wonderfully made in the image of God, you begin to see yourself through the lens of God's love. By seeking a loving relationship with God, you invite His presence into your health journey. You learn to treat your body with respect and care, not out of self-criticism, but from a deep understanding that your body is a sacred vessel entrusted to you.

May this month's prayers provide a time of deep connection with God's love for you. Open your heart, mind, and soul to the never-ending, reckless love that awaits you, and walk this path knowing that with God's love, anything is possible.

December 1
In His Image

"And have put on the new self, which is being renewed in knowledge in the image of its Creator."
Colossians 3:10 NIV

Dear God of Creation. My life bears witness to Your creativity, and ingenuity yet as I come before You today, I confess that I've sometimes undervalued Your masterpiece within me. I am truly sorry for not seeing myself with the same splendor and worth that You see. I acknowledge Your goodness and the truth that I am fearfully and wonderfully made (Psalm 139:14). I ask Your Spirit to renew my mind, creating new pathways of understanding as I dive deeper into the truth of just how much You love me, in the coming weeks.

Help me to see myself accurately through Your eyes. Where I perceive brokenness, reveal to me how You see me as whole and complete, lacking nothing (Colossians 2:10). When I feel less than, show me the mighty warrior You have made me, more than a conqueror through Christ (Romans 8:37). Where I view myself as a victim, change my perspective to see the victor who is always growing and learning, never losing.

Thank You for transforming my view and for Your everlasting love that envelops me (Jeremiah 31:3). I am grateful for Your work in opening my eyes. In Jesus' name, I pray. Amen.

December 2
Transcendent Peace

"Now may the Lord of peace himself give you peace at all times and in every way."
2 Thessalonians 3:16 NIV

Dear Jehovah Shalom, Your peace surpasses all understanding (Philippians 4:7). I come before You, grateful for the gift of Your transcendent peace that calms my nervous system and soothes my racing mind. In this sometimes chaotic world, I am thankful that You provide a peace beyond what it can offer (2 Thessalonians 3:16). You are my unshifting rock in the storm, my anchor in turbulent times, and my shelter from every evil.

Your promises of unfailing love give me the confidence to face each day with victory. You comfort me and remind me that I am the apple of Your eye (Zechariah 2:8). You work all things together for my good, and Your assurance that You will never leave me brings me peace. Yet, I admit that I still feel alone at times, and I confess that I cannot generate peace on my own.

Today, I praise You for Your goodness and love, asking that Your gift of peace continues to rest, rule, and abide in my heart. Thank You, Jesus, for Your unwavering peace. Amen.

December 3
His Steadfast Love

"Know that the LORD your God is God, the faithful God who keeps covenant and steadfast love …"
Deuteronomy 7:9 ESV

Dear Abba Father, Thank You for Your unfailing, steadfast love (Psalm 136:26). Despite knowing everything about me, You still love me beyond comprehension. Your love is a deep mystery, and I am eternally grateful.

"You have searched me, Lord, and You know me" (Psalm 139:1) and in spite of my flaws and failures, Your forgiveness and unconditional love remain. I am humbled by Your grace and mercy. Today, I seek a deeper experience of Your love. Holy Spirit, reveal any burdens or self-condemnation I may carry, knowing that Jesus has already paid the price with His precious blood (1 John 1:9). I surrender these to You, embracing Your love that surpasses any mistake or regret. Release me from the chains of self-condemnation, and help me fully accept Your steadfast love that continually draws me into Your presence.

Teach me to love You wholeheartedly, to extend compassion to others, and to embrace myself with the same acceptance. Thank You, heavenly Father, for Your unwavering love. May Your love transform me and overflow from me, bringing hope and healing to my life. In Jesus' name, I pray. Amen.

December 4
God's Gift of Patience

*"But you, O Lord, are a God merciful and gracious,
slow to anger and abounding in steadfast love and
faithfulness."*

Psalm 86:15 ESV

Dear Patient God, Your love is unwavering, and Your patience is boundless (Psalm 86:15). I am grateful for Your endless grace and mercy, which remind me that true fulfillment comes from embracing the journey rather than rushing towards results.

I often find myself striving for quick fixes and results that hold no eternal value. Yet, You gently teach me that life is a series of lessons and growth, where patience and wisdom are intertwined. Just as You are patient with me, guide me to be patient with myself. Help me extend the same grace and understanding to my own shortcomings that You generously offer me (Romans 8:28).

In Your peace and patience, I find strength and solace. Your presence is my refuge, reminding me that I am never alone. As I yield to Your guidance, may Your perfect will be revealed in my life, unfolding in divine timing (Romans 12:2). Thank You for Your immeasurable love and gentle hand that restores my soul. Grant me the wisdom to cultivate patience and focus on what truly matters. In Jesus' name, I pray. Amen.

December 5
His Overwhelming Love

"... If a man owns a hundred sheep, and one of them wanders away, will he not leave the ninety-nine on the hills and go to look for the one that wandered off?"
Matthew 18:12 NIV

Dear Loving God, You love me with an everlasting love (Jeremiah 31:3). I come before You in awe of Your boundless, relentless love that pursues me without end. Your love is a constant, enveloping presence that never fails or grows weary (1 Corinthians 13:8).

You sent Your Son, Jesus, to sacrifice Himself for my sins, bringing me into an awesome and intimate relationship with You. Through His blood, I am redeemed and forgiven. Nothing can separate me from Your love—neither height nor depth nor anything else (Romans 8:38). Your love embraces my brokenness and lifts me with grace, filling me with a peace beyond understanding.

Help me grasp the magnitude of Your love. Open my heart to see Your love in every part of my life. Teach me to walk in the assurance that Your love is constant and unchanging, even amidst life's challenges. Thank You for a love that is unconditional and healing, reaching the depths of my soul and restoring my spirit. In Jesus' name, I pray. Amen.

December 6
God's Ultimate Sacrifice

"... but God shows his love for us in that while we were still sinners, Christ died for us."

Romans 5:8 ESV

Dear Loving God, Thank You for Your limitless and reckless love. I am deeply grateful that You loved me even when I was still a sinner (Romans 5:8). I sought fulfillment in many things—food, shopping, and relationships—but found them empty compared to Your unconditional love.

I am sorry for not fully grasping the depth of Your sacrifice and for taking You for granted. Today, I bow before You, acknowledging the incredible gift of Your Son, Jesus Christ, who gave His life for me (Ephesians 2:8). This sacrifice overwhelms me with awe and gratitude.

I accept Your love and sacrifice with an open heart, knowing I can never earn it but can only receive it as a free gift. Help me to live in the reality of Your love daily, embrace Your grace fully, and share this love with others.

Thank You for loving me when I felt unlovable, guiding me when I was lost, and being my constant companion. I surrender my life to You, inviting You to transform me from the inside out (Ezekiel 36:26). May Your love guide my steps, heal my health, and shape my character. In Jesus' name, I pray. Amen.

December 7
God Rejoices Over You

*"The LORD your God is in your midst, a mighty one
who will save; he will rejoice over you with gladness;
he will quiet you by his love; he will exult over you
with loud singing."*

Zephaniah 3:17 ESV

Dear Precious Lord, You take my hand and guide me
gently (Psalm 139:10). Your love soothes my anxious
thoughts, and Your Word reveals the depth of Your love for
me. It brings me great joy to know You rejoice over me (Luke
15:10). Like a loving parent, You delight in me, seeing beyond
my flaws and embracing me with unconditional love. I confess
that I have sought validation from the world, letting my faults
define my worth, forgetting that my true value lies in You
alone.

Today, I embrace the truth that my worth is not defined by me,
but by You. I am fearfully and wonderfully made in Your image (Psalm 139:14). Release me from the chains of comparison
and the relentless pursuit of approval. Help me to accept myself
as You do, letting go of striving and hiding.

I am grateful for Your boundless love. Help me open my heart
to receive Your love fully, removing any barriers. May Your
love overflow within me (1 John 4:16), touching those around
me and reflecting Your grace. In Jesus' name, I pray. Amen.

December 8
But for the Grace of God!

"But God, being rich in mercy, because of the great love with which he loved us, even when we were dead in our trespasses, made us alive together with Christ—by grace you have been saved."

Ephesians 2:4-5 ESV

Dear God of Grace, I come before You in awe of Your boundless grace and immeasurable love. Thank You for not leaving me in the darkness of my transgressions but for lavishing Your mercy upon me. Your grace has redeemed, restored, and given me new life. I stand in wonder of Your love, which knows no limits (1 John 3:1).

Lord, I am humbled by the realization that I could never earn or deserve this incredible gift of salvation. May this truth guide my thoughts, actions, and words. Help me extend grace to others as You have to me, and fill my heart with compassion and forgiveness.

Remind me that Your grace is sufficient in times of weakness and doubt (2 Corinthians 12:9). May I find strength and comfort in Your unchanging love, knowing that I am held secure (Job 11:18). Thank You for the immeasurable riches of Your grace. May I continue to grow in my understanding and experience of Your grace each day, becoming a vessel of Your love to those around me. In Jesus' name, I pray. Amen.

December 9
Unselfish Love

"For God so loved the world, that he gave his only Son, that whoever believes in him should not perish but have eternal life."

John 3:16 NIV

Dear Selfless God, I seek You today with a heart full of gratitude for Your boundless love. Your love is beyond measure and comprehension. Despite my brokenness, You extended Your love to me, embracing me with open arms. You gave Your Son to save me from darkness and grant me eternal life (John 3:16; Colossians 1:13).

I am humbled by the magnitude of Your love. It is not based on my actions but on Your very nature, for You are love itself (1 John 4:8). You loved me even when I was lost in sin and selfishness.

Help me fully grasp and embrace the depth of Your love. Open the eyes of my heart to understand the enormity of Your sacrifice. Fill me with gratitude for the love You have lavished upon me (1 John 3:1). May Your love drive me to love myself and others as You have loved me. In moments of doubt or feeling unworthy, remind me that Your love is constant and unchanging. Teach me to trust in Your steadfast love, guiding my steps and transforming my life. In Jesus' name, I pray. Amen.

December 10
How He Loves Us

"I have been crucified with Christ. It is no longer I who live, but Christ who lives in me. And the life I now live in the flesh I live by faith in the Son of God who loved me and gave himself for me."

Galatians 2:20 NIV

Dear Holy Father, Oh, how You love me! Help me see myself and others through Your eyes, with pure love. Remind me that I am fearfully and wonderfully made, a masterpiece created by Your hands (Psalm 139:14; Ephesians 2:10). Teach me to embrace my uniqueness and cherish the fact that You created me in Your image (Genesis 1:27).

Guide my thoughts away from fault-finding and self-criticism. Let Your unwavering and unchanging love fill my heart, helping me to walk in self-compassion and to understand that Your love covers my imperfections (Galatians 2:20). May Your love overflow from within me, extending grace and forgiveness to those around me. Let my words and actions reflect the depth of Your love, allowing others to experience Your boundless compassion and find comfort in Your embrace.

Thank You, Heavenly Father, for the immeasurable love You have bestowed upon me. May I always remember the magnitude of Your love and let it guide and sustain me throughout my life's journey. In Jesus' name, I pray, knowing that I am forever cherished and loved. Amen.

December 11
Alive in Him

"Behold, I stand at the door and knock; if anyone hears My voice and opens the door, I will come in to him and will dine with him, and he with Me."
Revelation 3:20 NKJV

Dear Loving and Faithful Father, What a privilege to spend time with You today. You have breathed life into me and called me Your own. In so many past relationships, I felt unvalued and had to strive for love, but with You, Your love is unconditional and everlasting. Help me to fully embrace and be transformed by Your love (1 John 4:16).

I long to love You back with a fervent heart. Fill me with Your Holy Spirit, so my love for You radiates through my words and deeds, impacting my choices and decisions. God, Your love gives me strength, hope, and purpose. Help me live a life that is dead to sin (Romans 6:11) and alive in You each day. Guide me through life's challenges, keeping my focus on You.

Teach me to understand true love and reflect it in how I treat myself and others. May I show kindness, forgiveness, and grace, being a vessel of Your love and bringing healing to those around me. Thank You for the gift of life in You. I am alive with God and forever grateful. In Jesus' name, I pray. Amen.

December 12
God's Unconditional Love

"The LORD appeared to us in the past, saying: "I have loved you with an everlasting love; I have drawn you with unfailing kindness."

Jeremiah 31:3 NIV

Dear God of Love, I am amazed by the depth of Your love for me. It is incredible that nothing I do can increase or decrease Your love; it is perfect and unwavering. Please give me a heart-deep understanding of this boundless love (Jeremiah 31:3). Today, I lay my burdens, sins, joys, and struggles before You (Psalm 55:22).

In return, I receive Your unconditional love into my heart. It is like an ocean, vast and unending, filled with grace. Your love is limitless and pure, and in moments of weakness, remind me of its constancy. May Your love heal my past wounds, cleanse me from guilt (1 John 1:9), and restore my soul and body. Your love is my refuge and strength.

Thank You for loving me beyond comprehension and embracing me as I am. Help me live fully in Your love and reflect it to others. May Your love guide my steps (Psalm 32:8), fill me with compassion, and touch those around me. I am grateful for Your amazing love and pray in Jesus' name. Amen.

December 13
A Model of Love

"My command is this: Love each other as I have loved you."

John 15:12 NIV

Dear Daddy, You are great and greatly to be praised (Psalm 111:1). Thank You for showing me, through Your Son Jesus, what true love looks like—one that puts others first. Change my heart to reflect this kind of love. I admit it's difficult to love some people, but Your perfect love reminds me that even when I struggle, You still love me unconditionally (John 15:12).

Help me remember that Your love is constant and unwavering. I cannot do anything to make You love me more or less. I receive Your love and ask for the strength to love others as You have loved me. Enable me to see their worth and dignity, regardless of their actions or attitudes.

Grant me compassion to love those who are hard to love or who have hurt me. Help me to be selfless in my love, as You were on the cross, sacrificing Yourself for all humanity (Romans 5:8). May Your love flow through me, touching others through my actions, words, and kindness. Show me opportunities to serve and reflect Your grace and mercy. In Jesus' name, I pray. Amen.

December 14
Love is a Verb

"Beloved, let us love one another, for love is from God, and whoever loves has been born of God and knows God. Anyone who does not love does not know God because God is love."

1 John 4:7-8 ESV

Dear Abba Father, You never stop working, orchestrating Your plans and purposes (Ephesians 1:11). Your love is not fleeting but a solid foundation, a promise I can rely on, and a balm for my weary soul. Teach me to love as You do—sacrificially and intentionally. Help me see love as a verb, an action that requires effort and intention, not just words (1 John 3:18).

Grant me the strength to love even when it's difficult, to extend grace when it's undeserved, and to show kindness when it's not reciprocated. Let my actions embody Your love, reflecting Your character and nature. When I feel tempted to hold back or withdraw, remind me of Your perfect love that casts out all fear (1 John 4:18). Empower me to step out in faith and love boldly, knowing Your love within me is greater than any challenge I face.

May my love be an expression of Your love, drawing others to You. Let them see Your love reflected in my actions and be drawn closer to experiencing Your love for themselves. I pray all of this in Jesus' name, who demonstrated the greatest act of love through His sacrifice on the cross. Amen.

December 15
God Sings to You

"The Lord your God is in your midst, a mighty one who will save; he will rejoice over you with gladness; he will quiet you by his love; he will exult over you with loud singing."

Zechariah 3:17 ESV

Dear Good, Good Father, Your love is steadfast and secure, and I am overwhelmed by the realization that You sing over me. In the quiet moments, I hear Your gentle melody, a song of affection uniquely mine. Your voice, like a soothing lullaby, calms my weary soul and fills me with joy.

When the walls feel like they are caving in on me, Your song carries me through storms, reminding me I am never alone (Romans 8:35). Your love is my anchor, a melody that brings peace to my troubled mind. I find solace and strength in its harmonies. Your song speaks of forgiveness, washing away my sins and setting me free (Isaiah 61:1). It declares redemption, transforming my brokenness into wholeness. Through every note, You remind me that I am precious and cherished.

I long to join in the chorus of Your love, lifting my voice in gratitude and praise. With every breath, I want to sing of Your goodness and unending mercy (2 Peter 3:9). Let my life reflect Your love, bringing hope and healing to others. Thank You for embracing me with Your love and for the melody of Your heart. In Jesus' name, Amen.

December 16
Joy in The Journey

"And God will wipe away every tear from their eyes; there shall be no more death, nor sorrow, nor crying. There shall be no more pain, for the former things have passed away."

Revelation 21:4 NKJV

Dear Gracious and Compassionate Father, Thank You for the promise that You will wipe away every tear and that one day there will be no more pain or sorrow (Revelation 21:4). Your promises and grace sustain me, and I am grateful for the assurance of ultimate joy and peace in Your presence (2 Corinthians 1:20).

Lord, You see the depths of my heart and understand my struggles (Hebrews 4:14-16). Reveal any areas where I have not fully surrendered to Your will. Help me trust in Your goodness and submit to Your guidance, recognizing that joy comes from embracing Your plans for my life (Romans 8:28).

Teach me to see beyond my circumstances, understanding that joy is a deep contentment found in fellowship with You, not just a fleeting emotion. Even when happiness eludes me, let the inner joy from my relationship with You be my strength and resilience. Fill me with Your Holy Spirit, the source of true joy, and may that joy overflow into my life, bringing light and love to others. I surrender my journey to You and embrace the joy found in walking with You. In Jesus' name, Amen.

December 17
Rest in His Presence

"Humble yourselves, therefore, under the mighty hand of God so that at the proper time he may exalt you, casting all your anxieties on him, because he cares for you."

1 Peter 5:7 ESV

Dear God, You are the great I AM (Exodus 3:14), and I have nothing to fear because You are with me. I come to You with my burdens and rest in Your presence, casting all my cares on You (1 Peter 5:7). I realize I've clung to unhealthy patterns and mindsets that are no longer serving me. I surrender them to You, trusting in Your transformative power to heal me from the inside out.

Help me cease striving and controlling and step into Your rest beside the calm stream. I release my grip on these burdens, trusting You to carry them. In Your presence, I find rest and renewal. Replace my anxieties with Your perfect peace that surpasses all understanding (Philippians 4:7).

Thank You for Your faithfulness and unconditional love. May Your healing power flow through me, renewing my mind, body, and spirit. Guide me each step, reminding me that I can find rest and restoration in Your everlasting arms. I pray all of this in the mighty name of Jesus. Amen.

December 18
Amazing Love

"As the Father has loved me, so have I loved you. Now remain in my love."

John 15:9 NIV

Lord, Your love is amazing, beyond words. It's an endless ocean, deeper than any sea, and higher than any mountain. It reaches the depths of my soul and lifts me to new heights. Your love is the foundation of my faith, source of my hope, and strength in my weakness.

Your love is unconditional, forgiving, and everlasting. In moments of doubt, remind me of Your amazing love. When I feel unworthy, let Your love reassure me that I am deeply cherished. Help me grasp the breadth, length, height, and depth of Your love (Ephesians 3:18-19).

I surrender to Your love, knowing that through Your grace, I can receive such overwhelming love. May I never forget the price paid for my redemption (Hebrews 10:10).

Let Your love transform my thoughts (Romans 12:2), actions, and relationships. Teach me to love as You love, extending kindness and forgiveness to others. Open my eyes to see Your love in every moment of my life, guiding me on the path of righteousness (Psalm 23:3). Thank You for loving me beyond measure. In Jesus' name, I pray. Amen.

December 19
Seeking The Gift Giver

"For I know the plans I have for you," declares the LORD, "plans to prosper you and not to harm you, plans to give you hope and a future."

Jeremiah 29:11 NIV

Dear Daddy, You are the source of all goodness and love. I am grateful for the privilege of approaching You in prayer. I confess that I have sometimes sought earthly possessions and desires instead of pursuing a deeper relationship with You. Forgive me for my divided focus.

You have commanded me to seek Your Kingdom first (Matthew 6:33). I apologize for treating You as a means to an end, rather than seeking You for who You are. Help me to shift my perspective and align my heart with Your will. I desire to seek more of You and less of myself (John 3:30). Shape my desires to match Your perfect will, and guide me in obedience to Your commandments (Psalm 119:35). Let my deepest longing be to draw nearer to You, understand Your ways, and reflect Your love to others.

Replace my personal desires with an unwavering passion for You. May my thoughts, words, and actions honor and glorify Your name. Thank You for Your patience, grace, and love. Draw me closer to Your presence and guide me on the path to eternal life. In Jesus' name, Amen.

December 20
Overwhelming Victory with God

"No, in all these things we are more than conquerors through him who loved us."

Romans 8:37-39 ESV

Dear Victorious God, thank You for the triumph I have in You. By Your grace and power, I am more than a conqueror (Romans 8:37), overcoming all obstacles through Your strength. Your victory goes beyond mere success; it's a triumph that echoes throughout Your Kingdom.

Grant me wisdom to fully grasp and walk in this victory. Remind me of the power and authority I have in You (Luke 10:19). In times of doubt or weakness, reassure me that nothing can separate me from Your love (Romans 8:35). Height, depth, or any created thing cannot distance me from the love You've lavished upon me. I am secure in Your embrace.

Help me to understand that the battles I face are already won and to walk confidently in every circumstance. Let this truth transform my perspective and strengthen my faith. May I stand firm, knowing You are with me. Empower me to boldly live out and proclaim Your victory in my life. Thank You for allowing me to share in Your victory. With gratitude and faith in Your promises, I pray in Jesus' name. Amen.

December 21
In This is Love

"In this, the love of God was made manifest among us, that God sent his only Son into the world …"
1 John 4:9 ESV

Dear Precious Lord, I come before You in awe of the immense love You've poured out on me (Romans 5:5). You sent Your Son, not because I deserved it, but out of Your boundless love. Help me grasp the depth of this love, so it may transform my life.

In this is love: Jesus, You laid down Your life for us, the ultimate sacrifice to reconcile us with the Father. Your selflessness humbles me, and I'm deeply grateful. Let Your sacrificial love guide and inspire me as I navigate this world.

You call us to love one another as You have loved us (John 13:34). Empower me to embody this love daily. Teach me to show unconditional kindness and compassion (Philippians 2:3). Help me to see others through Your eyes and extend grace and forgiveness.

Lord, let Your love fill every part of me and overflow to those I encounter. Use me as a vessel of Your love to bring healing and hope to a hurting world. Thank You for Your boundless love. May I live each day reflecting this truth and letting Your love shine through me. In Jesus' name, Amen.

December 22
My Exceeding Joy

"To him who is able to keep you from stumbling and to present you before his glorious presence without fault and with great joy."

Jude 1:24 NIV

Dear Great God, I rejoice in Your abundant goodness and the surpassing joy You've given me. Your grace has ignited a flame of delight in my soul, and I am grateful for the joy that flows from knowing You intimately.

You are my source of unwavering joy. Your presence uplifts me, turning mourning into dancing (Psalm 30:11) and sorrow into praise. I am thankful for the unending wellspring of joy from my relationship with You. In seasons of celebration, may Your joy fill every heart and home. As we exchange gifts and enjoy festivities, remind us of the ultimate gift—Your Son, Jesus Christ. His birth brought immeasurable joy into the world and inspires us to share that joy with others.

I pray that those who have yet to encounter Your love experience the transformative power of Your joy. Break through their darkness and reveal the radiant joy found only in You. Let Your joy bring comfort, healing, and restoration to the weary and brokenhearted. May the joy of the Lord resonate throughout the world (Isaiah 52:8), spreading like wildfire and igniting a desire for Your presence. In Jesus' name, Amen.

December 23
His Mercy is New Every Morning

"The steadfast love of the Lord never ceases; his mercies never come to an end; they are new every morning."
Lamentations 3:22-23 ESV

Dear Faithful God, I praise You for Your limitless love and endless mercies. Each morning brings a fresh outpouring of Your grace and compassion (Lamentations 3:22-23). Your faithfulness remains constant in this ever-changing world.

I am in awe of how Your mercies renew each day, washing away my shortcomings and failures. I cling to the promise that Your love is unchanging and Your mercies are inexhaustible. I find comfort in knowing that, despite my stumbles, Your mercies are not dependent on my performance but on Your unchanging character (1 John 1:9).

Today, I surrender my heart anew and ask for Your guidance and strength to honor Your name. Help me to be a vessel of Your love and grace, touching those around me and drawing them closer to Your heart. I trust in Your mercy to carry me through any challenges I may face, rejoicing in the promise of a fresh beginning each morning (Psalm 30:5). Thank You for Your endless mercies. May I never take them for granted, but use them to grow in my relationship with You. In Jesus' name, Amen.

December 24
You are Here With Me

"The Word became flesh and made his dwelling among us. We have seen his glory, the glory of the one and only Son, who came from the Father, full of grace and truth."

John 1:14 NIV

Dear Ever-present God, I find great comfort in knowing You are always with me. You chose to manifest Your love and grace right where I am, intimately knowing every detail of my life (Psalm 139:1). Your presence is not distant but near, walking alongside me at every moment.

Help me recognize Your presence in all aspects of my life—through the kindness of others, the support I receive, and the small blessings that touch my heart. Let me not overlook the divine encounters in everyday moments. In times of darkness or uncertainty, remind me that You are here with me, in the midst of it all. Just as Jesus dwelled among us, You continue to be present through the Holy Spirit, comforting and guiding me through trials (Psalm 16:11).

Grant me the strength to be a vessel of Your love and light, offering help, compassion, and kindness to those around me. Let Your presence transform me, so others may see Your grace through my actions. Thank You for being so close, watching over me with Your comforting presence. May Your name be glorified as I walk with You every step of the way. In Jesus' name, Amen.

December 25
The Gift of Your Love

"Jesus replied: 'Love the Lord you God with all your heart and with your soul and with all your mind."

Matthew 22:37 NIV

Dear God of Love, I come before You with a grateful heart, amazed by the greatest gift of all—Jesus Christ. In a world focused on material things, I am reminded that the true treasure is Your profound love and sacrifice through Your Son.

Thank You for sending Jesus to walk among us, teach us, heal us, and redeem us. Through His life, death, and resurrection, He showed us the way to eternal life and reconciliation with You. In Jesus, we find hope (1 Peter 1:3), grace, and forgiveness, a beacon of light in our darkness.

As I reflect on this divine gift, I am overwhelmed by Your infinite mercy. You chose to send Your only Son to experience the joys and sorrows of human life (Philippians 2:7), all for our salvation. Such love is beyond comprehension.

Help me never take this gift for granted. Let me embrace the teachings of Jesus, and share His love with others. May His sacrifice inspire me to live a life that reflects His grace and guides others to witness Your love through me. Thank You for the gift of Jesus, the greatest gift of all (2 Corinthians 9:15). May I cherish and honor this gift daily. In Jesus' name, Amen.

December 26
I Love You This Much

"O righteous Father, even though the world does not know you, I know you, ..."

John 17:25 ESV

Dear Abba Father, I come before You with a heart full of gratitude. Your love is boundless and eternal (1 John 4:8), a constant source of comfort and strength in my life. I am in awe of Your unfailing goodness and offer You my deepest praise.

Thank You for revealing a love that surpasses understanding, a love that wraps around me even in my flaws and mistakes. I am so grateful for this experience of Your love. Forgive me, Lord, for when I've doubted or believed the lies that my errors are too great for Your love to reach.

Help me silence those doubts and remember that Your love has no boundaries. You showed this immeasurable love by sending Your Son to save me. With humility, I offer my life as a reflection of my love for You (Romans 12:1).

Guide me along the path of righteousness, strengthen me in weakness, and mold me according to Your will (2 Corinthians 3:18). May my life be a testament to Your redeeming love and grace, drawing others closer to You. In Jesus' name, Amen.

December 27
You are Pursuing Me

"For he satisfies the thirsty and <u>FILLS</u> the hungry with good things."

Psalm 107:9 NLT

Dear Unfailing God, thank You for Your unwavering pursuit of me, even when I stray. Your relentless love and grace always draw me closer to You. Help me to recognize Your presence in every aspect of my life.

When I feel empty, You are the Living Water that satisfies my soul (John 4:14). Fill my deepest longings with Your goodness and grace. Teach me to hunger and thirst for righteousness (Matthew 5:6), and guide me to make choices that honor You, including taking care of my physical health.

I confess I sometimes turn to food for comfort when I am not truly hungry. Grant me strength and self-control during these temptations. Remind me that true fulfillment comes from You alone, and help me find healthy ways to manage my emotions.

Guard my heart (Proverbs 4:23) and keep me aware of distractions that lead me away from Your truth. Guide me to engage in activities that nourish my spirit and bring me closer to You. Thank You for pursuing me with Your endless love. Help me respond with an open heart and live in a way that reflects Your glory. In Jesus' name, Amen.

December 28
Your Love is Sweet Enough

"How sweet are your words to my taste, sweeter than honey to my mouth!"

Psalm 119:103 ESV

Dear Sweet God, I am grateful for the boundless love and grace You show me each day. Your love uplifts my spirit and fills my life with joy and purpose (Jeremiah 15:16). Your words are sweeter than honey, guiding me towards righteousness and fulfillment (Psalm 119:103).

When tempted by sugary treats, I seek Your guidance (1 Corinthians 10:13). Grant me the wisdom and strength to choose healthier options, such as fruits or sugar-free alternatives. Help me remember that these choices support my well-being and journey towards optimal health. In a world that often glorifies sweet treats and sugary indulgences, give me discernment to enjoy them in moderation and reserve them for special occasions. Teach me that overindulgence neither satisfies my body nor benefits my finances. Keep my mind focused and aligned with my values.

I trust in Your love, knowing it extends to every part of my life, including my physical health. Guide me towards balance and strength, honoring my body as a temple with wholesome choices. With gratitude in my heart, I pray in Jesus' name. Amen.

December 29
Discernment and Moderation

*"Don't be drunk with wine, because that will ruin your life. Instead, be **FILLED** with the Holy Spirit."*
Ephesians 5:18 NLT

Dear Merciful God, thank You for guiding me with Your wisdom and love. Your word warns of the dangers of excess and calls me to live a balanced life (1 Peter 1:16). Help me avoid overindulgence and make wise choices that honor You.

Grant me a clear mind (1 Peter 5:8-9) to discern what is beneficial and what is harmful. Empower me with self-control to live a fulfilling life aligned with Your guidance. In times of celebration, may my decisions reflect Your values and bring joy without compromising my principles.

When faced with peer pressure or worldly temptations, strengthen me to stand firm in my commitment to godly living. Let Your love fill my heart and guide me to seek Your pleasure above all else. True fulfillment comes from living according to Your word and experiencing Your divine love.

I trust that You will answer me when I call out to You for help(Psalm 138:3). Thank You for the example of Jesus, who showed moderation and obedience to Your will. May His life remind me of Your grace and love. In Jesus' name, I pray. Amen.

December 30
Sweet Daily Surrender

*"Satisfy us in the morning with Your loving devotion,
that we may sing for joy and be glad all our days."*
Psalm 90:14 NIV

Heavenly Father, thank You for Your new mercies each morning (Lamentations 3:22). When my heart is overwhelmed, You guide me back to You (Psalm 61:2), where I find rest and peace. Your unwavering love assures me that I am never alone.

As I surrender this day to You, I embrace the joy that comes from relinquishing control and trusting Your divine plan. In this sweet surrender, I discover freedom from worry and anxiety, knowing You go before me, guiding my steps and strengthening me. Your presence fills me with courage in the face of challenges and temptations.

In the midst of chaos, I commit to keeping my eyes fixed on You (Psalm 141:8). Help me start each day with You on my mind, so my day may be blessed according to Your plan. I surrender my plans and desires to You, trusting that Your ways are higher than mine.

May my thoughts, words, and actions reflect Your love and grace to those around me. Thank You for the privilege of surrendering my day to You. In Jesus' name, I pray. Amen.

December 31
Gratitude for a Year of Faithfulness

*"See, I am doing a new thing! Now it springs up;
do you not perceive it? I am making a way in the
wilderness and streams in the wasteland."*

Isaiah 43:19 NIV

Dear Faithful God, thank You for Your unwavering love and faithfulness throughout this year. As I reflect, my heart overflows with gratitude for how You guided me through both trials and triumphs.

As I look to the year ahead, I recommit to focusing on You as I've seen your faithfulness this year. Help me keep moving forward with continual steady progress. This year has brought tests and joys, and through it all, You have been my rock and constant companion (Psalm 118:2). Thank You for Your steadfast love.

As I enter the new year, I do so with excitement, not for my own achievements, but for who You are—the Alpha and Omega, the beginning and end (Revelation 1:8). I will continue to trust in Your divine plan and surrender my plans, dreams, and desires to You. As I step into this new season, I am filled with hope and anticipation, knowing that Your love will continue to surround me, Your grace will sustain me, and Your blessings will overflow. With a heart full of gratitude and a spirit of surrender, I offer this final prayer of this year to You. In Your precious name, I pray. Amen.

Thank You

Thank you for being motivated, courageous, inquisitive, and committed to go deeper in your health journey and uncover the missing piece—Christ!

I pray that these principles have been as much of a blessing to you as they have been for me and the hundreds of thousands of women around the world who have experienced what it means to include God in their health and weight-releasing journey.

If you've been blessed by this book, then please don't keep it a secret!

There are millions of women who need to hear this message. Please take a moment to leave an honest book review so more people can discover this book as well.

This book has laid out a great foundation for you, but there's so much more for you to discover. Please keep in touch with me so that you can stay in this conversation and continue to make your health a priority—God's Way. Plus, I'll send you a free copy of my '*3 Steps to Overcoming Emotional Eating*' guide when you enroll for my weekly devotional message on successful weight loss, God's way.

Register for my weekly posts at cathymorenzie.com.

About the Author

Cathy Morenzie is CEO of and operates a ministry-minded health and weight-releasing company (weightlossgodsway.com) that has blessed hundreds of thousands of women around the world. She has been a voice for the faith-based health movement for over 35 years. She resides in Barrie, Ontario, Canada with her family. Cathy is a  highly sought-after international speaker and coach. She has given away 1 million free teachings through YouVersion devotionals and daily messages on YouTube.

Learn more at: cathymorenzie.com.

Follow Cathy at:

facebook.com/weightlossgodsway/
youtube.com/@CathyMorenzieWeightLossGodsWay
pinterest.com/cathymorenzie/
instagram.com/cathy.morenzie

www.ingramcontent.com/pod-product-compliance
Lightning Source LLC
Chambersburg PA
CBHW070859120626
46546CB00001B/67